Resisting Sherman

A Confederate Surgeon's Journal and the
Civil War in the Carolinas, 1865

Based on the diary of
Francis Marion Robertson, M.D.

edited by
Thomas Heard Robertson, Jr.

SB

Savas Beatie
California

Library of Congress Control Number: 2015933358
ISBN: 978-1-61121-260-0
e-book ISBN: 978-1-61121-261-7

First edition, first printing

SB
Published by
Savas Beatie LLC
989 Governor Drive, Suite 102
El Dorado Hills, CA 95762

916-941-6896
sales@savasbeatie.com
www.savasbeatie.com

FSC
www.fsc.org
MIX
Paper from
responsible sources
FSC® C011935

Savas Beatie titles are available at special discounts for bulk purchases in the United States by corporations, institutions, and other organizations. For more details, please contact Special Sales, P.O. Box 4527, El Dorado Hills, CA 95762, or you may e-mail us at sales@savasbeatie.com, or visit our website at www.savasbeatie.com for additional information.

Proudly published, printed, and warehoused in the United States of America.

Dedication

To Heard Robertson, my father, who instilled in me
an appetite for lifelong learning, a thirst for studying history,
and the idea for editing this little journal.

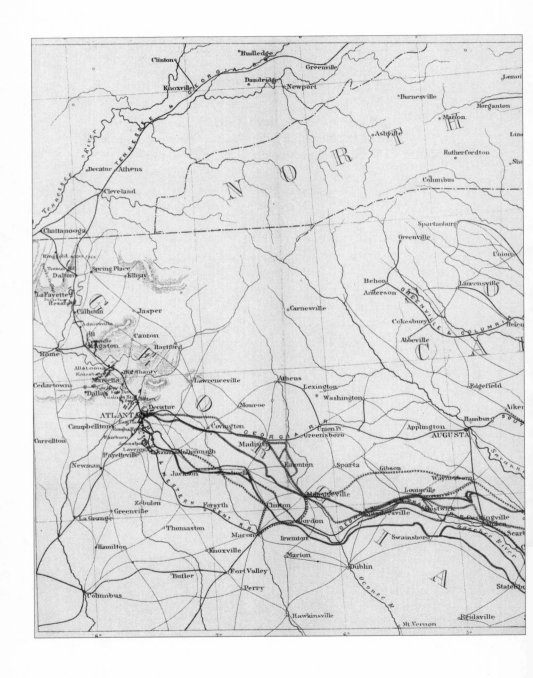

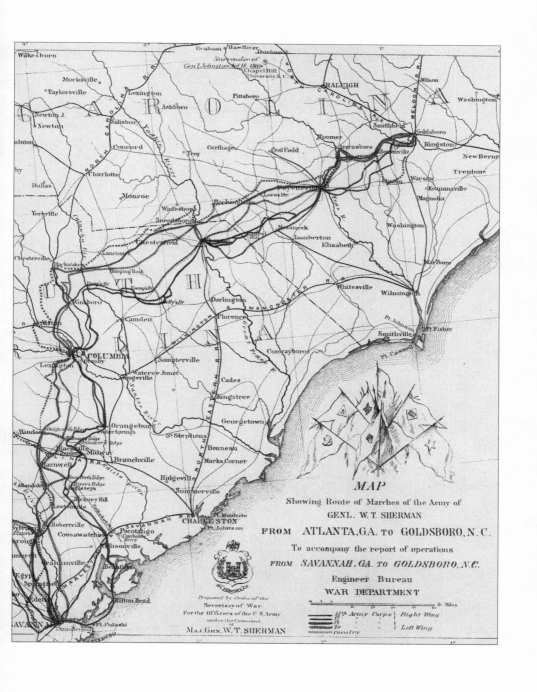

MAP

Showing Route of Marches of the Army of

GENL. W.T. SHERMAN

FROM ATLANTA, GA. TO GOLDSBORO, N.C.

To accompany the report of operations

FROM SAVANNAH, GA. TO GOLDSBORO, N.C.

Engineer Bureau

WAR DEPARTMENT

Prepared by Order of the
Secretary of War
For the Officers of the U.S. Army
under the Command
of
MAJ. GEN. W.T. SHERMAN

Table of Contents

Table of Contents (continued)

List of Maps

List of Illustrations

List of Illustrations (continued)

List of Illustrations (continued)

List of Illustrations (continued)

Editor's Note

An interest in history runs in the family. So it is with the journal of Confederate Surgeon Francis Marion Robertson. The doctor's great-grand-daughter Lily Taylor Robertson first transcribed the little hand-me-down volume in longhand for library use in the early 1960s. She stored the original diary in a nylon-stocking box lined with tissue paper, where it remained for about twenty years. Great-grandson Heard Robertson, my father, transcribed it again, this time in typescript form. As an avocational historian, he recognized its historical value and aimed to collaborate with his mother, Catherine Heard Robertson, to edit it for publication. Alas, the task was left unfinished, and the treasured original went back into the stocking box for another two decades. It has fallen to the next generation to see it published.

I scanned the typescript version prepared by my father into a computer program and corrected the text to conform to the journal's original language. The computer and the Internet have made research and editing a much easier process.

Dr. Robertson's journal covers about three months during the chaotic ending weeks of the Confederacy, including the evacuation of Charleston and his journey ahead of General William T. Sherman's advance through the Carolinas. I left his original spelling and punctuation intact, except in a few places where I have inserted bracketed information for clarification. I attempted to identify the persons and places mentioned in the text and have been mostly successful, with a few notable failures readers will soon discover. To help frame the larger context of the time, I have inserted entries at the

Original diary on contemporary traveling desk.
Thomas H. Robertson, Jr.

appropriate dates within the journal to cover various battles and events occurring elsewhere across the South, and have distinguished them using bold italics. A few of these entries refer to General Sherman's army, but I left the description of Confederate response to Sherman's advance mostly to the journalist himself.

The Prologue introduces many of the characters who appear in the journal, and covers the military and political background at Charleston, South Carolina, leading up to the evacuation described by Dr. Robertson. Some of the military episodes are punctuated by the involvement of the doctor himself and his sons and relatives. The Epilogue following the diary summarizes what happened to the Dr. Robertson and the diary's characters after the war ended.

Dr. Robertson included enough information about the people, places, and geography for me and my sisters, Cecilia Robertson Queen and Catherine Barrett Robertson, to trace his route during 2003 and 2004. To our delight, many landmarks and houses mentioned in the journal were still there after 140 years, and the history of that fateful period still lives in the minds and traditions of those we encountered along that route. I have included brief annotations in the footnotes about the modern context and the most likely routes and landmarks, and have distinguished this information from ordinary footnote text by bold typeface.

Working to identify the people, places, and events mentioned in the journal produced more stories than would seem possible from such a short volume. I have attempted to bring the story alive with sidebars on a variety of subjects suggested by the diary, including politics, food, song, milestones, and the Battle of Averasboro, which occurred during the time frame covered by the journal and involved at least one of the surgeon's sons. Many other stories in the Prologue, footnotes, and Epilogue amplify Dr. Robertson's eyewitness account of the final collapse of the Confederacy. I trust that they complement rather than detract from the original text.

Acknowledgments

Resisting Sherman is the work of many hands, beyond the thoughtful writing of the original diarist and my own explanatory narratives. I would like to highlight a few of the folks who were particularly helpful to me, at the great risk of leaving out other important ones who also contributed so well. If I missed anyone, please know that I deeply appreciate your assistance.

I have been greatly assisted in the research process by my two sisters, Cecilia Baker Robertson Queen and Catherine Barrett Robertson. We followed our forebear's actual 1865 route during retracement trips in 2003 and 2004. Catherine took photographs of many structures and venues, and later conducted relentless research into identifying people who appear in the diary and their genealogical connections. Cecilia followed up on various archival sources in South Carolina.

Russell K. Brown, Ph.D., led me to sources on many of the military figures. Frank Thompson furnished valuable information from New York City sources and identified Dr. Robertson's servant Henry Sutcliff. Curtis Worthington, M.D., and Jane Brown of the Waring Historical Library at the Medical University of South Carolina searched their archives and provided photographs and medical background. C. L. Bragg, M.D., gave me valuable information on anesthesia, dengue fever, and other historical medical practices. Bleakley Chandler, M.D., led me to historical medical journals and the subjects of yellow fever and dengue fever. Sarah Spruill of Cheraw Visitors Bureau furnished source material on Cheraw and the Pee Dee River area. Bill Surface of the Museum of the Cape Fear provided information on North Carolina troops and the Fayetteville area. Walt Smith of the Averasboro Battlefield Commission helped me understand the events of the battle on the ground and their geographic relation. Wade Sokolosky reviewed my Battle of Averasboro sidebar and helped me correct the details of military matters. Wayne Carver gave me considerable information on Armand Lamar DeRosset. Marvin L. Brown, Jr., whom we met by happenstance when we knocked on the door of his historic house, Edenwood, near Raleigh during our retracement tour, gave invaluable assistance. As a retired history professor from North Carolina State University, he shared his local history volumes, encouraged us to publish the diary, introduced us to the staff of the North Carolina Department of Archives, and furnished a copy of a fine historical map of Wake County. Ann Marion was a treasure trove of information on the families and history of Chester, and served as a fine guide on our tour of her town.

David Koch of the Presbyterian Historical Society helped identify many of the ministers mentioned in the diary. Ethel Robertson Boyle filled in genealogical gaps of the F. M. Robertson family. Lee Ann Caldwell, Ph.D., read the manuscript and offered suggestions for improvement. Erick D. Montgomery also gave me useful comments from his reading of the manuscript, furnished genealogical information on the relatives of Woodrow Wilson, and filled in other historical details.

I am indebted to the archivists who assisted me in obtaining illustrations from various institutions and private collections, including Karl Larson, history editor of Goodnight Raleigh, Bryan Collars of South Carolina Department of Archives and History, Mary Jo Fairchild of South Carolina Historical Society, Steve Engerrand and Gail DeLoach of Georgia Archives, Shelby Silvernell of Chicago History Museum, Nancy Glaser of Augusta Museum of History, and Jim Gerencser of Dickinson College. I am also thankful for my secretary Vicky Kiker who edited many of the images for clarity and otherwise spent ten years helping me with all manner of other editorial tasks.

George G. Robertson searched diligently (and unfortunately unsuccessfully) in the University of Tennessee Library for the newspaper account of Senator Henry Clay's 1844 campaign visit to Augusta. Both George G. Robertson and Jonathan S. Robertson proofread the text. Heard Robertson III wrote the musical arrangements, while Keith Shafer added a professional musician's review and prepared the musical scores for publication.

I appreciate the encouragement and good work of the managing director Theodore P. "Ted" Savas, marketing director Sarah Keeney, production manager Lee Merideth, and the rest of the talented staff at Savas Beatie in accepting, editing, designing, and producing my book.

I especially appreciate my wife, Lee Gostin Robertson, who has been so patient with me throughout the process, when I was absent at libraries, on the road, in books, on the Internet, or at the keyboard.

Thomas Heard Robertson, Jr.
Augusta, Georgia

Charleston was lost. And every citizen could sense it as soon as General William T. Sherman turned his army of 60,000 men toward Columbia. The Confederate troops would now have to hurry to get ahead of the Federals and join forces with their Southern counterparts in upper South Carolina and North Carolina. They would launch what turned out to be a last ditch effort to defeat their arch-foe Sherman. Lieutenant General William J. Hardee finally gave the order on February 16, 1865, to evacuate Charleston—too late, in the mind of Confederate Surgeon Francis Marion Robertson. Sherman was already at Columbia, headed north.[1]

Surgeon F. M. Robertson kept a daily journal during the fast-paced last campaign of the Civil War in the Deep South, from the evacuation of Charleston through the Confederate surrenders. His rank as an army surgeon made him the equivalent of a major of cavalry, a circumstance that, by itself, would not make him an expert on military strategies. But he was not unequipped to comment with some authority on military matters. He had been brought up as the son of a militia captain, attended the United States Military Academy at West Point, and commanded a company of militia himself in one of the Indian wars in Florida. His narrative looks critically at the decisions of the commanders from a middle-ranking officer's viewpoint, describes the army movements from the ground level, frequently invokes divine guidance, and places the military campaign within the everyday events of the citizenry with whom he came in contact. The salient military events leading up to the opening of Doctor Robertson's diary had begun a few months earlier.

---

1   Alfred Roman, *The Military Operations of General Beauregard in the War Between the States, 1861 to 1865*, 2 vol. (New York: Harper & Brothers, 1884), 2:349, 639.

General Hardee's army of approximately 7,000 men had evacuated Savannah on December 21, 1864, leaving the city to the Union army as the culmination of their march to the sea. General Sherman had then given the City of Savannah to President Abraham Lincoln as a Christmas present. Hardee had moved his troops up the railroad to Charleston, joining forces with the Confederate coastal forces there and assuming command.[2] General Pierre G. T. Beauregard, commander of the Department of South Carolina, Georgia, and Florida, and Hardee's superior, thought it was only a question of time before the Charleston area also would have to be evacuated. On December 27, 1864, he sent instructions to Hardee to make "silently and cautiously, all necessary preparation for the evacuation of Charleston, should it become necessary, taking at the same time, the proper steps to save the garrison." Even so, as late as February 11, 1865, General Beauregard and President Jefferson Davis still thought Sherman's objective might be Charleston. It seemed so. That night Union naval forces made offensive movements on James Island across the harbor, including an amphibious attack on Battery Simkins near Fort Johnson and a landing on the south end of the island the previous day. All the while they kept up their naval fire from the gunboats near the harbor. General Hardee thought these actions were merely demonstrations.[3]

Sherman's real objective was not to take Charleston, but was to join forces with General Grant near Richmond, Virginia. He began his march northward from Savannah through the Carolinas in the early part of January 1865, with an army that consisted of four corps totaling 60,000 men, 4,500 vehicles, and 30,000 horses and mules. His forces were organized into two wings: The left wing was the Army of the Cumberland, comprised of the XIV and the XX corps, while the right wing was the Army of the Tennessee, containing the XVII Corps and the XV Corps. A division of cavalry guarded the flanks and scouted ahead of the army.[4] The left wing marched toward Columbia, feinting toward Augusta by way of Barnwell and Windsor, and fighting a cavalry battle at Aiken

2 Charleston & Savannah Rail Road. See J. C. Swayze, *Hill & Swayze's Confederate States Rail-Road & Steam-Boat Guide* (Griffin, GA: Hill & Swayze, Publishers, 1862), 60, scanned version, University of North Carolina at Chapel Hill, 2001, http:docsouth.unc.edu/imls/Swayze/Swayze.html, accessed July 24, 2010.

3 Milby E. Burton, *The Siege of Charleston, 1861-1865* (Columbia, 1970), 311, 315-6; *The War of the Rebellion: A Compilation of the Official Records of the Union and Confederate Armies*, Pt. 2, vol. 47, 1,157, vol. 44, 994, 997-9, hereinafter cited OR; Roman, *General Beauregard*, 2:344-9.

4 Larry E. Nelson, *Sherman's March through the Upper Pee Dee Region of South Carolina* (Florence, SC: Pee Dee Heritage Center, 2001), 3; Jacqueline Glass Campbell, *When Sherman Marched North from the Sea: Resistance on the Confederate Home Front* (Chapel Hill: The University of North Carolina Press, 2003), 120n.

on February 11, 1865, against Confederate horsemen under Maj. Gen. Joseph E. Wheeler.[5] The right wing crossed the railroad toward Charleston at Hardeeville, and headed north, meeting resistance from a Confederate force under Maj. Gen. Lafayette McLaws at Rivers Bridge over the flooding Salkahatchie River. The Federals were delayed for several days in making the crossing, which they completed by February 4, 1865, after they had flanked the Confederates both upstream and downstream.[6]

The Salkahatchie River was typical of most of South Carolina's low country streams, flowing through a wide, low, swampy plain. Heavy rains and the resulting floods made the normally difficult stream crossings virtually impassable to such a large army. In fact, there were two significant floods during January 1865, and a third major one in March that bogged down the troops and wagon trains throughout Sherman's march through the Carolinas. These conditions slowed the Union army's progress as much as the Confederate resistance did.[7]

Sherman's plan for feeding and supplying his forces centered on foraging for food in the countryside, and commandeering supplies and equipment from the farms and towns along the route, similar to the methods he had employed during the march to the sea through Georgia in the months before. This system offered the opportunity for unscrupulous soldiers to take personal valuables and generally to plunder the residents along the way. In fact, most of the Union troops blamed South Carolina for causing the war through her rush to secede and fire the first shots, and they could not wait to punish the state and her citizens. Writing from Savannah to his superior General Halleck in Washington, Sherman observed, "The truth is the whole army is burning with an insatiable desire to wreak vengeance on South Carolina. I almost tremble at her fate but feel that she deserves all that seems in store for her."[8]

---

5   http://www.battleofaiken.org/history.htm, accessed October 31, 2004.

6   Roman, *General Beauregard*, 2:636; J. Tracey Power and Daniel J. Bell, *Rivers Bridge State Park Visitors Guide* (South Carolina Department of Parks, Recreation and Tourism, 1992), 1, 6-12.

7   Paul R. Speer and Charles R. Gamble, *Magnitude and Frequency of Floods in the United States, Part 2-A. South Atlantic Slope Basins, James River to Savannah River, Geological Survey Water-Supply Paper 1673* (Washington, 1964), 318-9; John G. Barrett, *Sherman's March Through the Carolinas* (Chapel Hill: The University of North Carolina Press, 1956), 46-7; Joseph T. Glatthaar, *The March to the Sea and Beyond: Sherman's Troops in the Savannah and Carolinas Campaign* (Baton Rouge: Louisiana State University Press, 1985), 108-10.

8   Nelson, *Sherman's March*, 2-3; Rosen, *Confederate Charleston*, 134; Maj. Gen. William T. Sherman to Maj. Gen. Henry W. Halleck, December 24, 1864, *OR*, 44:798-800.

Each day, groups of mounted soldiers went out as foragers in advance of the army, returning in the evening with "strings of chicken, bacon, turkeys and geese" pillaged from plantations that were occupied primarily by women and children. Some of these men got out of control, roaming the countryside aiming merely to plunder it. These were Sherman's "bummers," described by one Union army captain as "stragglers—not in the rear but in front of the army." The term came to mean a "ragged man . . . mounted on a scrawny mule, without a saddle, with a gun, a knapsack, a butcher knife and a plug hat . . . Keen on the scent of rebels, or bacon, or silverspoons, or corn, or anything valuable." By the time the last of the Union columns had passed through an area, the houses were "entirely gutted." Often what was left was "a heap of smoldering ashes."[9]

En route to the sea and ultimately headed toward a rendezvous with Grant, Sherman's immediate goal was to leave a population that would have to concentrate on regaining food and shelter for themselves, and, consequently, that would be less able to support further military operations in other states.

The home front thus became the battlefield, and the inhabitants along the way were terrified. Many of the white females, as heads of the households and managers of the plantations, were remarkably resolute in their support of the southern nation and passionate in their responses to the pillagers. Their tongues were their primary weapons against the invaders, and they often responded with intensity in defense of their homes and hearths. Black families were not spared thefts and indignities, either. They soon realized that few Union soldiers had real abolitionist sympathies. The roughnecks of Sherman's army would "go through a Negro cabin . . . with just as much freedom and vivacity as they 'loot' the dwelling a of a wealthy planter."[10]

North Carolinians were a bit less subject to abuses from zealous Union soldiers than were the citizens of South Carolina, the cradle of secession. North Carolina had been one of the last states to secede, and Sherman expected local support for his campaign from citizens with strong Unionist sympathies. In early March 1865, each wing of his army received similar instructions to the effect that "every effort will be made to prevent any wanton destruction of property, or any unkind treatment of citizens," and that a "marked difference should be made in the manner in which we treat the [North Carolina] people and the manner in which those of South Carolina were treated." Contrary to Sherman's expectations, however, the North Carolinians did not rush to

9 Campbell, *When Sherman Marched North from the Sea*, 44-5 and 124n. The Union Captain was George W. Pepper; Glatthaar, *The March to the Sea and Beyond*, 122-3.

10 Campbell, *When Sherman Marched North from the Sea*, 11, 13-14, 45, 50-51, 69.

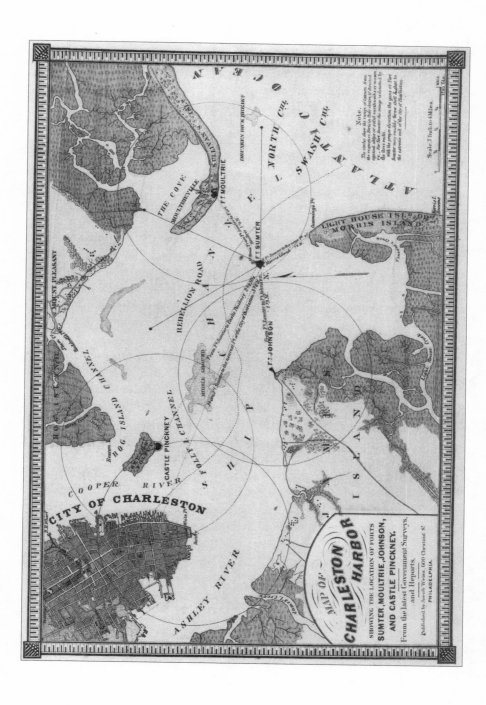

embrace his conquering army. Although it is true that many residents of the Tar Heel state had expressed discontent with the Confederate government, their dissension did not mean they would become disloyal to the southern nation.[11]

Beyond the Yankee invasion of the Carolinas, the war effort was also going poorly for the Confederates in other parts of the Deep South. The Army of Tennessee under Gen. John B. Hood fought to a bloody draw at Franklin, Tennessee, on November 23, 1864, and to a disastrous two-day loss at Nashville on December 15 and 16, 1864. The routed army retreated across the Tennessee River, entering camp at Tupelo, Mississippi on January 10, 1865. Within the previous six weeks, Hood's army had marched nearly five hundred miles, fought two disastrous battles, and ended up a wreck of an army. Probably half of the men were without shoes in the coldest winter Tennessee had known for years.[12]

General Pierre G. T. Beauregard, having left the command of the Confederate operations in South Carolina to General Hardee, hastened to Tupelo to give personal attention to the persistent rumors that Hood had suffered disasters in Tennessee. On January 15, 1865, he must have shuddered as he saw for himself the remnants of the army. "Very little—if anything—remained of its former cohesive strength. If not, in the strict sense of the word, a disorganized mob, it was no longer an army."[13]

Beauregard's orders were to return to the Carolinas with such troops as could be spared from the west. General Stephen D. Lee's Corps, under the command of Maj. Gen. Carter Stevenson, left for the Carolinas by way of Augusta on January 19, 1865, followed by Gen. Benjamin Franklin Cheatham's and Gen. Alexander P. Stewart's Corps by the end of the month. Eventually, about 5,000 soldiers joined forces with their countrymen to the east.[14]

Meanwhile in coastal North Carolina, the tides of war were also running against the Confederate forces. A combined effort of Union army and navy forces succeeded in overrunning Fort Fisher at the mouth of the Cape Fear River on January 13-15, 1865. The fort and nearby Confederate batteries at Smithville and Fort Anderson guarded the entrance to the port of Wilmington,

---

11 Campbell, *When Sherman Marched North from the Sea*, 75-76; General Order No. 8, *OR*, v. 46, pt. 2, 719; Special Order No. 63, *OR*, v. 46, pt. 2, 760-1.

12 Mark Swanson, *Atlas of the Civil War Month by Month: Major Battles and Troop Movements* (Athens: University of Georgia Press, 2004), 100-4.

13 Stanley F. Horn, *The Army of Tennessee: A Military History* (Indianapolis: The Bobbs-Merrill Company, 1941), 419-22; Roman, *General Beauregard*, 2:331-32.

14 Horn, *The Army of Tennessee*, 422-23; Roman, *General Beauregard*, 2:331-35; Swanson, *Atlas of the Civil War*, 104.

which was the South's most active port of entry for blockade-running ships. Following the fierce battle at Fort Fisher, the southern forces withdrew up river and into the interior of North Carolina. This left Charleston for a short time as the only seaport remaining in southern control.[15]

The loss of the port of Wilmington and, subsequently, of Charleston caused the Confederate commanders to adopt an overall desperate strategy to consolidate all available soldiers into a large army for a fight with Sherman. President Jefferson Davis appointed Gen. Joseph E. Johnston to command the force, to include General Hardee's command from Charleston, Gen. Braxton Bragg's force from Wilmington, and the remnant of the Army of Tennessee. If Johnston could rally and defeat Sherman before he was reinforced by the Union forces under Generals John M. Schofield and Alfred H. Terry pursuing Bragg from Wilmington, he might reinforce Gen. Robert E. Lee against Grant in Virginia to continue the fight, or at least to gain for the Confederacy better terms of peace.[16]

Since the very beginning of the Civil War, Charleston Harbor and surroundings had been a battleground nearly continuously. Immediately after South Carolina had seceded from the Union, newly elected president Abraham Lincoln had ordered the reinforcement with troops and supplies of the federal garrison at Fort Sumter at the mouth of the harbor. To avoid suspicion, the United States Navy employed a commercial vessel, the *Star of the West*, for the mission, rather than using a ship of war. With the soldiers out of sight below deck, the ship steamed up the channel leading to the fort and the harbor, just off the coast of Morris Island, on January 9, 1861. When it reached an on-shore artillery battery manned by cadets from the Citadel and by South Carolina militia troops, Maj. Peter F. Stevens ordered the guns to open fire. One of Dr. Francis M. Robertson's sons, Pvt. James Lawrence Robertson, was present in one of the militia companies, the Vigilant Rifles.[17] They directed the first shots

---

15 John Gilchrist Barrett, *North Carolina as a Civil War Battlefield 1861-1865* (Raleigh: Office of Archives and History, North Carolina Department of Cultural Resources, 2003), 63-4.

16 Chris E. Fonvielle, Jr., *The Wilmington Campaign: Last Rays of Departing Hope* (Campbell, CA: Savas Publishing Company, 1997), 433.

17 F. M. Robertson to [Congressman] W. Porcher Miles, Jan. 26th, 1864. "James, for whom I am making this application was at the attack on the "Star of the West," and has been uninterruptedly in service ever since." See *Compiled Service Records of Confederate Soldiers Who Served in Organizations from South Carolina*, for James L. Robertson, General Reference Branch, National Archives and Records Administration, Washington, D. C. "James Lawrence Robertson entered the service of S.C. at the age of 17 years, volunteered in the Vigilant Rifles under Capt. Samuel Y. Tupper, & was stationed on Morris Island, S. C. at the time that the 'Star of the West' attempted to re-enforce Fort Sumter. Served as a non-commissioned officer in the Marion Artillery & was present at the bombardment & capture of Fort Sumter & in all of the

across the bow of the ship, but aimed the following ones directly at the hull. The *Star of the West* soon turned away and sailed back to New York. These were the first shots of the growing hostilities that would soon break out into open warfare when South Carolina troops fired on Fort Sumter three months later.[18]

F. M. Robertson described the political and economic situation in South Carolina in a letter to a New York political acquaintance and former Whig, Samuel J. Anderson, on February 7, 1861:

> . . . I must frankly say to you, however, the Democracy of the North must not rely too much upon the hope of a reconstruction of the old Union. It cannot be done . . . There are other questions in my opinion more vital to the cotton States than slavery that should constitute an impassable barrier to her ever entering into another union with the North.
>
> I will explain. As long as cotton is king and the millions in Europe and Great Britain are dependent on it for employment and the civilized and uncivilized world for raiment so long will the institution of slavery exist and flourish in spite of the howlings and demented cries of the entire crew of abolitionists. For this I have no fears in or out of the Union. But as long as the Constitution contains a clause by which the South can be subject to unlimited taxation by an irresponsible majority in Congress through a tariff professedly for revenue but really to protect and build up the moneyed interest of one section at the expense of the other the cotton States will never consent to go back into the Union. I consider this question of equal if not greater importance than that of slavery. In all the compromises proposed not one word has been said to the South holding out the slightest hope of security on this point in future. . . .
>
> Can anything be gained by civil war? . . . . It would inevitably bring the North in conflict with England and France. We have little or no shipping to care for. England and France would carry our cotton under their flags and bring us wares and merchandise in return, and while the North was waging a bootless war on land letters of marque and reprisal would be sweeping her commerce from the ocean. . . . Let the South alone and suffer her to form her government in peace. . . . These are my views plainly and frankly expressed, and I feel satisfied that your judgment will assent to their correctness.

---

engagements on the Coast of S.C. & defense of Charleston S.C. Was appointed by President Davis as 2nd Lieutenant C. S. Army & assigned to duty in Co. I. 1st S.C. Regular Artillery. Was severely wounded at the battle of Averysboro N.C. on the 16th of March 1865." See Application for membership in United Daughters of the Confederacy of Margaret Wallace Robertson Moore (Mrs. John Moore), Paper #76, June 29, 1936.

18 Burton, *The Siege of Charleston*, 16-21; Robert N. Rosen, *Confederate Charleston: An Illustrated History of the City and the People During the Civil War* (Columbia, SC, 1994), 50-3.

Dr. Robertson continued to describe the military situation in Charleston harbor and added his hope for an amicable political resolution of the national crisis of separation that was brewing symbolically at Fort Sumter:

A word now about Fort Sumter and I will not inflict you further. We are all ready for the attack of that fortification. No movement will be made, however, until the action of the Southern Congress is known. If when it is demanded with other Southern forts by the commission from the Southern Confederacy it is not given up it will then be attacked and I can assure you it will be no child's play. The men who had the nerve to fire into the Star of the West with an armed force on board of her with the guns of Fort Sumter frowning upon them with threatening destruction can be trusted in times of danger. Our people are quiet, cool and determined. We can bombard it simultaneously from seven different points. It cannot be re-enforced.

I trust, however, it will not come to this. When it is evident that a Southern confederacy will be formed and recognized by foreign powers I hope there will be good sense enough at least among the leaders of the Republican party if not in the rank and file to see the wisdom of withdrawing the troops and arranging the terms of separation in an amicable manner and on the principles of justice and equality . . . . [19]

Two months afterward on April 12, 1861, before dawn, South Carolina artillery batteries opened fire on Fort Sumter under orders of General Beauregard. Two days later the United States forces under Maj. Robert Anderson surrendered the fort. For nearly four years thereafter, Southern troops manned Fort Sumter and held it firmly through three major Federal bombardments that leveled it to little more than a pile of brick masonry rubble.[20]

---

19 *OR*, Series 2, 2:610-12. Samuel J. Anderson was a former Georgian living in New York, who had formerly been Sheriff of Richmond County, Georgia, and who had served as Chief Clerk to Secretary of War George W. Crawford (of Georgia), as interim Secretary of War in the cabinet of President Millard Fillmore in 1850, and later as Clerk of the House of Representatives. Suspected as a disloyal person at the outset of the Civil War, he was imprisoned on August 27, 1861, by the new president Abraham Lincoln. Letters from F. M. Robertson, Alexander H. Stephens, and others were used as evidence against him. Anderson applied to Lincoln for release. He was let out of prison on October 11, 1861, upon swearing an oath of allegiance to the United States. Anderson ultimately met an unhappy end after the war, when he committed suicide in Atlanta in December, 1874. He left a note that included a peculiar bequest to General Robert Toombs: He left to him, "My pistol with my recommendation that he rid the world of his presence by imitating my example." See *OR*, Series 2, 2:604-618; *New York Times*, September 24, 1861 and December 26, 1874, http://www.hwwilson.com/Print/Facts%20Pres%20Sample.pdf, accessed November 11, 2008.

20 Burton, *The Siege of Charleston*, 42-3, 50-1.

Early in the war, Union forces overran and occupied most of the remote coastal islands of South Carolina that were inhabited by civilians. They captured the harbor of Port Royal Sound near Beaufort by taking Hilton Head Island and Bay Point of Saint Phillips Island that guarded the mouth. Another of F. M. Robertson's sons, Henry Clay Robertson, was serving with the quartermaster's department at Beaufort and assisted in providing flatboats and transportation for the Confederates retreating inland from Fort Beauregard at Bay Point on November 7, 1861.[21] The Federals subsequently occupied Saint Helena Island and Edisto Island to the northeast of Port Royal Sound toward Charleston.[22] Confederate forces, however, successfully defended the barrier islands closer to that city, including James Island, Morris Island, and Sullivans Island. These positions were strategically important for protecting the city, which was a major port of entry for blockade runners bringing supplies and munitions from overseas sources. Union military forces on land and sea spent considerable effort throughout the war in trying to close the harbor and take possession of the city.

In early June of 1862, the Union forces launched a campaign to approach the city by land by sending troops ashore on the southern end of James Island, which borders the southern rim of Charleston harbor. The Confederate defensive strategy for that island had been devised by Brig. Gen. William Duncan Smith. He implemented a system of "Advanced Forces" and "Grand Guards," as mobile pickets and supporting units that allowed rapid mobilization of limited Southern manpower to wherever the point of attack might be. The attack turned out to be near a small village of summer houses called Secessionville, where the Confederates had built an artillery battery across a narrow neck of land bordered by low-lying salt marsh on two opposite sides.[23] The fortification had been strategically placed beyond the range of the Federal naval guns aboard boats that could freely ply the nearby Stono River to the west. Union forces under Brig. Gen. Henry Benham attacked before daybreak on June 16, 1862, launching frontal assaults on the battery and flanking maneuvers on the Confederate right. The Southerners repulsed both movements in bloody fighting, after which the Federals retreated, and finally

21 *OR*, 6:22-31.

22 Burton, *The Siege of Charleston*, 99-100.

23 The Federals called the battery the Tower Battery. After the battle, the Confederates re-named it Fort Lamar after the Confederate commanding officer Thomas G. Lamar. See Patrick Brennan, *Secessionville: Assault on Charleston* (Campbell, CA, Savas Publishing Company, 1996), 305-6.

abandoned James Island by July 7, 1862.[24] The port of Charleston was saved, for the moment.

One Confederate officer who participated in the fighting later called the little known engagement at Secessionville one of the decisive ones of the war.[25] Gen. William Duncan Smith's superiors credited his strategy that flanked the Federal left with making possible the Confederate victory there. General Smith later became commander of the 1st Military District of South Carolina. But, his promising military career was short-lived, as he contracted the dreaded yellow fever later that Fall and died at the house of his uncle, Dr. F. M. Robertson, in Charleston on October 4, 1862.[26]

The Union forces, still intent on taking Charleston, tried a different approach on July 11 and July 18, 1863, when they launched major attacks against the Confederate position at Battery Wagner on the foreshore of Morris Island seaward of James Island. This position guarded both the ship channel approaching the Charleston harbor and the southern land approach to Fort Sumter. The attacks were combinations of ground assaults by troops under Maj. Gen. Quincy A. Gillmore and naval bombardments by gunboats under Rear Adm. John A. Dahlgren. During the first engagement the Confederate Surgeon Christopher Happoldt was taken prisoner, and Surgeon F. M. Robertson took charge of the medical arrangements on Morris Island.[27]

Both attacks failed to take the earthen fort, and the Union commanders finally realized that they could not overcome it by frontal storm. Instead they adopted siege tactics, digging approaches and parallels to bring their land troops slowly closer to the fort under cover of the trenches. All the while, the artillery

24 Brennan, *Secessionville*, 172, 252, 291.

25 Brig. Gen. (then Col.) Johnson Hagood, commander of the 1st S.C. Artillery battalion. See Burton, *The Siege of Charleston*, 99.

26 Brennan, *Secessionville*, 303, 306, 312; Newspaper account of the "Death of Brig. General Wm. Duncan Smith," *Savannah Republican*, October, 1862, copied from *Charleston Courier*, n.d. Article includes a long review of General Smith's career, his accomplishments, and his funeral; William Duncan Smith was the son of F. M. Robertson's wife Henrietta's sister Katharine Fullerton Righton Smith (Mrs. William Smith).

27 On July 11, 1863, Medical Director R. L. Brodie requested Brigadier General Thomas Jordan, Chief of Staff, to assign Surgeon F. M. Robertson at once to Morris Island after Surgeon Happoldt had been taken prisoner there. On July 13, 1863, Robertson requisitioned two wall tents and one army tent from Quartermaster C. H. Suber to shelter the wounded at Battery Wagner. See *Compiled Service Records, Confederate General & Staff Officers* for F. M. Robertson, South Carolina Department of Archives and History, Columbia, S. C., Microfilm Roll # 214; Joseph Ioor Waring, M.D., *A History of Medicine in South Carolina, 1825-1900* (Columbia: The South Carolina Medical Association, 1967), 242.

Brig. Gen. William Duncan Smith
Collection of Thomas H. Robertson, Jr.

barrage continued from large land
cannons and naval guns offshore, and
by September 7, 1863, not a single
Confederate artillery piece could
answer the Union threat. General
Beauregard ordered the battery evacuated that night.

The assaults on Battery Wagner
were among the most terrific and fierce
of the entire war. The attackers
suffered a tremendous number of
casualties, while the siege resistance
force endured some of the heaviest artillery fire ever experienced in a small area.
The small garrison, about 1,000 men strong at any one time, held off a force of
11,000 soldiers and a fleet of gunboats and armored vessels for fifty-eight days
and nights.[28]

While the siege of Battery Wagner was going on, the Federal forces also
began a major effort to capture Fort Sumter. They initiated a bombardment on
August 17, 1863, and within a few days reduced the brick fort to a shapeless
ruined mass. The Union commander, General Gillmore, demanded that the
Confederates surrender Fort Sumter and Morris Island or he would bombard
the City of Charleston. General Beauregard refused. On August 22, 1863, the
Federals opened fire on the already-disabled fort from five naval monitors.
Private Henry Clay Robertson, Francis Marion Robertson's son, was serving in
the garrison and was wounded during the attack that day. The Federals silenced
all of Sumter's big guns; then, thinking that only a token Confederate garrison
remained, made an amphibious assault on the night of September 8-9, 1863.
The garrison was not just a token force, as the Federals were surprised to find
out, and all of the attackers were either killed or captured.[29]

During the bombardment of Fort Sumter and the siege of Battery Wagner,
the Union forces took the opportunity to occupy a position near Morris Island

28 Burton, *The Siege of Charleston*, 179-80.

29 Burton, *The Siege of Charleston*, 183-97; Roman, *General Beauregard*, 610; *Compiled Service Records*
for Henry C. Robertson.

from which to fire artillery barrages into the City of Charleston itself. Making good on General Gillmore's threat, the Union artillery began directing cannon fire into the city on August 22, 1863. Some thought a meteor had fallen when the first shell landed in a churchyard in the wee hours of the morning, just north of the city market near the intersection of Pinckney and Church Streets. Dr. Francis Marion Robertson lived less than a block away at No. 1 Maiden Lane, where he also had his medical office in the rear of the garden at 30 Pinckney Street. The first shot fell in the rear yard of the church directly opposite his house, and the next one fell in his yard. Soon it became apparent that the explosion was a shell from a newly-invented rifled cannon or Parrott gun that could fire accurately at ranges previously thought impossible, including from the islands surrounding the harbor into the city of Charleston.[30] Mrs. Robertson soon moved to Summerville, out of harm's way, but ultimately got homesick and returned to her home where she remained until the end of the war.[31]

The shell came from the Marsh Battery that the Federals had constructed on the soft marshland between Morris Island and James Island in July 1863. The battery consisted of a single gun emplacement that they called the "Swamp Angel." With an effective range of 8,140 yards, this eight-inch Parrott gun could easily hit targets within downtown Charleston. The eight-ton Swamp Angel did not last long, however, bursting on the thirty-sixth round. Charleston then enjoyed a few months of relief before a new Union rifle battery was established, after the fall of Battery Wagner, on Cummings Point at the north end of Morris Island, slightly closer to the city. The effective range of these rifles was about 4.7 miles, placing a large area of the town in jeopardy of being hit by artillery shells, even beyond the neighborhood of Francis Marion Robertson and his family.[32]

---

30 "Your grandparents [F. M. and Henrietta T. Robertson] went to Charleston to live about 1845. The last time I saw them was in 1867, at which time I was shown where the first shell from Gilmore's "Swamp Angel" fell in rear of the church and directly opposite your grandparents house, the next falling in their yard." Letter, W[illiam] R[obertson] Boggs to Miss Pamela Robertson, February 18, 1900, copy in possession of Thomas H. Robertson, Jr., 2010; *Census of the City of Charleston, South Carolina for the Year 1861*, Electronic Edition, http:// docsouth.unc.edu/imls/census/census.html, 135, 167, accessed December 15, 2008; W. Chris Phelps, *The Bombardment of Charleston 1863-1865* (Gretna, LA: Pelican Publishing Company, 2002), 26-7; Samuel Gaillard Stoney, *This is Charleston*, (Charleston: 1944), 70, with marginal notes by Lily Taylor Robertson written to Catherine Heard Robertson, April 26, 1971, copy in possession of Thomas Heard Robertson, Jr., 2008.

31 "Your grandmother moved then to Summerville, but got home sick and returned to her home, where she stood it out until the end." Letter, W[illiam] R[obertson] Boggs to Miss Pamela Robertson, February 18, 1900, copy in possession of Thomas H. Robertson, Jr., 2010

32 Phelps, *The Bombardment of Charleston*, 26-7.

F. M. Robertson Residence, No. 1 Maiden Lane (circa 1937).
Library of Congress

Those citizens who had relatives elsewhere or could afford to leave Charleston, like Mrs. Robertson, went as refugees to inland locations, remote from the front line of fire. The city had had a population of about sixty-five thousand people at the beginning of the war, dwindling to about ten thousand inhabitants after the evacuation.[33] Most of those who remained belonged to the poorer classes who could not afford to escape. Some citizens had left as early as 1862 when the Yankees had threatened to take nearby James Island at Seccessionville. But many, who had ignored General Beauregard's earlier warnings to leave and had remained in the city, were now anxious to flee once the bombing started, jamming the railroads as refugees.[34]

Charleston was the location of one of five boards of medical examiners for the Confederate States Army Medical Department. The department had been established in 1861 and was organized similar to that of the United States Army.

33 J. T. Trowbridge, *The South: A Tour of its Battle-fields and Ruined Cities* (Hartford, 1866), 516.

34 Phelps, *The Bombardment of Charleston*, 28-9.

There were three ranks of medical officers: a Surgeon General to have the rank of colonel, Surgeons to rank as army majors, and Assistant Surgeons to be equivalent to captains. Each regiment was assigned a surgeon and an assistant surgeon. In addition to regular surgeons, the army employed contract surgeons, also called acting assistant surgeons, who were private doctors used to assist in caring for the sick and wounded, primarily in hospitals. At the beginning of the war, pay for a surgeon ranged from $162 to $200 per month, depending upon his length of service, plus allowances for expenses such as fuel and quarters. An assistant surgeon was paid $110 to $150 per month with similar allowances.[35]

Dr. Samuel Preston Moore of South Carolina was appointed Surgeon General on July 30, 1861, having served in the United States army as a surgeon during the Mexican War and thereafter. He organized the Medical Department of the Confederate armies and directed its operations efficiently throughout the war. Moore was something of a perfectionist and a strict disciplinarian with a brusque manner. He demanded that subordinates strictly adhere to army regulations in their communications to his office, leading some to find him unapproachable. One medical officer wrote, "I have been to see the Surg. Genl. but once, & shall not go again unless I am compelled."[36]

Army regulations required that every medical officer report to the Surgeon General and to the Medical Director of his corps "the date when he arrives at a station, or when he leaves it, and his orders in the case, and at the end of each month, whenever not at his station, whether on service or on leave of absence; and when on leave of absence, his post-office address for the next month."[37] Surgeon Robertson was careful to follow these regulations during his travels after the evacuation of Charleston.

The uniform worn by medical officers consisted of a gray tunic with black facings and a stand-up collar decorated with a star, and dark blue trousers with a black velvet stripe down each leg, outlined by a gold cord on each edge of the

---

35 H. H. Cunningham, *Doctors in Gray: The Confederate Medical Service*, second edition, (Baton Rouge: Louisiana State University Press, 1983), 21-2; F. M. Robertson's normal pay was $162.00 per month, plus an allowance for quarters of four rooms in Charleston, and forage for one and sometimes two horses. See *Compiled Service Records* for F. M. Robertson, Microfilm Roll #214.

36 Waring, *A History of Medicine in South Carolina*, 269-70; Cunningham, *Doctors in Gray*, 27-31.

37 Confederate States of America, *War Dept. Regulations for the Medical Department of the C. S. Army*, Regulation Numbers 53 and 54. University of North Carolina, *Documenting the American South*, electronic edition of *Regulations for the Medical Department of the C. S. Army* (Richmond: Ritchie & Dunnavant, Printers, 1862), http://docsouth.unc.edu/imls/regulations/regulations.html, accessed October 20, 2003.

Surgeon Francis Marion Robertson
*Courtesy of Waring Historical Library, Medical
University of South Carolina*

stripe. A cap with the letters "M.S." embroidered in gold, a green silk net sash, white gloves, and Jefferson boots completed the specified mode of dress.[38]

The regulations also provided that boards of medical examiners of at least three surgeons be appointed by the Secretary of War "to examine applicants for appointment of assistant surgeons in the regular army, and assistant surgeons for promotion. And no one shall be so appointed or promoted until so examined and found qualified. The board will scrutinize rigidly the moral habits, professional acquirements, and physical qualifications of the candidates, and report favorably, either for appointment or promotion, in no case admitting of a reasonable doubt." Assistant surgeons were to be between 21 and 25 years of age, and were eligible to be examined for promotion to surgeon when they had served five years.[39]

The need for examining boards came about because a large number of medical personnel was needed to staff the large army, but there were few trained military doctors available at the beginning of the war. Initially, medical officers were appointed based on their own recommendations of themselves. This situation led to an unacceptable level of incompetence in the performance of medical duties, stemming both from a lack of knowledge and from carelessness and neglect. The army medical boards re-examined all those previously appointed and likewise screened all new applicants.[40]

---

38 Cunningham, *Doctors in Gray*, 23.

39 *C. S. Medical Department Regulations*, Regulations 67-71.

40 Cunningham, *Doctors in Gray*, 31-35.

By 1864 there were five army medical boards in the medical department, located in Richmond, Charleston, the Trans-Mississippi department, and with the respective headquarters of Gen. J. B. Hood and Gen. E. K. Smith.[41] The members of the Board of Medical Examiners at Charleston included Doctors Eli Geddings, John Edwards Holbrook, Robert Alexander Kinloch, Francis Turquand Miles, and Francis Marion Robertson. Geddings was the president of the board until he resigned on February 7, 1865, citing his advanced age. In fact, most of the doctors on the board were older than normal combat age. At the end of the war, Geddings was 65 and Holbrook was older still at 70. Robertson was 58 and served as the secretary or recorder of the board. Miles and Kinloch were younger at 37 and 38, respectively, and they had seen military action in their several assignments.[42] All of these men were associated in one way or another with the Medical College of South Carolina, which closed for the duration of the war when the entire faculty entered Confederate service.[43]

Francis Marion Robertson was born near Calhoun's Mill on Little River in Abbeville District of South Carolina on December 12, 1806, the son of William and Pamela Moseley Robertson. Both his mother's and father's families had been part of the wave of emigrants who came south from Virginia and other states to settle the available lands of upcountry South Carolina and backcountry Georgia just after the American Revolution. The Robertsons and Moseleys came down at about the same time, and young William and Pamela were wed on January 30, 1806. Francis Marion was the firstborn of a brood that numbered six boys and five girls. He was named for a famous person, Gen. Francis Marion, the "Swamp Fox" of the Revolution, although he was not related to him by blood. He would repeat this naming practice with his own children.[44]

---

41 The locations of these boards are as of the Fall of 1864 as reported in "Confederate States Medical and Surgical Journal" of September and October, 1864; Cunningham, *Doctors in Gray*, General Appendix, 284-86.

42 Waring, *A History of Medicine in South Carolina*, 128, 235-37, 243-45, 253, 267-8, 290-91; Francis Turquand Miles was Captain of the Calhoun Guards of the Charleston Battalion and was wounded at the Battle of Seccessionville. He saw further service at Fort Sumter. He resigned his command in January, 1864, and received a commission as a surgeon on the Board of Medical Examiners. See also W. Chris Phelps, *Charlestonians in War: The Charleston Battalion* (Gretna, LA: Pelican Publishing Company, 2004), passim; Cunningham, *Doctors in Gray*, General Appendix, 284-86.

43 All of the medical schools in the south except for Virginia closed down during the war. See Cunningham, *Doctors in Gray*, 35 and 36n.

44 Obituary of Francis Marion Robertson, M.D., "Transactions of the South Carolina Medical Association," 1893, 16-18, copy in files of Waring Historical Library, Medical University of South Carolina.

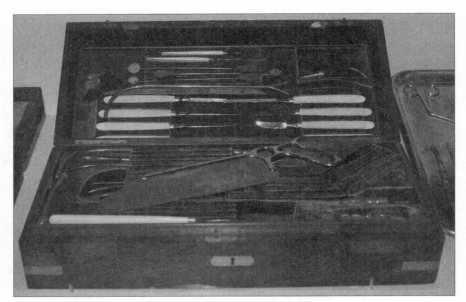

Surgical Instrument Kit of Dr. Henry Campbell
Used by permission, Robert B. Greenblatt, M.D., Library, Georgia Regents University, Augusta,
on loan to Augusta Museum of History, 2013.

Francis became exposed to military affairs from an early age. His grandfather John Robertson had been a lieutenant in the Virginia Continental Line during the Revolutionary War. His father served as the captain of a company in Lt. Col. William Austin's Regiment beginning in 1811. Drawn from drafted citizens of South Carolina, this militia unit was called to service at the very end of the War of 1812.[45]

Francis began his education at the feet of his father, who was a civil engineer and teacher. William Robertson made a "remarkabley correct" survey of the entirety of Abbeville District in 1817 for the map in *Mills' Atlas of South Carolina* that was published in 1825.[46] He also taught arithmetic, algebra, trigonometry, and surveying on the square at Abbeville.[47] Francis attended the

45 *Compiled Service Records*, Austin's Regiment S. C. Militia, 1812, for William Robertson, Jr., National Archives and Records Administration, Washington, D.C.

46 Robert Mills, *Atlas of the State of South Carolina*, 1825, reprint edition with an introduction by Gene Waddell (Easley, SC: Southern Historical Press, 1980), ii, vi.

47 John A. Chapman, *History of Edgefield County from the Earliest Settlements to 1897* (Newberry, SC: Elbert H. Aull, 1897), 244; Lowry Ware, *Old Abbeville: Scenes of the Past of a Town Where Old Time Things are not Forgotten* (Columbia, SC: ACMAR, 1992), 2, 8.

renowned school of the Reverend Moses Waddell, D.D. at Willington, which became well known for the many leaders that emerged among its graduates. In 1820, William Robertson and a group of leading Abbeville District citizens requested Secretary of War John C. Calhoun to appoint Francis to the United States Military Academy at West Point. William wrote, "at this time [Francis] is making great progress in Trigonometry, and in the course of this Winter, I shall be enabled to make him well acquainted with Algebra and Mathematics generally as far as conic sections. I am not apprised of the proper period at which he should enter the academy, but I presume that about two years hence would be time enough. . . ." Calhoun obliged by appointing his young neighbor to West Point in 1822.[48] Francis studied at the academy during the years 1822 through 1826, but did not graduate, resigning effective February 14, 1826.[49] His fellow students at West Point included the future United States commander of Fort Sumter, Robert Anderson, in the class ahead of him; future Confederate States generals Joseph E. Johnston and Robert E. Lee, three classes his junior; President Jefferson Davis, two years younger; and Gen. Leonidas Polk, one class behind.[50]

William Robertson's military and various professional endeavors caused the family to move several times. Sometime between 1822 and 1824, he had moved the family to Hamburg, South Carolina, where he was associated with Henry Shultz, who had founded the town in 1821 on the Savannah River opposite Augusta, Georgia. By 1826, he had settled across the river in Augusta. Robertson was associated with the South Carolina Canal and Rail Road Company, which built the railroad from Charleston to Hamburg. At 136 miles in length, it was the longest in the world at the time of its completion in 1833.[51]

48 William Robertson, Jr. to Hon. J. C. Calhoun, Sec War, Oct 17th 1820, with appended recommendation signed by "our mutual friends," 15 Abbeville District citizens, "U.S.M.A. Cadet Application Papers (1805 to 1866)," microfilm copy in West Point Library, original at National Archives and Record Service, Washington, D.C.; John C. Calhoun was a distant relative of young Francis, a half brother-in-law of the boy's grandmother Mary Ann Robertson Moseley.

49 Kenneth W. Rapp, Assistant Archivist, USMA Archives, to Catherine H. Robertson, November 28, 1977.

50 United States Military Academy, *Register of Graduates*, Classes of 1825, 1826, 1827, 1828, and 1829, including non-graduates.

51 "Family Record," manuscript of Marriages, Births, Deaths, from Constance S. Robertson Estate Papers in possession of Thomas H. Robertson, Jr. (2008). Cites the birth of Lewis Ford Robertson as being in Hamburg, S.C. on January 3, 1825; Francis Marion Robertson, "We are Passing Away," Upon the death of his Father, William Robertson (1786-1859) in *The Southern Presbyterian*, Charleston, S.C. July 23rd, 1859, typescript in possession of Thomas Heard

Francis Marion Robertson returned from West Point in 1826 to his family in their new home in Augusta, where he studied medicine under the training of Dr. Lewis DeSaussure Ford, his preceptor.[52] He continued his medical training at the Medical College of South Carolina at Charleston, completing his education with a thesis on remittent fever and graduating in 1830.[53] He immediately began to practice medicine in Augusta. The next year he married Henrietta Toomer Righton of Charleston.

Still interested in military matters, he joined a local militia company, the Richmond Blues, and was elected its captain. Under his leadership, this unit was one of the first to answer the call of duty in the winter of 1836 when President Andrew Jackson called for state troops to volunteer for service in fighting the Seminole Indians in Florida. Robertson led the Blues through three months of marches through central Florida with the army of Gen. Duncan L. Clinch, at one time serving as commanding officer of all the volunteer troops. The Adjutant General commended him for his service and for that of the Richmond Blues, writing, "I take this occasion to express to you the entire satisfaction of the Department with the very high testimonials of handsome service rendered by the very efficient company which you commanded, during the Seminole

---

Robertson, Jr. (2013). He states, "In 1826, while a resident of Augusta, Georgia, the deceased became a subject of Divine Grace . . ."; *Aiken Standard*, April 30, 1985, 3.

52 Dr. Lewis DeSaussure Ford (1801-1883). Only five years older than his student F. M. Robertson, Lewis D. Ford was fast becoming an eminent medical expert, particularly emphasizing epidemic diseases and fevers. Born in New Jersey and educated in the field of medicine in New York, Dr. Ford ultimately settled in Augusta. "It was a guiding principle of his life to do good, and daily as he taught the students he inculcated the lesson of unselfish devotion to duty on them. 'The virtue of benevolence,' he told them, 'lies at the foundation, while it forms the crowning glory of the medical character.'" He was one of the founders of the Medical College of Georgia (part of Georgia Regents University, 2013). [H]e "practiced his noble profession with a generous tenderness of heart that makes his name venerated throughout the city." He served on City Council of Augusta for a number of years, was elected mayor in 1846 and was reelected in 1847. During the war years, Dr. Ford was surgeon of the First Georgia Hospital in Richmond, Virginia. F. M. Robertson's brother Lewis Ford Robertson was named for the venerable physician. See Charles C. Jones, Jr. and Salem Dutcher, *Memorial History of Augusta, Georgia* (Syracuse, N. Y.: D. Mason & Co., Publishers, 1890; reprint edition, Spartanburg, S. C.: The Reprint Company, 1966), 275-6.

53 "An Inaugural Dissertation on Remittent Fever Submitted to the examination of the Dean and Professors of the Medical College of So. Ca. For the degree of Doctor of Medicine By Francis M. Robertson of Augusta Georgia 1830," copy in Waring Historical Library, Medical University of South Carolina.

campaign, as expressed by the Generals, and other brother officers with whom you have been associated in Florida."[54]

His wife, Henrietta, was not so happy about his military service. He had left her in a strange town with a two-week-old baby. He made peace with her by promising to "to resign my command and wipe my hands of military matters. This my dearest you may rest assured I will do."[55] He did not wait very long to break his vow, for soon after he resumed his medical practice, he served as an acting assistant surgeon at the United States Arsenal at Augusta. His position was a civilian one, where he, as a private medical doctor, acted under contract as a military assistant surgeon for a fee. As it turned out, Robertson's more serious promise breaking about wiping his hands of military matters would come later.[56]

F. M. Robertson was always interested in politics and became active in the Whig party. When Senator Henry Clay of Kentucky was running as the party's candidate for president, he visited Augusta and made a campaign speech in late March 1844. William T. Gould led him to the rostrum carrying a wooden, black and gold baton, and F. M. Robertson introduced him to the crowd gathered at the court house.[57]

In 1846, Dr. Robertson moved to Charleston with Henrietta and six children and established a successful medical practice in the larger coastal city. He lectured on medical subjects, primarily obstetrics, at the Charleston Summer

54 Brevet Brigadier General Roger Jones, Adjutant General, to Capt. F. M. Robertson, June 4, 1836. Original letter in collection of Augusta Richmond County Historical Society, Special Collections, Reese Library, Augusta State University. See Thomas Heard Robertson, Jr., "The Richmond Blues in the Second Seminole War: Letters of Captain Francis Marion Robertson, M.D.," in *Military Collector & Historian*, Volume 54, No. 2, Summer 2002. Original letters in Collection of Augusta Richmond County Historical Society, Special Collections, Reese Library, Georgia Regents University.

55 Francis Marion Robertson to Henrietta Toomer Righton Robertson, March 17, 1836. Ibid.

56 Letter: Benjamin King, Acting Surgeon General, to Doctor F. M. Robertson, Acting Asst. Surgeon, U. S. Arsenal, Augusta, Georgia, April 30, 1838, acknowledging receipt of semi-annual returns of public property and quarterly report of sick; email: Bill Wells of Georgia Regents University, Augusta, to Thomas H. Robertson, Jr., November 4, 2008.

57 Edward J. Cashin, *The Story of Augusta* (Augusta: Richmond County Board of Education, 1980), 93; Senator Henry Clay wrote to F. M. Robertson, March 10, 1844, from Shady Grove near Columbus, Georgia, outlining his proposed itinerary through Georgia, specifically to Augusta and beyond, referenced as having been printed in *Jonesborough Whig and Independent Journal*, (Jonesborough, Tennessee, March 27, 1844) in Melba Porter Hay and Carol Rearden, ed., *The Papers of Henry Clay: Volume 10, Candidate, Compromiser, Elder Statesman January 1, 1844-June 29, 1852*, Google Books edition (Lexington, KY: University of Kentucky Press, 1991), 3. Although this original newspaper is catalogued in the Library of the University of Tennessee, Knoxville, the search for it has been fruitless.

Advertisement for Michel's
Anatomical Rooms
Courtesy of Georgia Murphy Johnson

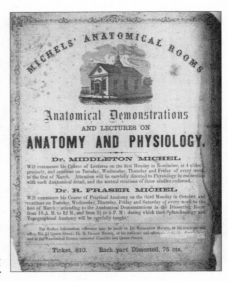

Medical Institute, which was a private school conducted by the brothers Middleton and Fraser Michel, M.D., from 1848 to 1861. They held classes for several months each year in Michel's Anatomical Rooms as a preparatory school for students intending to enter the public Medical College of South Carolina.[58]

Dr. Robertson was a pioneering researcher on the subject of chloroform and ether as anesthetic agents for surgery, and conducted the first instance of chloroform inhalation in South Carolina in an operation on a child in 1850. By the time of the Civil War, chloroform and ether were nearly universally used as surgical anesthetics, notwithstanding folklore about soldiers' biting bullets or getting drunk as they met the surgeon's knife.[59] Dr. J. Julian

58 Waring, *A History of Medicine in South Carolina*, 86-89, 265-6; Emmet B. Carmichael, "Richard Fraser Michel," in *Alabama Journal of Medical Science*, v. 2, no. 2, 1965, 223; Michel's Anatomical Rooms were located at 9 Franklin Street in 1861. See *Charleston Census, 1861*, 89. Middleton Michel, M.D., served during the war years as consulting surgeon at Manchester and Richmond, Virginia, and was an editor of the *Confedereate States Medical and Surgical Journal*, 1863-64. Fraser Michel, M.D., was a demonstrator at the Summer Medical Institute led by his brother. He entered Confederate service with the First South Carolina Artillery on Morris Island, and later served as a surgeon with the Army of Northern Virginia. See Waring, *A History of Medicine in South Carolina*, 265-7. Coincidentally, Middleton Michel and F. M. Robertson are both great-great-grandfathers of the author, Thomas H. Robertson, Jr., maternal and paternal, respectively.

59 F. M. Robertson to J. McK. Gage, M.D., October 15, 1850. *James McKibbin Gage Papers*, University of North Carolina at Chapel Hill, Southern Historical Collection, #1812-z, folder 3, scans 48-51; "The first instance of chloroform inhalation in the state, that we have any notice of, was for the performance of a lithotomy on a child 7 years old, in the presence of Drs. Fitch, Mood and Geddings in Charleston, May 15th, 1850, by Dr. F. M. Robertson. The calculus [a stone formed in the body] weighed one ounce and was four and seven-tenths inches in circumference." *Transactions of the South Carolina Medical Association*, 43rd Annual Session held in Sumter, South Carolina, April 19 & 20, 1893, 62, copy in Waring Historical Library, Medical College of South Carolina; Ira M. Rutkow, M.D., "Anesthesia during the Civil War," *Archives Of Surgery* (Chicago, 1960) [Arch/Surg] 1999 Jun; v. 134 (6), 680.

Chisholm, Robertson's colleague at the Medical College of South Carolina, believed chloroform to be "wonderful in mitigating the suffering of the wounded," and prescribed its administration when he edited *A Manual of Military Surgery for Use of Surgeons in the Confederate Army* in 1861.[60]

Robertson was a devout Christian, and the depth of his faith becomes obvious to the reader through the numerous religious references with which he punctuated his journal. His daily entries often appear on two levels: his accounts of the events of his sojourn, and his religious thoughts, prayers, and reflections. The practical narratives have an aristocratic, sometimes snobbish tone, while his religious passages leave no doubt of his complete faith in the power of the Almighty.

At the outbreak of the Civil War, Francis Marion Robertson served for a time with the 16th Regiment of South Carolina Militia as a surgeon and as captain of Reserve Company No. 4, comprised of old men from 45 to 60 years old and young boys, ages 16 to 18.[61] On February 5, 1862, he was appointed to the rank of Surgeon in the Confederate Medical Department to take effect from October 26, 1861, and was assigned to the Army Board of Medical Examiners on January 6, 1862. In addition to his duties as Recorder of the board, he served in 1862 as supervisor of the Surgical Department of Marine Hospital. The next July he saw field service at Battery Wagner, in charge of medical arrangements on Morris Island. The following September he received the additional duty of "consultation with medical officers in all important surgical operations."[62]

Complementing his own army service, Dr. Robertson also had five sons in various parts of the Confederate army, ranging in age from 19 to 31 years old at the time his diary narrative begins in early 1865, plus a sixth soldier whom he included in describing his "domestic circle."[63]

---

60 J. T. H. Connor, "Chloroform and the Civil War," http://findarticles.com/p/articles_qu 3912/is_200202/ai_n9408156/print?tag_artBody:col1, accessed November 24, 2008; J. J. Chisholm, *A Manual of Military Surgery for Use of Surgeons in the Confederate Army* (Richmond, Va.: West & Johnston, 1861), 380-1; Alfred Jay Bollett, M.D., *Civil War Medicine: Challenges and Triumphs*, (Tuscon, AZ, 2002), 76-83.

61 "Sixteenth (16th) Regiment South Carolina Militia Charleston District, 4th Brigade 2d Division," n. d., http://www.geocities.com/screbels_1864/SM1660.html, accessed October 23, 2003.

62 *Compiled Service Records*, for F. M. Robertson, 1 Regt. S. C. Militia, South Carolina Department of Archives and History, Columbia, S. C., NARS Microcopy #267, Microfilm Roll # 146; *Compiled Service Records* for F. M. Robertson, Confederate Medical Department, NARS Microcopy # 331, Roll # 214.

63 "Diary of Surgeon Francis Marion Robertson," February 19, 1865.

William Francis Robertson, M.D., 31, performed medical duty in hospitals and in the field during the war, initially as an assistant surgeon in the 6th Regiment South Carolina Infantry in 1861 and later as a surgeon in Stark's Battalion of light artillery in the Army of Northern Virginia. By 1864 he was serving with a company stationed on Johns Island, South Carolina.[64]

Joseph Righton Robertson, 29, began his Confederate service in April, 1862, with the 1st Battalion of South Carolina Infantry, called the Charleston Battalion, where he served as 2nd Corporal of Company D, under Captain Francis Turquand Miles. He was almost immediately detached by order of Brigadier General Pemberton. By early 1864, he had reached the rank of major and served as Commissary of Subsistence, providing foodstuffs for the army units stationed on Sullivan's Island.[65]

Henry Clay Robertson, 23, was named after the presidential candidate whom his father had introduced in Augusta in 1844. He was a young mechanic when he and John Toumey provided transportation for the Confederate troops withdrawing from Port Royal Sound at Beaufort on November 7 and 8, 1861. He had recently enlisted in Capt. J. Gadsen King's Company, 1st Battalion South Carolina Artillery, on September 6, 1861. Early the next year, this unit became Company F of the 1st Regiment of South Carolina Artillery, stationed primarily at Fort Sumter. Pvt. Robertson was wounded on August 22, 1863, during the sixth day of the first major Union bombardment of the fort. He spent six months on the sick list and was discharged from service on February 2, 1864, due to the dislocation of his upper femur joint. On September 27, 1863, while on sick furlough, Henry managed to be married to Mary Elizabeth Mikell in Aiken, where her family was living as refugees from Edisto Island.[66]

James Lawrence Robertson, age 21, was named after Capt. James Lawrence, famous for his dying order while commanding the USS *Chesapeake* in the War of 1812: "Don't give up the ship!" Jimmie, as he was sometimes called,

64 Waring, *A History of Medicine in South Carolina*, 291; *Compiled Service Records* for William F. Robertson; Letter: John Meyer Miller to Margaret Smith Miller, December 4, 1864, in Thomas Heard Robertson, Jr., *Miller Family Letters 1837 to 1894*, second edition, privately published, June, 1994, copy in Reese Library, Georgia Regents University, Augusta.

65 *Compiled Service Records* for J. R. Robertson; *OR*, v. 28, pt. 2, 231, v. 35, pt. 1, 129-33, 506-8, 520-2.

66 Roman, *General Beauregard*, v. 2, 610; Henry's work at Beaufort was under the Quartermaster's Office, Provisional Forces of the Third Military District, commanded by Maj. Edward Willis. His connection with Major Willis would continue in the latter days of the war and afterward. *OR*, 6:29-30; *Compiled Service Records* for Henry C. Robertson; genealogical typescript titled "Family Register, Lyman Hall Robertson and Constance Truxton Robertson," n. d., in possession of Ethel Robertson Boyle, Conyers, Georgia, 2004.

Pvt. James L. Robertson, October 1862.
Courtesy of Isabelle Robertson Maxwell

had been a student at the College of Charleston before the war. In January, 1861, at the age of 17, he volunteered with the South Carolina militia company Vigilant Rifles of Charleston under Capt. Samuel Y. Tupper. He served with that unit on Morris Island supporting the battery of Citadel cadets at the shelling of the *Star of the West*, the first shots in the prelude to war. He enlisted in Capt. E. L. Parker's Company of South Carolina Light Artillery, known as Marion Light Artillery, on April 28, 1862, serving as a private and then a corporal throughout most of the war. In October 1863, he applied to Secretary of War James A. Seddon for an appointment as a second lieutenant in the 1st South Carolina Regular Infantry, or with any other unit that had a vacancy. Although his appointment was ordered November 28, 1863, and in spite of strong endorsements from Generals Johnson Hagood, J. F. Gilmer, and P. G. T. Beauregard, and from Congressman William Porcher Miles, his application languished for over a year for lack of an available position. He was finally appointed Second Lieutenant of the 1st South Carolina Regular Artillery on November 4, 1864, taking the oath of office on February 1, 1865, just in time to participate in the final campaign of the war at his new rank and assignment in Company I.[67]

The youngest son, Duncan Clinch Robertson, was a new recruit in December 1864, at age 19. Like two of his older brothers, he got his name from a famous figure, in this case Gen. Duncan L. Clinch, his father's former commanding general in the Second Seminole War in Florida. Duncan enlisted

---

67 *Compiled Service Records* for James L. Robertson, including letter F. M Robertson to Congressman W. Porcher Miles, January 26, 1864; Photograph of Robertson taken in Artillery uniform by Pelot & Cole, Portraits, 628 Broad Street, Augusta, Ga., inscribed on reverse "Jan. 1865 James L. Robertson 2nd Lieut. Co. I 1st S.C. Regular Artillery, C.S.A.," in possession of Isabelle Robertson Maxwell, 2015; Margaret Wallace Robertson Moore, Application for membership in the United Daughters of the Confederacy, notarized June 29, 1936, transcript by Joseph Righton Robertson, Jr., Ph.D., 1991; Catherine Heard Robertson, "Corrected Line of William Robertson 1705-1774 to 1969," genealogical manuscript (with annotations by Thomas Heard Robertson), original in possession of Thomas H. Robertson, Jr., 2013.

as a private in Capt. J. B. L. Walpole's Company of Stono Scouts, South Carolina Cavalry, which would soon become part of Gen. Wade Hampton's cavalry command in the final campaign.[68]

The sixth soldier in the Robertson household is known to the reader of the diary only as "Joe, almost left alone and helpless without a friend."[69] Why might he have been described in that way? Was Joe an orphan? When Surgeon Robertson wrote to Congressman William Porcher Miles in January 1864, to request his political help to push forward the appointment of his son James as a second lieutenant he added a postscript to his letter: "I have five sons in the army, and a sixth who, unless the war terminates sooner than I expect, will also shoulder his musket in our glorious cause."[70] His son Duncan must have been the sixth, because he had not yet enlisted in the Stono Scouts and would not until the following December. Therefore, Joe must have been older than Duncan, or more than 18 years of age. And, considering that Dr. Robertson already had a 29-year-old son named Joseph Righton Robertson, then, "Who is Joe?" The search for further identification of Joe has been fruitless.

Besides the soldier sons, Robertson's family members included his wife Henrietta and daughter Marion Robertson Silliman. Henrietta is reported as having stood it out in Charleston after the bombardment began, but the family must have been living at least intermittently in Summerville, about twenty miles north of the city. Son Henry Robertson spent the Fall of 1863 in General Hospital No. 1 in Summerville, recuperating from the wound he had received at Fort Sumter, and his first child was born in that town in 1864.[71] Jimmie Robertson applied for leave to go there in 1864.[72]

---

68 *Compiled Service Records* for Duncan C. Robertson; genealogical typescript titled "Family of the Grandparents of Lyman Hall Robertson ...," n. d. in possession of Ethel Robertson Boyle, Conyers, Georgia 2004.

69 "Diary of Surgeon Francis Marion Robertson," February19, 1865.

70 F. M Robertson to Congressman W. Porcher Miles, January 26, 1864, in *Compiled Service Records* for James L. Robertson.

71 *Compiled Service Records* for Henry C. Robertson. The son was Francis Marion Robertson [II], b. October 27, 1864. See Yates Snowden, Henry Gardner Cutter, *History of South Carolina* (Lewis Publishing Company, 1920), 4:244.

72 Writing to Capt. E. L. Parker from Church Flats on January 3, 1864, James L. Robertson requested "leave of absence to visit Summerville, S.C. on business of importance." See *Compiled Service Records* for James L. Robertson. Further indication that the family was living outside of Charleston is the fact that Surgeon F. M. Robertson was paid by the Confederate Quartermaster for quarters in the city consisting of four rooms, fuel, and fodder for one or two horses during 1862 and 1863. See *Compiled Service Records* for F. M. Robertson.

Dr. Robertson also wrote in his diary of a third female in his "domestic circle"—"darling Annie."[73] Like the elusive Joe, Annie has also not been found in the Robertson family tree. Annie might have been the female identified in the 1870 Census as A. M. Wilson, age 16, who was residing with the Robertsons at that time. Miss Wilson would, therefore, have been born about 1854, approximately the same time when teen-age daughter Marion wrote to her temporarily absent mother Henrietta, ". . . Father took them [the children] and the babie over to the island this evening. the babbie rode from the boat in the buggy with Father and he brought her in the house fast asleep. . . ."[74] Could this "babbie" have been Annie? And, was she an orphan? Because Dr. Robertson specialized in obstetrics and diseases of women and children, he would have been in the right place to take in an infant in need. In spite of these tantalizing clues, further identification of Annie has not been successful.

The family circle also included at least one slave, Henry Suttliff (or Sutcliff), about 24 years old. He accompanied Surgeon Robertson as his personal servant on his war-end journey after the evacuation of Charleston.[75]

In early February 1865, Gen. P. G. T. Beauregard had been urging Gen. William J. Hardee, commanding the forces at Charleston, to make haste with the withdrawal from the city, so that he could safely remove his troops and avoid having his command cut off by Sherman's army. The initial plan was to make a stand against Sherman at Columbia. On February 2, 1865, General Beauregard convened a council of war with generals D. H. Hill, G. W. Smith, and W. J. Hardee at Green's Cut Station, Georgia, on the Savannah and Augusta Railroad near Briar Creek, where they decided on the strategy.[76] On February

---

73 "Diary of Surgeon Francis Marion Robertson," February 19, 1865.

74 Marion Robertson to Henrietta Robertson, n. d. circa 1855, in Constance S. Robertson Estate Papers in possession of Thomas H. Robertson, Jr., 2013.

75 The exact spelling of Henry's surname is obscure in the original diary, appearing to be "Suttliff" or "Scotliff." Most likely it should be "Sutcliff," as he appears in the *1870 U.S. Census*. It is unusual for a slave to have had both a given name and a published surname. It is possible that Henry was not a slave at all, but a free black man. His 1865 employer, F. M. Robertson, is not listed as a slave-holder in Charleston in the *1860 U.S. Census*. Nevertheless, it seems likely that Henry is a slave, as he does not appear in the *1860 U.S. Census*, nor the *1861 City of Charleston Census* as a "free person of color" head of household. Moreover, the latter shows no free colored residents on Dr. Robertson's street (if Henry actually lived there). The summary entry for Maiden Lane shows a total of 20 white persons and 16 slaves, living in the 3 houses on that street. According to the *1870 U.S. Census*, Henry Sutcliff was a native South Carolinian, and was 30 years old in July, 1870; therefore, he was born about 1840.

76 Roman, *Beauregard*, 337-39; Green's Cut Station is located about 26 miles south of Augusta, Georgia. See Swayze, *Hill & Swayze's Confederate States Rail-Road & Steam-Boat Guide*, 58.

11, 1865, he directed General Hardee to begin executing the plan agreed upon at the Green's Cut conference, and on February 14, 1865, Beauregard issued a memorandum to the Charleston commander detailing the different evacuation routes for the various detached units defending the city. By this time, though, Hardee had become very ill, possibly with typhoid fever it was feared, and valuable time was lost in getting him to begin the withdrawal. Maj. Gen. Lafayette McLaws hastened to Charleston to take command and personally supervised the evacuation on the night of February 17-18, 1865.[77]

The Confederate army at Charleston consisted of only approximately 13,000 men, including many artillery soldiers whose combat experience was mostly manning batteries of big shore guns. Many of these soldiers were converted to infantry service for the campaign that followed the withdrawal from Charleston. For General Hardee, the immediate objective was now to get ahead of Sherman in upper South Carolina. This effort would turn out to be a race for the bridge over the Great Pee Dee River at Cheraw.[78]

As the Confederate commanders still debated their strategy of evacuation, Surgeon Francis Marion Robertson set out on a journey that would last for three months and would lead him over more than nine hundred miles through four states. The reader now joins Dr. Robertson on Saturday, February 11, 1865, as he prepares to leave Charleston and then departs by rail on the day before the general evacuation by the army.

---

77 Burton, *The Siege of Charleston*, 317-8; Phelps, *The Bombardment of Charleston*, 131-3; *OR*, v. 47, pt. 2, 1179-80; Roman, *General Beauregard*, 2:341-50, 639.

78 Nelson, *Sherman's March*, 4-5; Joseph E. Johnston, General, C.S.A., *Narrative of Military Operations Directed during the Late War between the States* (New York: D. Appleton and Company, 1874), Appendix: W. J. Hardee, "Memoranda of the Operations of my Corps, while under the command of General J. E. Johnston in the Dalton and Atlanta, and North Carolina Campaigns," 582.

Chapter One

Charleston and Cheraw

"I am now satisfied that Sherman is pushing for Lee's rear. . ."

The movements of Sherman in the direction of Columbia rendered the evacuation of Charleston a military necessity. If he intended to cut the communications with Charleston, by the different Rail Roads, we were shut up in Charleston, cut off from all supplies, and the loss of the army would be inevitable. Hence, in this event, the evacuation was necessary; and its prompt execution became a matter of great importance. If on the contrary, it was Sherman's design to push on to Columbia, destroy every thing there and make a rapid march upon Genl Lee's rear, and cut his communications by Rail Road, the evacuation was still more important, in order to combine and concentrate our forces to give him battle, and check his further progress. The evacuation having been determined on, our Board was ordered to Columbia. Events were hurried so rapidly upon one another, that I was compelled to go to Cheraw, and then await the movements of Genl Hardees army.[1]

---

1 Maj. Gen. William Tecumseh Sherman was the Union commander in Georgia and South Carolina. Gen. Robert Edward Lee was the Confederate commander of the Army of Northern Virginia. Surgeon F. M. Robertson was a member of the Army Medical Board to examine applicants for appointment as assistant surgeons in the regular army. The board was constituted to convene at Charleston, January 6, 1862, by Special Order No. 4, Adjutant & Inspector General's Office, Richmond. See *Compiled Service Records*, Confed. Gen. & Staff officers, for F. M. Robertson, Microfilm Roll # 214, S. C. Department of Archives and History, Columbia, SC. Lt. Gen. William J. Hardee was the commander of the Confederate forces at Charleston. Listed as W. J. Hardee, Hardee's Corps Lt. Gen. in Janet B. Hewett, ed., *The Roster of Confederate Soldiers 1861-1865*, 16 vols., (Wilmington, NC, 1995).

[**Saturday, February 11, 1865**]—I left Summerville, with my family, for Charleston on Saturday the 11th Feby 1865; and left Charleston with my servant Henry Suttliff on Thursday the 16th and reached Florence at 9 o'clock that night.[2] Finding it impossible to get to Columbia, I remained at Florence until Friday the 17th and telegraphed Genl Hardee and communicated with the Surgeon General by mail.[3] Genl Hardee replied, and ordered me to remain in Florence or go to Cheraw. I left for Cheraw the same evening and arrived there on Saturday the 18th at 4 o'clock A.M. got a bed at the Hotel and rested comfortably until breakfast.[4] Met a number of friends and some of the citizens with whom I had been previously acquainted, and made other pleasant acquaintances—Mr. H. H. Williams of Charleston,[5] was very kind to me. In the course of the morning I met my friend Chancellor John A. Inglis,[6] who insisted on my going to his residence, about a mile and a half from the town, and making

2   Henry Sutcliff, either a slave or a free black man, about 25 years old. Dr. Robertson travelled via the North-Eastern Rail Road, from Charleston to Florence, where it connected with the Cheraw & Darlington Rail Road and Wilmington & Manchester Rail Road. See J. C. Swayze, *Hill & Swayze's Confederate States Rail-Road & Steam-Boat Guide*, 61.

3   Samuel Preston Moore, Surgeon General of the Confederate Army. Joseph Ioor Waring, M.D., *A History of Medicine in South Carolina, 1825-1900* (Columbia, SC, 1967), 269. Listed as Samuel P. Moore, Gen. & Staff Gen. in Hewett, *Confederate Soldiers*. Surgeon General Moore required subordinates to adhere strictly to Army regulations which required each medical officer to report "the date when he arrives at a station, or when he leaves it, and his orders in the case . . . ." See Confederate States of America, *War Dept. Regulations for the Medical Department of the C. S. Army*, Regulation Numbers 53 and 54, in University of North Carolina, *Documenting the American South*, electronic edition of Regulations for the Medical Department of the C. S. Army, (Richmond, 1862), http://docsouth.unc.edu/imls/regulations/regulations.html, accessed October 20, 2003.

4   Cheraw is at the northern end of the Cheraw and Darlington Rail Road line. See Swayze, *Confederate States Rail-Road & Steam-Boat Guide*, 16.

5   Mr. and Mrs. Henry H. Williams. They were in Cheraw as ". . . refugees from Charleston." They had apparently been in Cheraw for some time, because their daughter Nannie B. had been married to Samuel R. Brown there on June 9, 1863, and their son Gilbert Williams had been confirmed June 14, 1863, at St. David's Church in the town. See letter: Sarah C. Spruill to Thomas H. Robertson, October 21, 2003; Brent Holcomb, ed., *St. David's Parish, South Carolina, Minutes of the Vestry 1768-1832 Parish Register 1819-1924* (Easley, SC). In Charleston, the Williamses had lived at No. 1 Liberty Street. See Census of the City of Charleston, South Carolina for the Year 1861, electronic edition, http://docsouth.unc.edu/imls/census/census.html, 129, accessed December 15, 2008.

6   John Auchincloss Inglis (1813-1878), one of four chancellors of the Court of Equity in South Carolina. The title Chancellor is the equivalent of Judge. In 1860, Inglis had served as a delegate from Chesterfield County to the secession convention of South Carolina, where he was chairman of the Resolutions Committee and presented the Ordinance of Secession that was adopted December 20, 1860.

it my home until I received orders from the War Department.[7] In the evening I found myself comfortably seated by a good fire, with the Chancellor, his wife and daughter—his two sons being absent—one in the Army and the other in the Navy.[8] His residence is very pleasantly situated near the town. I have a delightful room, all to myself, and have access to a fine miscellaneous library, which is in the house.[9] Mrs. Inglis is a quite amiable lady—"going about doing good" among our soldiers—deeply interested in our cause, and devoted to her household matters. Her daughter is a sweet amiable girl—not grown. She is going to school in the Town. Altogether, I could not have fallen into better hands; for I am as comfortable as I could be, separated as I am from my darling wife and children, and without the means of receiving any intelligence from them. May the Lord take care of them.

February 11, 1865—Battle of Aiken, South Carolina. Confederate forces stopped the Federal advance toward Graniteville, South Carolina and Augusta, Georgia.[10]

7   The Inglis family's plantation home, called "The Woodlands." The house was burned by Sherman's troops a few days later. The Inglis residence in the Town of Cheraw, located at 226 Third Street, was spared. See Cheraw Visitors Bureau, *Guide to Cheraw Historic District*, Site 31, and Exhibits in Cheraw Lyceum Museum. **Route: The site of the house is on Old Society Hill Road approximately at the intersection of Chesterfield Highway and Society Hill Road (South Carolina Highway 9 and Road 152).**

8   His wife was Laura Prince Inglis and his daughter, Miss Laura Prince Inglis, 16 years old. For detailed accounts of the Inglis and Prince families in Cheraw, see "Memoirs of Laura Prince Inglis (unmarried)," "Reminiscences or Remnants of Recollection, Written by Charles. L. Prince, Son of William L.T. and Mary P. Prince, Cheraw, S.C. Baltimore Md., Sept. 26th, 1931," and "Memories of Miss Laura Inglis, by Thomasine McCown Haynes," in Adeline Godfrey Pringle Merrill, ed., *All in One Southern Family, Volume II: Life in Cheraw* (Charleston, 1996), 6-14. His son Lawrence Charles (Charlie) Inglis was in the Army, and son John Henry Inglis was a midshipman in the Confederate Navy. See Register of Officers of the Confederate States Navy 1861-1865, Historical Data Systems, comp., *U. S. Civil War Soldier Records and Profiles*, [database on-line] (Provo, UT, USA: Ancestry.com Operations, Inc., 2009), accessed November 26, 2012, and National Park Service, *U. S. Civil War Soldiers, 1861-1865*, [database on-line], (Provo, UT, USA: Ancestry.com Operations, Inc., 2007), accessed November 26, 2012.

9   The library had over 4,000 volumes. See Merrill, *Life in Cheraw*, 7.

10 Mark Swanson, *Atlas of the Civil War, Month by Month, Major Battles and Troop Movements*, (Athens & London, 2004), 106.

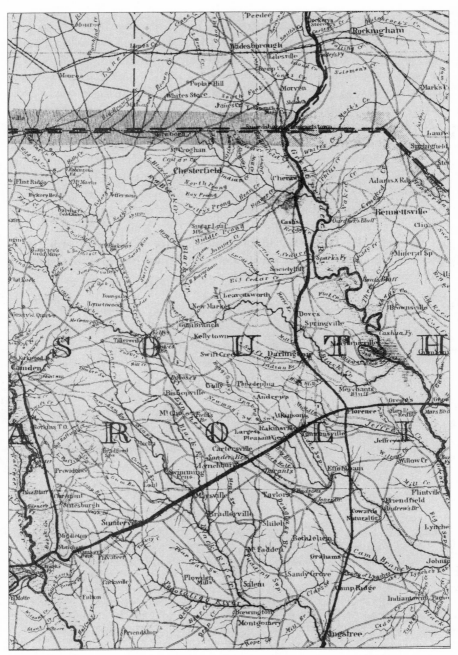

Florence to Cheraw, S.C., and Rockingham, N.C. Detail from U.S. Coast Survey, 1865.
State Department of Archives and History, Raleigh, N.C.

Henrietta Marion Robertson Silliman
Collection of Thomas H. Robertson, Jr.

February 15, 1865—General Sherman's army arrived at the west bank of the Congaree River opposite Columbia, South Carolina. After two days of bombardment, the city fell and was burned that night.[11]

Sunday the 19th—Went to the Presbyterian Church with the family, and heard a good practical sermon from the Rev. Mr. Corbett.[12] I did not go in this afternoon, but spent the remainder of the day in reading and meditation. I walked alone in the woods towards sundown. It was a mild, clear and beautiful evening. All was calm and serene around me. The laws of nature seemed to be in harmonious action—no jarring—no discord—all proclaimed the perfection and magisty of the laws which the Divine Omnipotent had impressed upon the physical world. How great the contrast on turning to that moral world, in which man stands preeminent, among God's creatures for good or for evil. What sin—what wickedness—what discord—what a conflict of the baser passions—what strife—what bloodshed—Oh that the wickedness of the wicked would come to an end! It was during this solitary walk that I felt the full force of the sudden and rude shock which had, in a moment, severed all my domestic ties and driven me as a wanderer and refugee from my home and all its comforts, and those earthly endearments, which approximate the domestic circle, on earth, to that Heavenly inheritance which the blessed Redeemer has promised to His followers. When I thought of my afflicted wife,[13] broken in spirits and bodily

11 Swanson, *Atlas of the Civil War*, 106.

12 The Reverend William B. Corbett, Minister of the [First] Presbyterian Church of Cheraw 1859-1869. Program for "First Presbyterian Church, Cheraw, South Carolina, 175th Anniversary Service, September 21, 2003."

13 Henrietta Toomer Righton Robertson (1805-1873).

health; of my dearest Marion[14] and darling Annie,[15] left in the power of a relentless enemy, with no means of ascertaining their condition—when I thought of my dear boys—one in the hands of the enemy,[16] the others in different parts of our Army—of my young and tender Duncan,[17] with the physical frame of a mere child; of Joe[18] almost left alone and helpless without a friend, of Righton[19] and Henry[20] separated from their dear families—of

14 Dr. Robertson's "dearest Marion" is his daughter Henrietta Marion Robertson Silliman (November 18, 1839–July 18, 1865).

15 "Annie" is perhaps A. M. Wilson (b. ca. 1854), who was living with the Robertson household in 1870, according to the U. S. Census. Annie has not been further identified.

16 This "boy" is probably Surgeon William Francis Robertson, M.D. (1834-1875), age 31, named after F.M.'s father and himself. He had most recently been serving with a unit on Johns Island. See John Meyer Miller to Margaret Smith Miller, December 4, 1864, in Thomas Heard Robertson, Jr., *Miller Family Letters 1837 to 1894*, second edition, privately published, June, 1994, copy in Reese Library, Georgia Regents University, Augusta. Listed as W. F. Robertson Conf. Lt. Arty. Stark's Bn. Surg., W. F. Robertson Gen. & Staff Asst. Surg., William F. Robertson SC 6th Inf. Asst. Surg., William F. Robertson Gen. & Staff Surg. in Hewett, *Confederate Soldiers*.

17 Pvt. Duncan Clinch Robertson (1845-1898), age 19, in Captain J. B. L. Walpole's Company of Stono Scouts, South Carolina Cavalry, part of General Wade Hampton's cavalry command. He was named after Brig. Gen. Duncan Lamont Clinch (1784-1849), Capt. F. M. Robertson's commander when Robertson led the Richmond Blues, a volunteer company of Augusta, to Florida in the Second Seminole War, 1836. For further information, see Thomas H. Robertson, "The Richmond Blues in the Second Seminole War: Letters of Captain Francis Marion Robertson, M.D.," *Military Collector & Historian*, Vol. 54, No. 2, Summer 2002, 50-63; and unabridged edition of the same article, manuscript in collections of Reese Library, Georgia Regents University, Augusta. Listed as Duncan Robertson SC Lt. Arty. Garden's Co. (Palmetto Lt. Btty.), Duncan C. Robertson SC Cav. Walpole's Co. in Hewett, *Confederate Soldiers*.

18 "Joe" is a member of F. M. Robertson's "domestic circle," but has not been further identified.

19 Maj. Joseph Righton Robertson (1836-1916), age 29, staff officer serving as Commissary of Subsistence. He was named after F. M. Robertson's father-in-law. Listed as J. R. Robertson Gen. & Staff Maj. CS, J. R. Robertson, Anderson's Div. Maj. CS, J. R. Robertson, Gen. & Staff in Hewett, *Confederate Soldiers*. Major Robertson lived in Charleston at 5 Glebe Street, which was owned by the Corporation of Saint Philip's Church. See *Charleston Census*, 1861, 91.

20 Pvt. Henry Clay Robertson (1841-1892), age 23. Henry was medically discharged from the army after having been wounded at Fort Sumter, August, 1863. He was named after Senator Henry Clay of Kentucky, Whig Party candidate for President of the United States in 1844, whom F. M. Robertson introduced on his campaign visit to Augusta, Georgia in March 1844. He was probably serving in or with 7th South Carolina Reserves in this campaign, or perhaps 15th South Carolina Infantry (Regulars); listed as Henry Robertson SC 5th St. Troops Co. G, Henry Robertson SC 7th Res. Co. C, Henry Robertson SC 15th Inf. Co. K, Henry C. Robertson SC 1st Arty. Co. F, in Hewett, *Confederate Soldiers*.

2nd Lt. Jas. L. Robertson, Augusta, Georgia in the uniform of an artillery officer. Photo dated at Augusta, Georgia January, 1865.
Courtesy of Isabelle Robertson Maxwell

Jimmy,[21] in a command which would be made to bear the brunt of battle in case of an engagement—my soul was shaken with anguish, and I wept as for a departed first born. Amid this solitude, where no ear could hear and no eye could see, but the omnipotent and omnipresent God, I poured out my soul in earnest prayer to that God Redeemer who is ever gracious to the repentant and contrite sinner. He, and He, alone, knows when, if ever, upon earth these broken ties are to be reunited. Let us abide His time and bow to His dispensations and chastenings. If they are not to be reunited here, may He grant each one of us a reunion in that world of peace and blessedness, where there is no more war—no strife—no tears and anguish, but perfect happiness, and fullness of joy in Christ Jesus our Lord.

Monday, the 20th passed off with the usual wild rumors about the movements of the enemy and our own troops. It is certain that Charleston has been entirely evacuated, and that Sherman has passed through Columbia—not a word of positive information can be obtained. The indications are that our troops will pass this place as rapidly as possible, for Charlotte, N. C., to unite with Genl Beauregard.[22]

---

21 2nd Lt. James Lawrence Robertson (1843-1922), age 21, 2nd Lt. in company "I" of 1st South Carolina Regular Artillery. James was named after United States naval hero Capt. James Lawrence (1781-1813), famous for the order that he gave in the naval engagement off the coast of Boston during the War of 1812 from which came the slogan, "Don't Give Up the Ship." James L. Robertson is the great-grandfather of Thomas Heard Robertson, Jr. Listed as James L. Robertson SC Lt. Arty. Parker's Co. (Marion Arty.) Cpl., James Robertson SC 19th Inf. Co. C, J. L. Robertson SC 1st Arty. 2nd Lt., J. L. Robertson SC Mil. Arty. 1st Regt. Parker's Co. in Hewett, *Confederate Soldiers.*

22 Brig. Gen. Pierre Gustav Toutant Beauregard. See Mark L. Bradley, *Last Stand in the Carolinas: The Battle of Bentonville* (Campbell, CA, 1996), 21. Listed as G. T. Beauregard Gen & Staff Gen in Hewett, *Confederate Soldiers.*

From the developments since I left Charleston, I am satisfied it would have been better to have evacuated Charleston soon after the fall of Savannah if not before. If reinforcements had been sent from Virginia in time, the evacuation might have been avoided. Without these reinforcements, the evacuation became a positive necessity; and if it had been done sooner, Sherman might have been defeated and driven back to Savannah or Port Royal, before reaching the So. Ca. Rail Road. There is a want of decision of character and prompt action, some where. In every critical juncture, we hesitate too long, and act too slo[w]ly after the step has been decided upon. May God overrule our blunders and mistakes for His glory and our good.

Tuesday 21st—No positive information from Charleston or Columbia. I mean as to the particulars after the evacuation of those two cities. I went over to Bennettsville with Mr. Townsend and Miss Joze, to see Jane.[23] We had a pleasant ride of fourteen miles. I found her well and very comfortably fixed. She had been in utter ignorance as to matters in Charleston, and was very much excited when she met me. I placed her in full possession of all the information about the family. It seemed to relieve her very much, though she was deeply afflicted at our seperation and dispersion. I spent the afternoon with her, and then took tea at Mr. Townsend's, and remained at his house that night. I spent the morning of the 22nd with Jane, and left at half past ten o'clock for Cheraw, when I arrived in time to take dinner with Mr. Williams, and return to the Chancellors to tea.

February 22, 1865—General Robert E. Lee (with President Jefferson Davis's approval) appointed General Joseph E. Johnston as Commander of the Department of South Carolina, Georgia, and Florida, replacing

---

23 Jane is Jane Righton Yates, F. M. Robertson's sister-in-law, sister of Henrietta Toomer Righton Robertson, who married Samuel Yates June 11, 1811, "Register of the Independent Congregational Church of Charleston, SC 1784-1815," in *Historical and Genealogical Magazine*, vol. 33, no. 1 (Jan. 1932), 29-54; "I know three of your grandmother's sisters, Mrs. Yates (Ma Jane) was the oldest . . .," W[illiam] R[obertson] Boggs to Miss Pamela Robertson, February 18, 1900, copy in possession of Thomas H. Robertson, Jr., 2014; "Is Aunt Jane still in Bennettsville?" Letter: Lillie [Mrs. Joseph Righton Robertson, nee Constantia (Lily) Whitridge Taylor] to Mother [Mrs. James Henry Taylor, nee Eliza Ann Tyler], Graniteville, August 9, 1865, original in possession of Thomas H. Robertson, Jr, 2014. Townsend is a common name in the Bennettsville, Marlboro County, and Pee Dee Area of South Carolina. The exact identities of Mr. Townsend and Miss Joze are not determined.

John A. Inglis's law office, Cheraw (2003).
Courtesy of Catherine Barrett Robertson

General P. G. T. Beauregard. General Braxton Bragg led the final withdrawal from the Wilmington area of coastal North Carolina.[24]

Thursday 23rd—Went to town this morning with the Chancellor and his daughter. Hoped to hear something from Charleston; but nothing more definite than yesterday. Only the troops connected with the Quartermaster, Commissary and Engineers departments have arrived. Can learn nothing of the Boys, but understand that our troops are passing on this way. I am now satisfied that Sherman is pushing for Lee's rear, and I am afraid he will get to Charlotte before Hardee can unite with Beauregard. I think Richmond is bound to be evacuated. We shall see. I only remained an hour in Town and walked back, and am now seated in the Chancellor's library penning these notes. I hear several trains[25] passing the house, and hope to get some definite information this evening on the return of the Chancellor from Town. It is reported that Wilmington has, also, been evacuated. If so, we are, now, cut off from

24 Swanson, *Atlas of the Civil War*, 106.

25 Wagon trains, not railroad trains, as there was no railroad near the house.

communication with Richmond, except by way of Fayetteville, N. C. This will delay my dispatches from the War Department. I shall remain here until I do receive some communication from the Surgeon General.

Friday the 24th—Some soldiers belonging to the 5th, 32d and 47th Georgia Infantry[26] came to the house yesterday evening asking for something to eat, and offering to purchase potatoes &c. The family kindly furnished them with food. If these men are without food, then there is a great fault somewhere, and it should be speedily corrected, as the whole country has been stripped of subsistence by the government, and commissary stores are now accumulated in large quantities at Florence and this place. This matter should be looked into, and the people, who have barely reserved sufficient subsistence for the non combatants thrown upon them, should be relieved from straggling bands, by a proper enforcement of discipline and care, on the part of the officers. If they are not without food, then this wandering from house to house is a wanton breach of propriety and, I fear, is the evidence of that lack of principle, which should be the true characteristic of a patriot and good soldier. While some of them behaved respectfully, it was evident that others exhibited signs of disaffection and discontent not creditable to the soldiers of a great state contending, side by side, with our little commonwealth, in this struggle for the high and sacred right of self-government. I could see a lurking satisfaction in speaking of Sherman's uninterrupted march through South Carolina; and one of them, evidently, took pleasure in letting the Chancellor know that he was of the opinion that the Yankee troops would overrun and devastate this entire region of country. Alas poor human nature. What low and malignant sentiments does war often develope in the human character! The furnace clears away the dross and brings out the fine gold. I fear it cannot be said, of some, who have been through the furnace of affliction, and trial, during this war, that the dross has been consumed and the fine gold made to shine. May God, in mercy, overrule, ever, our baser passions for our good.

It commenced raining last night and has continued uninterruptedly, and is still raining. Harrisons Brigade of McLaws' Division arrived by several trains last evening and are encamped near the Town. The other troops are to follow as rapidly as possible. The Chancellor's son[27] arrived this morning about 4 o'clock. He is a member of Charles' Battery of Light Artillery. The company has stopped

---

26 These units made up Harrison's Brigade of McLaw's Division, commanded by Col. George P. Harrison. See Bradley, *The Battle of Bentonville*, 424.

27 Charlie Inglis. Listed as Laurence C. Inglis SC 2nd Arty. Co. D Cpl., L.C Inglis SC 8th Inf. Co. C, in Hewett, *Confederate Soldiers.*

at Darlington Court House, some distance below this, on the Rail Road, to have their horses shod, and he will remain at home until the Battery comes up. He met my son Righton with Rhett's Brigade at St. Stephens Depot on the Santee. He was well, and had his commissary train in safety at that point.[28] I am truly thankful to hear of the safety of Righton. I still hope to hear something of the others—especially of my dear Duncan. I feel deeply concerned for him. The other boys have had some years experience in the field, and understand taking care of themselves. He is so tender and inexperienced that I tremble for him. I commit him, in faith, into the hands of a just and merciful God. May He take care of him, and give him strength and grace according to his day of trial.

I fear, from what I can gather from the straggling soldiers, that our troops are greatly dispirited, and are beginning to fail in self reliance. Oh for a living and energizing faith to bring our people up to the high standard of our cause. "Give ear, O shepherd of Israel, thou that leadest our people like a flock, thou that dwellest between the Cherubims, shine forth. Before" our Rulers and Generals, "stir up thy strength, and come and save us. Turn us again, O God, and cause Thy face to shine; and we shall be saved. O Lord God of hosts, how long wilt thou be angry against the prayer of thy people? Thou feedest them with the bread of tears; and givest them tears to drink in great measure. Thou makest us a strife unto our neighbours; and our enemies laugh among themselves. Turn us again, O God of Hosts, and cause thy face to shine; and we shall be saved."[29]

Saturday 25th Feb'y 1865

It continued to rain all night, and at intervals during the day. Twelve members of the Washington Artillery[30] who were sick and broken down were

28 The commissary probably consisted of foodstuffs and supplies aboard a railroad train on the Northeastern Rail Road just south of the Santee River.

29 *The Holy Bible*, Psalm 80, 1-7. Surgeon Robertson re-aimed the message of Psalm 80 at the current war situation by substituting the words "Our Rulers and Generals" for the biblical original text, "Ephraim and Benjamin and Manasseh."

30 These soldiers were probably part of the remnants of the Washington Light Artillery company that had been formed in Augusta, Georgia, in 1854, during the wave of militant sectionalism that followed the Compromise of 1850. (This Washington Artillery should not be confused with the well known five-company battalion from New Orleans, most of which served with the Army of Northern Virginia.) The Georgia Washington Artillery had been present at the Union surrender of the Augusta Arsenal on January 23, 1861, when their soldiers fired a 21-gun salute with two of their cannon. The battery entered Confederate service on April 11, 1861, and included among its officers Lt. George T. Barnes, great-great-grandfather

sent forward from Kingstree by rail, and came to the house yesterday evening and requested to have some rations cooked. They also asked permission to occupy some out building until their Battery arrived. The Chancellor was full, or he would gladly have accommodated them in the house. He opened his gin house to them, had their meals cooked, sent them some extra provisions, and had all their clothing washed and ironed. Some of their socks were entirely worn out in the feet—nothing but the tops remaining. Mrs. Inglis is the president of a ladies association, in Cheraw, for suffering destitute soldiers. She will tomorrow go into the town and bring out socks for those who are needy. These are the most decorous and orderly men that I have seen, and have exerted themselves, with success, in preventing depredations from being committed by the unprincipled stragglers who are continually prowling about seeking what they may devour. In a casual conversation I learned that Edward,[31] the son of my old and valued friend James H. Taylor[32] was one of the party. I immediately sent for him. He was delighted to see me, and told me that he saw Righton at the Santee Bridge as he came up. He had had chills, but had missed them, and was doing well. I offered him funds, but he told me he had sufficient. I told him to call on me, at any time, for money or assistance in any other way. I hope the party will be greatly refreshed by their stay at the Chancellor's. The Chancellor went to Town with his son, but could hear nothing positive about the movements of troops. In fact, we are entirely cut off, except by way of Fayetteville, and the mail is not daily. Ed Taylor requested me to let my servant Henry go to Town to make some purchases for his party. I told him to make use of him in any manner he wished during the stay of the party here. It continued to rain up to a late hour.

---

of Thomas H. Robertson, Jr. The company served with the Army of Tennessee, but by the time of the campaign in the Carolinas, the unit was greatly diminished. It had been reduced to a company cadre, which served its last known field duty as a unit at Atlanta. When that city was evacuated in September, 1864, the cadre moved to Macon, Georgia. See Russell K. Brown, "Augusta's 'Pet Company': The Washington Light Artillery," *Richmond County History*, v. 26, no. 2, Winter 1996, Richmond County Historical Society.

31 Edward Taylor, Maj. Joseph Righton Robertson's brother-in-law.

32 Father-in-law of F. M. Robertson's son Joseph Righton Robertson, who married Taylor's daughter Constantia (Lily) Whitridge Taylor, May 18, 1859. Taylor lived at No. 7 Rutledge Street, Charleston. See *Census of the City of Charleston, South Carolina for the Year 1861*, Electronic Edition, http://docsouth.unc.edu/imls/census/census.html, 198, accessed December 15, 2008.

Presbyterian Church of Cheraw, Session House (2003).
Courtesy of Catherine Barrett Robertson

Sunday 26th Feby: 1865

The rain ceased some time during the night. It cleared off quite pleasant, and rather warm. Rode into church with Mrs. Inglis, her daughter and son. Heard a sermon from a chaplain of one of the regiments now here. His text was from the 3d chapter of Amos and a part of the 6th verse—"Shall there be evil in the City and the Lord hath not done it?" He made a practical application of this text to our condition as a nation struggling for existence. Urged us to recognize God in all that was passing—to consider our disasters as punishment for our sins, and urged the people to repentance and faith. He justly rebuked the spirit of despondency, which he characterized as the grave of energy and perseverance, and called upon all to repent, and look to God in faith, as he felt assured he would yet save us.

While I grieve over the loss of our dear old city, yet I am afraid the fraud, extortion, speculation and idolatry for gold which has been engendered by blockade running, have had much to do with the demoralization of our people and Army. It may be that God found it necessary that this nest should be broken up, in order to purge away the effete matter, and bring out the true patriotism and courage of the people. Such sifting scatters the chaff before the wind, and leaves the rich grain uncontaminated. If this be His design, then its evacuation is a blessing in disguise, and we shall yet live to bless the hand that has applied the chastening rod.

Troops are arriving all the time. The artillery has been arrested by the rise in Thompson Creek, a few miles from Town, but it will probably be got over today. Genl Hardee and staff arrived about 12 o'clock today. I saw him for a few moments, but had no opportunity of holding any conversation with him. He gave orders for McLaw's Division to be got in readiness to move at any moment. I heard that my son Mjr. J. R. Robertson had arrived this morning. I soon found him at the Depot. He looks well, and appears cheerful. He had not heard anything of his family, whom he left at Graniteville.[33] He left Jimmy and Joe behind, and thought they would be up today or tomorrow. They were both well. He heard of my dear Duncan. He was behind with the Cavalry, but would probably be up tomorrow or the next day. He understood that he was well and in good spirits. He had swapped horses. I am curious to know what kind of a trade he made, and whether he got a better horse. Right was informed, by some one, that the Stono Scouts had been taken as Genl Hardee's body guard. I hope soon to see Duncan and the other boys.

There was information received in Town today, that the enemy had occupied Camden, and had advanced as far as Lynch's Creek on the road to this place.[34] I presume, like all rumors, it has grown in direct portion to distance from the first starting point. If there is a column of the enemy in that direction, they are evidently attempting to intercept or anticipate Hardee's move in the direction of Charlotte or Greensboro, N. C.

Righton saw his dear Mother the evening of the day on which I left. They were all well. Thank God for this much. May He be ever near to sustain and support her amid the trials upon which she was about to enter. I should be too much rejoiced if I could only convey to her the intelligence of my whereabouts and health. But this, at present, is impossible. It is not usual for me to dream of

---

33 His family consisted of his wife Constantia (Lily) Whitridge Taylor Robertson, two children, John Frederick, age 4, Henry Clarence, age 2, and another one on the way, James Taylor Robertson, who would be born March 2, 1865. Joseph Righton Robertson had been working for a Mr. Halsey in Graniteville, probably in a mercantile business. See letters, F. M. Robertson to Joseph Righton Robertson dated July 27, 1865, and August 9, 1865, originals in Constance Sevier Robertson papers in possession of Thomas H. Robertson, Jr., 2014; Righton Robertson's father-in-law, James H. Taylor, had been one of the original stockholders of the Graniteville cotton mill in 1846, many of whom had been Charlestonians. See *Minutes of Graniteville Manufacturing Company, 1846-1919*, 3 vols., original and photocopy in possession of Weldon Wyatt, Sage Valley Golf Club, Graniteville, South Carolina, 2014.

34 Lynch's Creek or River is approximately 30 miles southwest of Cheraw, about half way between Camden and Cheraw.

those from whom I am seperated; but, last night I had a dream, in which I was carried back to my dear wife. I saw her distinctly—embraced her, when I entered the room, and imprinted upon her dear lips one of those prolonged and ardent kisses that was usual with me after a season of seperation. It was a moment of true happiness; to see her and caress and converse with her as of old. But it was all a dream, and awaking, the vision fled. However, even in a dream to be blessed, is something to be thankful for.

Monday 27th Feby: 1865

Various rumors are afloat this morning. There has been some fighting upon Lynches Creek by Butlers Cavalry—four or five Yankee waggons and thirty seven prisoners were sent in.[35] It is supposed that Sherman has changed his course, having been foiled in his effort to reach Charlotte and Genl Lee's rear, and is now making for a water base—either Wilmington or Charleston. If to the former, I think it probable I shall have to leave here in a hurry. I must patiently await the development of events, and trust in the good providence of God.

I met Dr. Duncan[36] today, who informed me that he saw my dear wife at Mr. Carrington's,[37] the day after I left. All seemed to be quiet. Thank God for this intelligence. Troops have been arriving all day—Rhett's Regiment came in this evening, and encamped near the Town.[38] I saw my son James. He was well and I expect to bring him home with me tomorrow to spend the day—that is if the movement of the enemy does not prevent it. It commenced raining about dark, and continued up to the time I went to bed. Information was received today of the appointment of Genl Jos. E. Johnson [sic] to the command of the troops operating against Sherman.[39] His order, assuming command, was read

35 Butler's Division, Maj. Gen. M. C. Butler, commanding, from the Army of Northern Virginia. See Bradley, *Battle of Bentonville*, 447.

36 Quartermaster. Listed as A.S. Duncan, SC 3rd Res. QM Sgt. in Hewett, *Confederate Soldiers*.

37 Probably at William Carrington's residence, 30 Coming Street, or office at 278 King Street. See *Charleston Census*, 1861, 71, 120.

38 Rhett's Brigade of Taliaferro's Division, commanded by Col. Alfred M. Rhett, and made up of 1st South Carolina Infantry (Regulars), 1st South Carolina Heavy Artillery, and Lucas's South Carolina Battalion. See Bradley, *Battle of Bentonville*, 423; listed as Alfred Rhett SC 1st Arty. Co. B Col. in Hewett, *Confederate Soldiers*.

39 Gen. Joseph Eggleston Johnston; listed as J. E. Johnston Gen. & Staff, A. of TN Gen. in Hewett, *Confederate Soldiers*. Surgeon Robertson consistently refers to him in the diary incorrectly as "Johnson" instead of "Johnston."

John Auchincloss Inglis, Author of Secession
Wanted: Dead or Alive

The Chancellor is very much exercised as to the proper course for him to pursue. He was a member of the convention and introduced the Ordinance of Secession. He has gone to Town tonight, to be with his family and consult as to the best course to pursue in case our army retires from this point. I feel very much for him and his excellent family.

Surgeon F. M. Robertson
February 28, 1865

John Inglis was a wanted man with a big price on his head, as the Federal army approached Cheraw, South Carolina, in late February 1865. They suspected him of having been the author of South Carolina's Ordinance of Secession that ultimately led to the war, and placed a bounty of $10,000 on his head (dead or alive).[1]

John Auchincloss Inglis (1813-1878) was one of four chancellors of the Court of Equity in South Carolina. The title chancellor is the equivalent of judge. As a young man he had moved to Cheraw from Baltimore to become principal of Cheraw Academy. He subsequently practiced law and became a chancellor.

Continued on page 46

1 *The Cheraw Chronicle* Bicentennial Edition, July 1, 1976, and other historical interpretation and exhibits in Cheraw Lyceum Museum, which occupies the former Chancery Court Building in Cheraw, S.C.; John Amasa May and Joan Reynolds Faunt, *South Carolina Secedes*, (Columbia, 1960), 162-3; Nelson, *Sherman's March*, 37-8.

---

on parade this afternoon. It produced a tremendous shout along the line. It will infuse new energy into our officers and soldiers.

Anderson Walton[40] and my nephew, Robert Robertson,[41] came to see me this evening, I was very glad to see the dear child. He is just seventeen; and has the spirit and patriotism of his dear father. Had he been living he would now have been, side by side, with his brave son in this great contest.

---

40 Anderson Watkins Walton (b. 1817). See Walton genealogy in Daughters of the American Revolution, Vol. II Richmond County Records, 335-7. Probably the same as A. W. Walton, clerk at Clayton & Kennady, clothing merchants, Augusta, Georgia, and residence at 84 Reynolds Street. See R. A. Watkins, *Directory for the City of Augusta and Business Advertiser for 1859* (Augusta, GA.: R. A. Watkins, 1859), 141, Google Books edition, accessed October 13, 2012; listed as A. W. Walton GA 1st (Symon's) Res. Co. I 1st Lt. and A. W. Walton, GA Inf. 1st Loc. Troops (Augusta) Co. C in Hewett, *Confederate Soldiers*.

41 Robert Walton Robertson (b. 1849), of Augusta, Georgia, son of Surgeon Robertson's brother William Alexander Robertson (1817- ca. 1857) and Mary Louisa Walton; listed as Robert W. Robertson GA 1st (Symon's) Res Co. I. in Hewett, *Confederate Soldiers*.

Charleston and Cheraw 45

John A. Inglis's Town House in Cheraw (2003).
Courtesy of Catherine Barrett Robertson

Tuesday Feby 28th 1865

It continued to rain the most of the day. I went out to Rhett's Brigade this morning, and brought James to the Chancellors with me. He spent the day and took dinner with me. I had some clothes washed for him and gave him a chance of shaving and washing. After furnishing him with some funds, and a fine pair of English shoes, which Capt. Peck[42] gave me, I carried him back to the encampment of his Regiment.

The Chancellor came home quite excited this evening. He learned that our forces were engaging the enemy at Purvis' Bridge on Thompsons Creek, about five miles and a half from Town, on the Camden Road. When I went with James

---

42 Probably Thomas C. Peck, Gen. & Staff Capt. AQM, as listed in Hewett, *Confederate Soldiers.*

Chancellor John A. Inglis
Courtesy of Archives and Special Collections,
Dickinson College, Carlisle, Pennsylvania

Continued from page 44

In 1860, Inglis had served as a delegate from Chesterfield County to the secession convention of South Carolina, where he was chairman of the Resolutions Committee and presented the Ordinance of Secession for consideration by the assembly.[2] Inglis said that the model for the resolution was a short draft submitted by fellow Chancellor Francis Hugh Wardlaw of Abbeville and Edgefield.[3] Other compelling evidence suggests that the model for the ordinance was a similarly brief text written by W. Ferguson Hutson, a Charleston lawyer.[4]

No matter who the actual author was, Inglis was the man who had introduced the brief resolution on the afternoon of December 20, 1860. It simply repealed the State's 1788 ratification of the United States Constitution and dissolved the union between South Carolina and the other states. It had passed unanimously.

Inglis and F. M. Robertson were acquainted through the Presbyterian Church. In 1861 they had been elected by their respective presbyteries to attend a General Assembly in Augusta, Georgia, to establish a new Presbyterian Church in the Confederate States of America. Robertson was appointed by the Charleston Presbytery as a Ruling Elder to attend the General Assembly. Similarly, Inglis was elected by the Harmony Presbytery as a delegate to attend the convention.[5]

John A. Inglis did escape the fury of Sherman's army when he fled Cheraw on March 2, 1865. The Yankees had to settle for burning his plantation house. His house in town was spared.

2 Charles H. Lesser, *Relic of the Lost Cause: The Story of South Carolina's Ordinance of Secession*, 2nd edition, (Columbia, 1996), 3-7

3 Chancellor Wardlaw was also an acquaintance of F. M. Robertson from the time when the young Wardlaw had been a pupil of Capt. William Robertson in mathematical subjects in Abbeville in 1815. The Chancellor's father, James Wardlaw, had endorsed F. M. Robertson's application for admission into West Point in 1820. See Chapman, *History of Edgefield County*, 244; and William Robertson, Jr. to Hon'l J. C. Calhoun, Sec War, Oct 17th 1820, with appended recommendation signed by "our mutual friends," 15 Abbeville District citizens, "U.S.M.A. Cadet Application Papers (1805 to 1866)," microfilm copy in West Point Library, original at National Archives and Record Service, Washington, D.C.

4 Charles H. Lesser, *Relic of the Lost Cause*, 6-7.

5 See Resolution of the Charleston Presbytery meeting at Columbia, July 24, 1861, and Paper adopted by Harmony Presbytery at Sumterville, July 24, 1861, in F. D. Jones, D.D. and W. H. Mills, D.D., editors, *History of the Presbyterian Church in South Carolina since 1850*, published by The Synod of South Carolina, (Columbia, SC, 1926), 90-93.

Chancery Court, Cheraw (2003).
Courtesy of Catherine Barrett Robertson

to his Regiment, I found that the remainder of McLaws Division,[43] a portion of Elliotts Brigade[44] and some artillery had gone to the bridge. There could have been no fighting up to 2 o'clock, as a waggon train crossed the bridge at that hour, and saw nothing of the enemy. One of the men told me that he was

43 Named for Maj. Gen. Lafayette McLaws, native of Augusta, Georgia; listed as Maj. Gen. Lafayette McLaws, PACS in Hewett, *Confederate Soldiers*.

44 Elliott's Brigade of Taliaferro's Division, named for Brig. Gen. Stephen Elliott, Jr., commanding.

informed that they were some twenty miles off. More prisoners came in today from Lynch's Creek. If the enemy advances, I presume our forces will make a stand at Thompsons Creek unless they (the enemy) mass in too strong a force. It is of vital importance that this point should be defended and held, as most of the rolling stock and engines from all the Rail Roads in this state, and some of the Georgia Rail Roads, are at the terminus of the Darlington and Cheraw Road. There is no possibility of getting them off, without running them back into a portion of the country open to the enemy.[45]

The Chancellor is very much exercised as to the proper course for him to pursue. He was a member of the convention and introduced the Ordinance of Secession. He has gone to Town tonight, to be with his family and consult as to the best course to pursue in case our army retires from this point. I feel very much for him and his excellent family. I am alone in the house, and will remain with my faithful servant Henry until the morning. I will then go into Town and, if necessary, make further arrangements, as to my future movements. I have never felt my condition as an exile from home more keenly than I do tonight. When O, when will this suspense end, and I be united with my dear family once more. How gloomy everything appears now. But let me not murmer. It is God's will. Oh for grace to make me to say His will be done. If I could only be assured of the safety of my dear Duncan and Joe, how rejoiced I should be. But why do I indulge in these feelings and expression. The same good providence, that has been over them thus far, can protect them amid all dangers, both seen and unseen. If our whole army succeeds in reaching here without loss by capture it will be a merciful providence. The hasty evacuation of the City, the weather and the roads, have all conspired against it.

Wednesday, lst March 1865

Had a comfortable and quiet nights rest alone with Henry in my room. The Chancellor came out to breakfast. I moved into Town today with my trunk and blankets. Mr. H. H. Williams kindly invited me to his house. I called on Genl Hardee today to know what it was best to do. He seemed to think that it would be best to endeavor to strike the Rail Road either at Charlotte or Salisbury in

45 Cheraw was located at the northern end of the Cheraw and Darlington railroad line and the head of navigation of the Pee Dee River. These circumstances limited the Confederate army's capability for transporting supplies further north to the capacity of their wagon trains, which amounted to only a portion of the vast quartermaster and commissary supplies and munitions that had been brought up from Charleston. They took what they could and destroyed or left behind the rest.

Lieutenant General William J. Hardee
Library of Congress

North Carolina, and place myself in direct communication with the Surgeon Genl. He issued an order directing the Board to report to Genl Johnson. This leaves us at liberty to go when we please by the most practicable rout, which, in this present state of doubt and uncertainty, is a most difficult matter to decide. The enemy retreated from Genl McLaws front near Purvis' Bridge on Thompson Creek, and are reported to be attempting to cross into North Carolina in the direction of Wadesboro and Rockingham. Under these circumstances, it will be unsafe for a small party to attempt to reach Genl Johnson in that direction. I have concluded to wait the movements of this army. If I go with it, I shall reduce my baggage, leaving my trunk with Mr. Williams, and join Rightons mess, and endeavor to get a horse. I pray that providence may point out the best course. How perplexing.

The Marion Artillery came up yesterday. Some uneasiness was felt about them. I have not yet seen Joe and William Francis.[46] The Stono Scouts left Florence yesterday, and will, no doubt, be up today or tomorrow. Genl Hardee told me he intended to keep them with him. I told Coln Roy,[47] if I left before seeing Duncan, I would leave some funds for him in his hands. The Genl. kindly said tell him (Duncan) if he requires anything, at any time, call on me, and I will furnish him. May the good providence of God be over the dear child.

Thursday, March 2d 1865

It is still raining, and cold. The enemy is reported in full force beyond Thompsons Creek. If our army makes any stand, it will simply be to cover the

---

46 William Francis Robertson (1834-1875). Joe is unidentified.

47 Acting Adjutant General Thomas B. Roy; listed as T. B. Roy Hardee's Corps Lt. Col., AAG, in Hewett, *Confederate Soldiers*.

retreat of our forces across the river, and to protect the removal of the Quartermaster and commissary stores. I have made my arrangements to continue with the Army, as the safest way of reaching Genl Johnson's Head Quarters. Mr. Williams has kindly offered me a small buggy and a tolerable good horse. This outfit will carry what baggage I can take with me, and enable me to leave the army, with my servant, when it is safe to cut loose from it. I shall accompany Rightons waggon and mess with him. My friend, the Chancellor, left this morning with Genl Prince, his brother-in-law.[48] I feel very deeply for him. He will make for some safe point in North Carolina. Firing was heard in the front this afternoon. The Chancellor returned this afternoon and took his daughter and two nieces out with him. Gilbert Williams also left the town.[49] It would not surprise me if we are ordered to move tonight.

48 Gen. William L. T. Prince, brother of John A. Inglis's wife, Laura Prince Inglis.

49 Son of H. H. Williams.

Chapter Two

Rockingham, Carthage, and Fayetteville

"We behold a dense mass of human beings, horses, artillery, waggons,
and attendants all pressing to one narrow bridge."

Friday, **March 3rd 1865**—I was aroused at half past one oclock A.M. by a message, from Righton, that the trains were in motion, and I must join his waggon immediately. I packed up in a hurry, and was off in a moment, for the field—crossed the bridge[1] at daylight—made four miles over terrible roads and stopped to feed and breakfast at 10 o'clock A.M. We had scarcely unhitched our animals when heavy artillery firing, with musketry, was heard in the direction of Cheraw. Supposed to be an engagement between our rear guard and the advance of Sherman. We resumed our march at 12 o'clock and continued it until 2 o'clock P.M., when we encamped for the night, to allow the trains, and troops in the rear, to come up. We encamped upon a high pine ridge on a dry soil. It has rained slightly during the day and continues cloudy. I shall anxiously await the news from the fight in Cheraw. The firing ceased at 2 o'clock P.M. I have just heard that the contest at the bridge was rather warm. The Yankees pressed into the Town, on the Camden road in double quick, and commenced shelling our pickets, as soon as they entered it. Our men fell back slowly to the bridge and passed over. Butler's Cavalry all got over safely except a few. There was a warm contest to prevent our troops from burning the bridge. They brought their field pieces to the bluff on the Cheraw side, and shelled the bridge, hoping to drive away our troops and extinguish the fire. In this they failed, and the entire bridge was soon enveloped in flames and totally consumed. There were some casualties among our men,

---

1 The bridge over the Great Pee Dee River.

but I could not learn the particulars. Theodore Barker was slightly wounded by a shell.[2]

Saturday March 4th 1865—I slept last night under my buggy. Our tent was not pitched as we expected to be disturbed during the night by the enemy. I used my wool robe as a bed, kept on all my clothes, covered with two blankets, and put the buggy cushion under my head. Fortunately it did not rain. All was quiet during the night, except the lumbering of the waggon trains passing to and fro with subsistence and ammunition. We were up at 3 o'clock A.M., fed our horses and got breakfast—fried bacon, and corn bread—and made a start at half past four o'clock. It was so dark, and the roads so bad that it was necessary to have torches carried in front of the teams. This with the numerous campfires through which we had to pass, for several miles, before daylight, gave the whole scene the appearance of an immense torch light procession. Our route to Rockingham in North Carolina, about twenty-two miles from Cheraw, was a fatiguing and disagreeable one.[3]

We reached the Town about 2 o'clock P.M. It is a small village with a few good houses and quite a fine church, judging from external appearances. There are some factories and mills in the vicinity. Heavy firing was heard in our rear, about 9 o'clock this morning. Coln Rhett's Brigade protects our rear.[4] I learned

2   T. G. Barker, Adjutant-General of Butler's Brigade of Cavalry. See Raymond P. Boylston, Jr., *Butler's Brigade: That Fighting Civil War Cavalry Brigade from South Carolina*, (Raleigh, 2001), 263; listed as Theodore G. Barker. SC Inf. Hampton Legion Adj. and Theodore G. Barker. Butler's Cav. Div. Maj. in Hewett, *Confederate Soldiers*.

3   **Route: The "fatiguing and disagreeable" route generally follows modern U.S. Highway 1.**

4   Col. Alfred M. Rhett (1829-1889) was a native Charlestonian, the son of United States and Confederate States Senator R. Barnwell Rhett. He was a Harvard graduate and became a well known duelist, police chief, trial justice, and rice planter. He commanded the 1st Regiment of South Carolina Artillery (Regulars) and was in charge of Fort Sumter during the unsuccessful bombardment by Federal monitors in 1863. Upon the evacuation of Charleston, his regiment and the Lucas Battalion (Regulars) were formed into a brigade under his command and hence known informally as "Rhett's Brigade." On the march through South and North Carolina, Rhett's Brigade was usually assigned the difficult position of rear guard of the forces under Lt. Gen. Hardee. See obituary of Alfred Moore Rhett, "Find A Grave Memorial," www.findagrave.com/cgi-bin/fg.cgi?page=gr&GRid=12915254, accessed February 5, 2015; Capt. Charles Inglesby, *Historical Sketch of the First Regiment of South Carolina Artillery (Regulars)*, n. d., 15, 24.

from Capt. Gilchrist[5] of Gen. Hardee's staff that it protected from the enemy shelling our picket line from the bluff at Cheraw. He also informed me that the enemy had burned a large portion of Cheraw, and were putting down pontoons for the purpose of crossing. It rained nearly the whole day. We encamped about a mile north of the Town.[6] I have been suffering with a severe headache since twelve o'clock.

Sunday March 5th 1865—I suffered very much last night. My head continued to ache most violently, and after getting to bed in the open air—I had a severe chill, and passed a very uncomfortable night. I took neither dinner or supper, except a cup of warm coffee. I had some sleep during the night, and got up at daylight, free from headache, but very much exhausted. How often did I think of home, and all its tender and endearing associations, during the night. What a solace it would have been, in the moments of my agony, to have felt the soft and soothing hand of my dear wife, pressing my aching forehead. But no such privilege was mine—no sympathizing voice to whisper comfort and encouragement to my agonized heart. It is thus that God often deals with us, and by depriving us of our earthly treasure and comforts, points us to Heaven as the only secure and certain resting place for the afflicted soul.

Resumed my journey with the Army towards Bostwicks Mills, about fourteen miles from Rockingham, in the direction of Asheboro.[7] Weather clear windy and cold. Heard artillery firing in our rear about 11 o'clock. What a terrible thing war is—and above all this war. Besides the destruction of human life, and the utter devastation of the Country, it seems to wipe out the existence of God and the Sabbath. I was surprised at the number who did not really know that it was the Sabbath. Swearing is a crying sin in the Army. How shocking, on this sacred day, to hear the terrible oaths that are poured forth on all sides. How I feel the privations of home and Sabbath privileges. My dear wife—my darling

---

5   Acting Assistant Adjutant General Robert C. Gilchrist, listed as R. C. Gilchrist. Hardee's Corps AAAG, Robert C. Gilchrist. SC Hvy. Arty. Gilchrist's Co (Gist Guard) Capt., and Robert C. Gilchrist. SC Arty. Manigault's Bn., Co. E Capt. in Hewett, *Confederate Soldiers.*

6   Dr. Robertson added "Capt. Page was" in pencil between the lines here, without completing the sentence. "Capt. Page" was probably Peyton N. Page, assistant adjutant general, listed as Peyton H. Page Gen. & Staff Capt. and P. N. Page Gen & Staff AAG. in Hewett, *Confederate Soldiers.*

7   **Route: The route extends generally along modern U. S. Highway 220, and probably along S. R. 1317 to Bostick's Mill on Little Mountain Creek northwest of Ellerbe, North Carolina.**

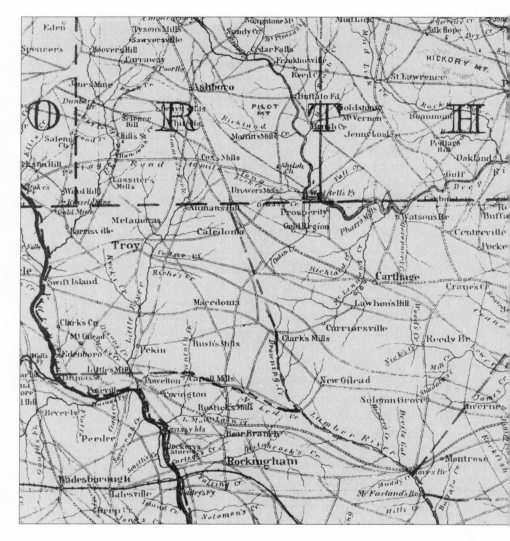

Marion and Anny—Lily and Mary and their sweet children.[8] Shall I ever see them all again? My constant prayer is that we may all be spared, and be permitted to meet in old Charleston once more. No intelligence from them yet.

8   Marion is Henrietta Marion Robertson Silliman, daughter of Dr. Robertson; Anny is unidentified; Lily is Constantia Whitridge Taylor Robertson, wife of Joseph Righton Robertson; Mary is Mary Mikell Robertson, wife of Henry Clay Robertson. Lily's sweet children are John Frederick Robertson, age 4, and Henry Clarence Robertson, age 2. Did Dr. Robertson know that Lily had given birth to another son, James Taylor Robertson, just three days earlier? Mary's sweet child is Francis Marion Robertson, age 4 months.

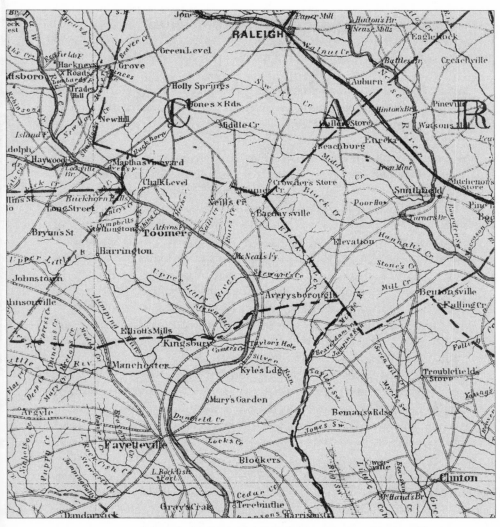

Rockingham to Raleigh, N.C. Detail from U.S. Coast Survey, 1865.
State Department of Archives and History, Raleigh, N.C.

I have only seen one Richmond and one North Carolina paper since leaving Charleston, and none since leaving Cheraw.

Marched through a miserable country today. Pine barren, broken and hilly, our route lying upon a range of ridges, of considerable elevation, sloping to the right and left in valleys or ravines—soil sandy and unproductive. This region appears to be very sparsely populated. It also seems to be uncultivated. In fact, for miles, no living creature was seen even of the domestic kind, and no bird or wild animal of any description was met with. We hear vague conjectures as to our ultimate point of destination. But the soldiers and officers, outside of the Generals military family, know nothing of these matters. We simply halt and bivouac when ordered, and mount and march when & where directed.

March 6, 1865—General Joseph E. Johnston assumes command of the North Carolina Department, in addition to the Department of South Carolina, Georgia, and Florida.[9]

Monday March 6th 1865—Left Bostwicks Mills this morning at sunrise, but, before the train had fully started, an order came to halt for further instruction. About 11 o'clock we started again, and after having proceeded about five miles to Baldwins Mills, the train was seperated. Up to this time it appeared that our destination was Greensboro or High Point via Ashboro. Now it was evident that we were to make a rapid push for Fayetteville. A portion of the supply train, with provisions, remained to issue rations to the Army up to the 10th inst. inclusive, and were then to join us.

The main body of the Army made for the old Morgantown Road leading direct to Fayetteville, while the other portion with the waggon trains and reserve artillery took a circuitous route, by a neighborhood road, crossing the Morgantown Road, making for the road from Highpoint to Fayetteville at a place called Carthage, about twenty-two miles from the point at which we seperated. This movement was, probably, adopted for two reasons. First the better to forage our animals, and secondly, to facilitate the rapid movement of the Army to Fayetteville, by separating the trains; and, for its better protection, to throw the main body of the infantry and cavalry between the enemy—who were also passing on to the same point—and the supply trains and reserve artillery.

I accompanied the train to Carthage. Our route was, at first, in a northwesterly direction. We passed over barren sand hills similar to those of the day previous, and then turned to the north and northeast, and struck the Morganton Road leading to Fayetteville. We proceeded only a few miles on this road to McKenzies Bridge on Drowning Creek, where we encamped for the night.[10] Our main army encamped on the same road a few miles to our right as we faced the northeast. At Drowning Creek, we found clay and water-worn pebbles cropping out in abundance, also stratified rocks formed the bed of the

---

9 Swanson, *Atlas of the Civil War*, 108.

10 **Route: The route is likely along State Roads 1527, 1003, 1523, and 1522, which is the old Morganton Road.**

creek. The ridge, over which we had passed, seemed to form the watershed dividing the streams that flow into the Pee Dee from those which empty into the tributaries of the Cape Fear.[11] It is an exceedingly poor and sterile region. For the first time we pitched our wall tent. We took a bountiful supper of bacon, rice, biscuit, fritters and coffee with sugar (genuine). At this place a woman sold syrup to our soldiers at $8 per quart. Can we wonder that depredations are sometimes committed by our soldiers, when such prices are extorted from them?

Tuesday March 7th 1865—We started this morning at 6 1/2 o'clock. Left the Morganton Road by taking a left-hand neighborhood road leading to Carthage.[12] We soon struck the same character of country that we had passed over the day previous, with the exception that the hills loomed up almost into mountains. Passing along the Summit of the ridge or backbone, we could see for miles around—nothing but hill upon hill and forests of pines stretching as far as the eye could see. During the march over this region, not a living wild animal could be seen and only one or two houses that were inhabited. For the first fifteen miles not a stream or standing pool could be seen, in consequence of which our animals suffered very much, as the day was warm, notwithstanding a white frost in the morning. The pines and a few scattered scrub oaks were the most stunted and diminutive that we had seen.

We soon saw Carthage from over three miles distant, as we were passing along one of the highest ridges that we had encountered during the day. The town was situated on an opposite ridge of equal elevation. Its appearance in the dim distance was picturesque and imposing. How often does "distance lend enchantment to the view"![13]

The character of the country over which we had passed for the last two days gave no earnest of a city of magnificence so near at hand, though the name called up the historic records of the great city founded by Dido and famed for

11 Drowning Creek is the main headwater of the Lumber River, which, in turn, is a major tributary of the Little Pee Dee River. Our diarist is somewhat mistaken, because he has yet to cross the drainage divide into the watershed of the Cape Fear River.

12 **Route: The neighborhood road seems to follow State Road 1137 (or perhaps 1140), then 705 and 1261 to Carthage.**

13 A quotation from Scottish poet Thomas Campbell (1777–1844): "'Tis distance lends enchantment to the view, And robes the mountain in its azure hue." See http://www. encyclopedia.com/doc/1O214-distance.html, accessed September 8, 2010.

untold luxury, commercial refinement & wealth.[14] As we proceeded we soon began to descend into a valley or ravine. Here the red clay and water worn pebbles were found in abundance and evidence of good farms became apparent. At the bottom of the descent, we found a clear rapid stream passing over the outcropping stratified rocks. The land on each side of this stream appeared to be productive, judging from the remains of the previous crop and the number of fields in which the sprouting wheat was visible.

After crossing this stream and ascending the opposite ridge, we came to the outskirts of the Town at 2 o'clock P.M. having completed twenty miles in seven hours and a half. We were, as usual, delayed some time before a camping ground was selected. We drove through the Town and parked our train on the outskirts, but within a stones throw of the Court House. The reserve artillery parked where we first halted at 2 o'clock without entering the town. We again pitched our wall tent. Had good appetites and made a hearty dinner and supper together. A word now about this city of Dido's. Truly may I say it was distance that lent enchantment to the view from the opposite ridge. Who under the sun could have given such a name to such a place. The North Carolinians are famous for boro's; and certainly, Foxboro, Coonboro or Terrapinboro would have been much more appropriate. The Town is perched upon the top of a barren sand ridge. A few scattered and dilapidated houses, with a miserable Court House and Jail, the doors of the latter wide open, inviting criminals to come in, or saying to those already in duress, "go in peace." The rest of the houses were closed. What a name, and what a city. Carthage is certainly a high-sounding name, and was of old a renowned city, famous in the annals of commerce for mercantile greatness and the refinements, luxury, and learning of its citizens.

When I entered the place in advance of our column, I found a group of young and able bodied men near the Court House somewhat excited and talking as though they had just recovered from the effects of a stampede. They told me that there were only about twenty-five residents in the Town. When asked about the empty houses, I was told that they were only occupied on public occasions. The fact is, I ascertained that they had taken our Army for Sherman's approaching columns, and I have no doubt decamped at our approach. This too is the great region for deserters, and it may be that a portion of these had left in anticipation of our arrival. All questions were answered with

14 Dido was the mythical queen of the City of Carthage, who fell in love with the Trojan Aeneas. He ultimately left her for his mission of founding Rome, whereupon she committed suicide with Aeneas's sword atop a funeral pyre. See Virgil, *Aeneid*, Book 4; North Carolina's Troy is located about 35 miles west of Carthage.

a nervous agitation which showed that they were ill at ease. The most of these able bodied men professed to be Colonels, Lieut. Colonels, Majors, Captains and Lieutenants of Militia, all of whom even within conscript age are classed in the State reserves by the laws of North Carolina. Some of our war-worn and weatherbeaten soldiers questioned them rather closely and intimated that such chaps should be forced into the Army at the point of the bayonet, if their consciences could not be pricked by the point of honor and patriotism. We looked, in vain, for the Dido of this modern Carthage. The only one to whom the appellation could apply was a fat woman with a smooth wide face, with black eyebrows and gray hair. But, to dispel the romance, she had a small stick in her mouth and a box of snuff in her hand. The unmistakable ensigns of that feminine genus called dippers. This was mathematically demonstrated, when she dipped the stick into the snuff, and carried it to her mouth. It was thrust as far back as possible between the teeth and the cheek and then suffered to remain, when she continued to talk and emit the tobacco juice from time to time with an unrivaled masculine squirt. Whatever may have been the accomplishments of the people of ancient Carthage, the masculine and feminine occupants of this modern city, consisted in the former, drinking apple jack[15] and the latter, using snuff a' la dipper. This is a common practice in this part of the country. Go where you will, you meet with the stick and the snuff box in the hands of females. Old Virginia certainly owes them a debt of gratitude on the score of increasing the consumption and enhancing the value of her staple commodity.

We, however, met with some kindhearted people even here. I have not washed or taken off my clothes since leaving Cheraw. I was kindly furnished with a room, wash basin and towels by a gentleman. I took a thorough washing and astonished my body and friends with a clean white shirt and collar. What a comfort and a luxury it is to feel clean. One man here who professed to be a warm advocate of our cause and a great friend to our soldiers sold them apple brandy at $40 per bottle. I must owe our individual the justice to say that he invited our mess to sleep and eat in his house, and when we declined on the ground that we had dined and supped bountifully and had a comfortable tent, he extended it to the soldiers personally. I do not remember his name.

Wednesday, March 8th 1865—Left the renowned city of Carthage at 6 1/2 o'clock A.M. and bid adieu to the consuming of apple jack and feminine representation of the dipper class. The road to Fayetteville had once been a

---

15 An alcoholic drink derived from apples.

Plank Road, Carthage (2003)
Courtesy of Catherine Barrett Robertson

plank road, but was now in a dilapitated condition; but with the labor of the pioneer corps under the engineers, which preceded us, it was better than the ordinary dirt road.[16] It rained all day. Made nineteen miles and encamped at a place called Johnsonville. It consisted of one house and a store. It rained and blew at such a rate that we could, with difficulty, get dinner and supper, which are usually compressed into one. Our mess had purchased some chickens at $5 a piece, and eggs at $3 per dozen—and we finally had rather a better dinner than usual. The house was occupied by a Mrs. Morrison, whose husband was in Genl Lee's army. She kindly gave Major Black[17] and myself a bed to sleep in, and put Major Scriven[18] on the floor on a comfortable pallet, and would not receive a cent from either of us.[19] This was very kind, but she not only dipped but actually had a quid of the genuine Virginia weed stored away in her cheek. I was on the point of asking her if she had a tumor in her cheek, when it suddenly shifted to the opposite side, and saved me from an unpleasant dilemma.

Thursday March 9th 1865—Left our camping grounds at half past six o'clock A.M. intending to go within two miles of Fayetteville, which would

16 The Fayetteville and Western Plank Road stretched 129 miles from Fayetteville to Bethania, seven miles short of Salem. Built in 1851 and 1852, it earned large profits through the mid-1850s, but later declined as the use of railroads as means of trade increased. See North Carolina History Project, "Fayetteville and Western Plank Road," (Raleigh, 2012), http://www.northcarolinahistory.org/encyclopedia/70/entry, accessed October 12, 2012. **Route: The former plank road is now North Carolina Highways 24 and 27.**

17 Acting Assistant Inspector General S. L. Black; listed as S. L. Black. Hardee's Corps Maj. AAIG, and S. L. Black. SC 15th Inf. Co. C. in Hewett, *Confederate Soldiers.*

18 Probably Maj. John H. Screven, Quartermaster Department; listed as John H. Screven. SC 1st Mtd. Mil. Screvens's Co. Capt. John H. Screven Gen & Staff, QM Dept. Maj., and John Screven GA Inf 18th Bn. Co. A. Maj. in Hewett, *Confederate Soldiers.*

19 One might speculate that the travelers had been attracted to this house by the glow of a flickering candle in a window, a traditional way of signaling that a home would open its doors to take in weary travelers who might need shelter for the night.

make the days march twenty miles.[20] About a mile from camp we came to a very high hill. The elevation was so great that we could see for miles to the right and left. The view to the left took in a larger space, as it extended into the deep river region, where the North Carolina coal fields are worked. A railroad—now in full operation, extends from Fayetteville to Egypt, a point at which the mines are worked.[21] When our men heard the whistle of the locomotive as it passed within a few miles of our encampment last night, they set up a universal shout that resounded from hill to hill amid the pine forests.[22] We crossed this road[23] three miles and a half from our encampment and then again at the depot, after which we continued with the road on our left all the way to Fayetteville. Thirteen miles from Fayetteville came to a fine plantation, with a stately old fashioned mansion, belonging to a Mr. McDirmid.[24] Everything wore the

20 **Route: The march follows modern North Carolina Highways 24 and 87.**

21 High production mining operations of the Deep River Coal Bed began in 1852, when the main shaft of the Egypt mine was sunk to a vein at 430 feet. The first coal was brought up in 1855, but reliable delivery to market was a problem because of poor navigability of Deep River. When the Civil War began, the young government expedited the construction of a railway, the Western Rail Road, from Fayetteville, the head of navigation on the Cape Fear River, to a point within two miles of the Egypt mine, opening the way for coal to get to market at Wilmington and elsewhere. The coal was used by the Confederate Navy vessels and by blockade runners. It had an unfortunate property of producing yellow smoke when it burned, leaving a dreaded telltale trail of Deep River coal that might disclose the locations of vessels at sea. See Michael Hetzer, "The Coal Demon of Deep River," *The State* Magazine, June 1987, electronic edition, http://freepages.history.rootsweb.ancestry.com/~pfwilson/coal_demon_of_deep_river.html, accessed October 10, 2003; John A. Oates, *The Story of Fayetteville and The Upper Cape Fear*, (Charlotte, 1950), 94, 415, 541, 751; James R. Vogt, "Map of North Carolina, 1861-1865," copy in Museum of the Cape Fear, Fayetteville, NC.

22 A continuously blowing railroad whistle often signified a southern military victory, and local residents of towns would gather at the depot to meet the train and hear the news. See Memoirs of Laura Prince Inglis in Adeline Godfrey Pringle Merrill, ed., *All in One Southern Family*, Volume II: Life in Cheraw (Charleston: 1996), 6.

23 The Western Rail Road.

24 Daniel McDiarmid (1803-1873), one of the most successful planters of the region, whose plantation produced an estimated 30,000 bushels of corn at the beginning of the war. He also contracted for a lengthy section of the Western Plank Road with his large slave labor force. See James Sprunt, *Chronicles of The Cape Fear River, 1660-1916*, second edition, (Raleigh, 1916; reprint edition, Wilmington, 1992), 624. Mr. McDiarmid was the "... owner and developer of Ardnave Plantation. The main part of the present house was built during his early ownership. The kitchen, as was then the custom, was in the yard. The quarters, at some distance from the house, were referred to as being on 'The Street.' The huge rooms of the house were furnished with handsome furniture, and steel engravings hung on the walls...Ardnave was a world within itself, becoming one of the great ante-bellum estates of Cumberland County." See *The Fayetteville Observer*, July 17, 1966, narrative by Mrs. James C. (Kate Robinson) McDiarmid of

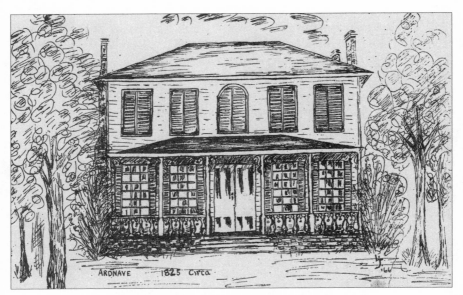

Mr. McDiarmid's House at Ardnave Plantation
Courtesy of Araminta McDiarmid Nixon

aspect of plenty and comfort. He was one of the descendants of the old Scotch Presbyterians, and was a staunch advocate of our cause. His wife and daughters could not do enough for the soldiers.

The table was spread, and all who came hungry went away filled, without money and without price. Although they expected Sherman or Kilpatrick[25] in our rear, yet it made no difference. Their expressions of sympathy and generous liberality were free and unstinted. As one of the Batterys of the reserve artillery stopped to get forage for the horses, one of the men brought in a battle flag in

North Wilkesboro and sketch, "The McDiarmid Family Home," from Lucille Miller Johnson, *Hometown Heritage*, (Fayetteville: Col. Rowan Chapter, Daughters of the American Revolution, 1978), copy furnished by Araminta McDiarmid Nixon, June, 2010. Daniel McDiarmid was the third son of the Reverend Angus McDiarmid, a minister of the Presbyterian Church who was born in 1757 on the Island of Islay, Scotland…and came to North Carolina about 1794. Mr. and Mrs. Daniel McDiarmid (nee Ann Eliza Wright) had daughters Catherine, Janie, and Mary, along with sons Archibald Knox and William James. Telephone communication, Robert White of Jacksonville, Florida to Thomas H. Robertson, Jr., October 4, 2003; Note, Araminta McDiarmid Nixon to Thomas H. Robertson, Jr., n.d., received October 27, 2003, in possession of the author. **Route: Mr. McDiarmid's house at Ardnave is no longer standing (2014).**

25 Brigadier General (Brevet Major General) Hugh Judson Kilpatrick, commander of the Third Division of Union Cavalry. See Wittenberg, *The Battle of Monroe's Crossroads*, 3; Bradley, *The Battle of Bentonville*, 422.

an unfinished state, and asked if one of the ladies would give the finishing touch to it. One of them at once took it in hand, and before they were ready to start it was completed and only awaited an opportunity to be unfurled to the breeze in the face of the foe.

My horse was very lame for the want of shoes. I have procured a set from the Quartermaster, but have no nails nor any one to put them on. Asked Mr. McDirmid if there was a blacksmith shop near. He said he had one with a boy to do his plantation work. Upon ascertaining my wants, he had the boy called, had nails made and my horse shod and could not be prevailed upon to take a cent in payment.

On the centre table, in the parlor, I found bibles, other religious books and the Presbyterian Hymnbook; and while my horse was being shod, I had an opportunity of refreshing myself by their perusal. He readily turned over to the Quartermaster all the corn and long forage which was required for our animals, and we all left the good man and his household wishing that our country had thousands upon thousands of such families, and with the sincere prayer that the merciless Yankees might pass them by unharmed.

It has been cloudy and threatening to rain all the morning. Soon after leaving Mr. McDirmids we crossed Little River, a rapid and beautiful stream which rises in the hilly region through which we have been passing for several days, and empties into the Cape Fear above Fayetteville. As it traverses some portion of the piney woods there are no indications, by growth or otherwise, of the nearness of any stream. The banks are perpendicular and abrupt, and without being aware of its potency you come immediately upon a bold and rapid river. At this point there are some factories from which the place is called "Manchester."[26] After crossing the river, I found the country still hilly and sandy. It took me some time to pass the reserve artillery, and before doing so it commenced raining. I arrived at camp—two miles from Fayetteville—at 4 o'clock P.M. One train had arrived at 2 o'clock. The army encamped about four miles from us.

The rain increased to a perfect torrent, so that our tent was completely flooded and it was impossible to keep a sufficient fire to cook anything more than a little bacon and rice. There was a large house near and our mess obtained permission to occupy a room on the floor with our blankets. The house was occupied by a Mrs. Carver and two daughters. She was a widow, whose sons

---

26 Named after Manchester, England, an early manufacturing city with substantial cotton mills, which made it the world's largest cotton market, and thus an important place, well known to southern cotton producers.

"Power, plunder, and extended rule."

Surgeon Robertson equates the Union logic of war with that which was being espoused by a set of Union opponents of President Abraham Lincoln's conduct of the war.

Following the long series of Federal military disasters leading up to and including their defeats in the battles of Fredericksburg and Chancellorsville in 1863, there arose a movement within the Army and the Federal Congress that reached a fever pitch in its call to displace President Lincoln, in effect, by the appointment of a dictator to direct the war effort. Members of Congress called for appointing a vigilant "committee on the conduct of the war" to watch and supervise Lincoln's movements and decisions. Supporters of this cabal included (a) political activists who sought increased Federal military victories and preservation of their personal and party power, (b) commercial zealots who desired spoliation and plunder of the South, and (c) religious abolitionists whose sympathy for the slave had degenerated into envenomed hostility toward his owner. These aggressive enemies of Lincoln in the North and within his own party summed up the logic of war in the comprehensive formula, "Power, plunder, and extended rule."

This phrase summarized the vindictive motivation that the seceding Southerners both expected and feared from the Union, if they should lose the war. The collection of attitudes has later been described by historians as the radical Republican philosophies.

So Lincoln, faced with fire in both his front and rear, finally concluded that he must assert himself. Lincoln exclaimed, "This state of things shall continue no longer. I will show them at the other end of the Avenue whether I am President or not!" From soon after this moment, "his opponents and would be masters were now, for the most part silenced; but, they hated him all the more cordially."[1]

In the end, after the southern surrender and Lincoln's assassination, the worst apprehensions of white Southerners about "power, plunder and extended rule" at the hands of the Republican North and the carpetbaggers would largely come true.

---

1 Ward Hill Lamon, *Recollections of Abraham Lincoln, 1847-1865,* (Chicago: A. C. McClurg and Company, 1895), Google Books edition, 2005, accessed August 10, 2010, 179- 184.

were in the Army.[27] They were very kind. Insisted on my taking some supper with them and fixed me up a bed. Notwithstanding it was one of the old fashioned ones with a bed cord instead of slats, I had an excellent nights rest. They have evidently stripped the house of everything valuable, and simply left a few old articles, intending to remain, hoping to save the house from the torch. I hope their efforts were successful. Unfortunately these kindhearted and patriotic ladies belonged to the dipper class, as the tin snuff box and short sticks were unmistakable evidence of the fact. But let this pass—they were kind to all the soldiers, for the house was filled that stormy night, and many a poor fellow was saved from a wet shirt, who, otherwise, would have been compelled to

---

27 Mrs. Carver, her daughters, and sons have not been further identified.

Fayetteville Market House (2003)
Courtesy of Catherine Barrett Robertson

My Soul, Be On Thy Guard

Let the pure and heavenly example of the women of our country cheer us on to greater endurance and more unreserved devotion. Let our watchword be that of the Christian women: "Then watch and fight and pray . . ."

Surgeon F. M. Robertson
March 10, 1865

My Soul, Be On Thy Guard

Words: George Heath, 1781
Music: *Heath*, from Mason and Webb's *Cantica Laudis*, 1850,[1] arranged and with a descant by Thomas Heard Robertson III, 2013.

1 The Christian women's poetic words comprise verse 2 of a hymn that begins, "My soul, be on thy guard," by George Heath. This hymn does not appear in subsequent Presbyterian hymn books, but may be found in the *Hymnal of the Episcopal Church*, Edition of 1940, at No. 555.

brave the peltings of the pitiless storm, with the saturated earth for a bed and the dark clouds for a covering.

March 10, 1865—Battle of Monroe's Crossroad, North Carolina.[28]

Friday 10th March 1865:

Though I rested well last night, I find myself a little out of sorts this morning. Had to take a quarter of a grain of morphine[29] to quiet the uneasiness in my bowels. Artillery firing heard in the rear of our Army, early this morning, on the Morganton road. It is Sherman's Army pressing our pickets. It ceased in half an hour. Genl Johnson and Genl Hardee met here day before yesterday and held a conference. Johnson left for Raleigh yesterday evening. Our army is to pass through Fayetteville today and burn what public property that has not been removed, and destroy the bridge.[30]

As I find myself more unwell, and have been greatly exposed to the weather for several days past, I determined to take the direct road to Raleigh, in advance of the Army.[31] The reserve Artillery and waggon train commenced crossing early this morning. I went through the Town about half past ten o'clock, merely stopping to get some paregoric,[32] and crossed the bridge.[33]

In coming into the Town I lost without perceiving it in time my horse collar. I was indebted to a kind gentleman for a very good shuck collar, which answered very well. He would take no pay for it.

---

28 Swanson, *Atlas of the Civil War*, 108. For a complete account of this engagement, see Wittenberg, *The Battle of Monroe's Crossroads*.

29 Morphine is an important pain-relieving drug derived from the sap of the seed pods of the common opium poppy.

30 Fayetteville was the location of a significant manufactory of arms, which the Confederates did not want to fall into the hands of the Federals. The rifle-making machinery and stores of the Fayetteville Arsenal would be shipped out at three o'clock in the morning of March 11th via the Western Rail Road to a hiding place at the Egypt Coal Mines. Many of the stores were carried by wagon to Greensboro. See Oates, *Fayetteville and The Upper Cape Fear*, 283-284; John M. Murphy, M.D. and Howard Michael Madaus, *Confederate Rifles & Muskets: Infantry Small Arms Manufactured in the Southern Confederacy, 1861-1865* (Newport Beach, CA, 1996), 219.

31 **Route: The direct road toward Raleigh begins on modern U.S. Highway 301.**

32 A camphorated tincture of opium, used especially to relieve pain or diarrhea, or as an expectorant or cough medicine.

33 The bridge over the Cape Fear River, located at the upstream limit of viable commercial navigation.

Mr. Murphy's House (2003)
Courtesy of Catherine Barrett Robertson

It has been said that war knows no Sabbath. So in relation to the appointments of the State; it heeds them not. This is the day set apart, by our government, for fasting, humiliation and prayer, and while this mighty host is passing through the streets, the church bells are sounding to assemble the people to humiliation and prayer.[34] At the same time the booming of artillery in our rear tells of the deadly strife in which the blood of our sons is being poured out as a sacrifice upon the altar of our country. While these commingling sounds fall upon the ear, we behold a dense mass of human beings, horses, artillery, waggons, and attendants, all pressing to one narrow bridge. The loud crack of the teamsters whip startles you amid the din around you. Another, with the most horrid curses, shouts to his jaded team to urge them out of the way of those who curse and shout in the rear. The giddy laugh, the obscene jest, and idiotic howl of the reeking drunkard add their portions to this horrid scene. This was Fayetteville as I rode through it this morning of the evacuation. One redeeming—one heavenly trait shone above all this medley of moral inconsistencies. At numerous houses along the streets, the soldiers were met by

---

34 Jefferson Davis and the Confederate Congress had proclaimed March 10, 1865, as a national day of fasting and prayer to "acknowledge their dependence on his [God's] mercy," and to shore up the sagging morale in the army and on the home front. See George C. Rable, *God's Almost Chosen Peoples: A Religious History of the Civil War* (Chapel Hill, 2010), 363-365, Google Books edition, accessed January 12, 2013.

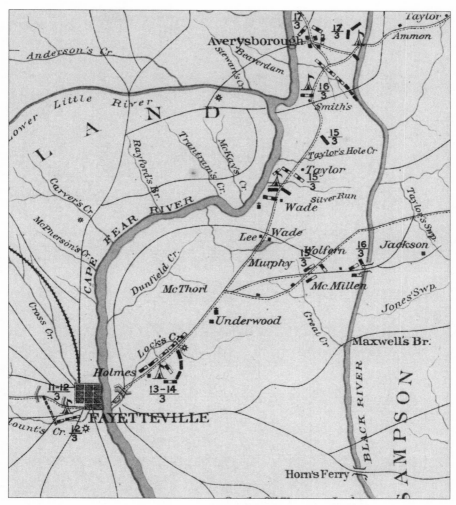

U.S. Military Map, Fayetteville to Averasboro.
Collection of Thomas H. Robertson, Jr.

ladies offering them refreshments as they passed along. An abundance of everything was, freely, tendered by these ministering angels. One would have supposed that the certain prospect of the occupation of the city by the "hell hounds" who had sacked and burnt Columbia, Cheraw and other places, would have deterred them from making these open demonstrations of "aid and comfort" to our retreating soldiers; but not so. Rising superior to all selfish considerations they dared to do their duty in defense of their beloved land. Cannot this spirit shame the skulkers from their hiding places, and paralyze the tongues of those craven creatures, who, upon the fall of a city or Town, are ready to brand their consciences by taking the infamous oath of allegiance to

John Anderson, My Jo

Mr. Murphy's wife was seventy-four years of age. The old couple, who seemed to be devoted to each other, reminded me of Burn's heartstirring song "John Anderson my Joe."

Surgeon F. M. Robertson
March 10, 1865

John Anderson, My Jo

Words: Scottish poet Robert Burns (1759-1796)[1]
Music: Scottish folk tune,[2] arranged by Thomas Heard Robertson III, 2013.

1 "Best Love Poems Network: Romantic poems for poetry lovers!," www.bestlovepoems.net/-classic_love_poems/john_anderson_my_jo_robert_burns, accessed August 11, 2005. In Scottish vernacular, *jo* means sweetheart and *pow* means head of hair.

2 http://www.folkinfo.org/songs/displaysong.php?songid=657, accessed October 13, 2012.

Abraham Lincoln and thus write a libel upon their own veracity and patriotism. If "consistency is a jewel,"[35] how much brighter and purer is that jewel of true patriotism which unreservedly, and without stint, devotes life fortune and sacred honor to a country contending for the right of self government, against those who have trampled the constitution in the dust, repudiated Christianity, and fight only "for power, for plunder and extended rule"?[36]

Let the pure and heavenly example of the women of our country cheer us on to greater endurance and more unreserved devotion. Let our watchword be that of the Christian women:

"Then watch and fight and pray,
The battle ne'er give o'er,
Renew it boldly every day,
And help Divine implore."[37]

After crossing the bridge and passing the reserve Artillery and waggon train, which was not completed until I had passed over four miles of horrible road, I quickly made my way to a Mr. Murphy's just ten miles from Fayetteville.[38] It rained nearly the whole way. When I rode up to the gate and

35 Ancient adage from an obscure origin.

36 This quotation is a summary of the logic toward the war and the South held by the radical Republicans and others of the Union who were aggressively opposed to President Lincoln's policies and conduct of the war beginning in 1862. The logic of the phrase is more fully explained in the sidebar, "Power, plunder, and extended rule." See Ward Hill Lamon, *Recollections of Abraham Lincoln, 1847-1865* (Chicago, 1895), Google Books edition, 2005, accessed August 10, 2010, 179-184.

37 These poetic words comprise verse 2 of a hymn that begins, "My soul, be on thy guard," by George Heath. [Presbyterian Church in the United States], *Parish Psalmody: A Collection of Psalms and Hymns for Public Worship* (Philadelphia, 1844), No. 435, p. 520, Google Books edition http://books.google.com/books?id=tJ ibeXR7YIC&pg=PA10&lpg=PA10&dq=%22My+s oul+be+on+thy+guard%22+presbyterian&source=bl&ots=KB-qufkGsK&sig=DcAVdL4 BhDz4VGSnl2n24wOlF8Q&hl=en&ei=PFJ6TOzdBIOBlAe52sHsCw&sa=X&oi=book re sult&ct=result&resnum=4&ved=0CBsQ6AEwAzgK#v=onepage&q&f=false, accessed August 29, 2010. This hymn does not appear in subsequent Presbyterian hymn books, but may be found in the Hymnal of the Episcopal Church, Edition of 1940, at No. 555. See Albert Edward Bailey, *The Gospel in Hymns: Backgrounds and Interpretations* (New York, 1950), 139, 591.

38 John Murphy (1781-1865). **Route: Mr. Murphy's plantation plain-style house is still nicely preserved (2013), at 5902 Dunn Road (U.S. Highway 301) opposite Rich Walker Road (Road 1719)**. Personal communication, Mr. and Mrs. Ted Taylor with Thomas H. Robertson, October 4, 2003; telephone communication, Mrs. Sylvia Lucas, aunt of Ted Taylor. She formerly lived in the house and was the current owner on that date. See

alighted from my buggy, I was met in the yard by the old gentleman. After hearing who I was and my desire to rest at his house until morning, he invited me into a roaring fire which was truly grateful to a man sick, weary, cold and wet. He is a native of North Carolina and is now eighty-four years of age. His father, a Scotch Presbyterian and elder of the church, settled in this very spot before the Revolutionary War. He also is an elder of the Presbyterian Church.

I arrived here about two o'clock P.M. It had ceased raining and the sun is coming out brightly. By resting this afternoon and getting a good nights rest, I hope to resume my journey in the morning greatly refreshed. In the course of the afternoon, Dr. Duncan[39] came by in his old fashioned peddlers waggon drawn by two mules, and stopped to get some corn and fodder. He is suffering from abscesses and is going in advance to avoid the annoyance of the extended waggon train and reserve artillery. Mr. Murphy let him have all the corn he wanted, but his fodder was all at his plantation on the river except a small quantity for his own immediate use. When Duncan asked what was to pay, he inquired if he belonged to the army, and upon being informed that he was the Quartermaster of Col. Goodwins Brigade of So. Car. Reserves, he told him not a cent, as he would prefer our army to have it than to allow it to fall into the hands of our enemies. Mr. Murphy's wife was seventy-four years of age. The old couple, who seemed to be devoted to each other, reminded me of Burns heartstirring song "John Anderson my Joe".[40] But alas, how soon might this stream of domestic happiness, which flowed in so near its peaceful termination, be suddenly and rudely interrupted by the vandals who were pressing on in our rear. In their wild and reckless sweep over our land, they spare neither age sex or condition. All are alike subject to their brutal insults and merciless robery. I shall make it a point to institute some inquiries about these good old people after the enemy has passed along. When sick and weary, how one sighs for the loved ones at home; and Oh! how we miss those tender cares and comforts to which we are accustomed. But I must not murmur. Still I cannot refrain from saying Oh! that my dear devoted wife and children were near me. When, when, Oh when shall this be?

---

http://awt.ancestry.com/cgi-bin/igm.cgi?op=GET&db=ssassybritches&id=I04468, accessed October 12, 2003.

39 Quartermaster. Listed as A.S. Duncan, SC 3rd Res. QM Sgt. in Hewett, *Confederate Soldiers*.

40 "John Anderson, My Jo," poem by Scottish poet Robert Burns (1759-1796). The text of the poem and the music of its folk tune are presented in the sidebar "John Anderson, my Jo."

Capt. McCorkle[41] of the Navy with some operatives and a few waggons passed by this evening on their way to Raleigh.

41 Capt. David Porter McCorkle, Confederate States Navy. He had run the Naval Ordnance Works at New Orleans until just before that City's evacuation in 1862. He moved the ordnance and laboratory stores to Atlanta and established shops on leased properties. On June 4, 1864, Gen. Joseph E. Johnston ordered him to remove to Augusta, Georgia. McCorkle wrote to his supervisor, Catesby ap Roger Jones, on June 8, 1865, "I am moving the boilers and engines to-day. All the lathes, planes, steam hammer, etc., are already shipped, and, to crown all, they have given an order to move the hospitals, and I can not get cars enough to move." In November, he was still at work building a foundry and other temporary structures, but was not at that time actually producing ordnance. See *OR* Series 2, 2:250, 548, 901; *OR* Series 1, 21:755-758; also http://en.wikipedia.org/wiki/David_Porter_McCorkle, accessed October 13, 2012.

Chapter Three

Raleigh, Richmond, and Greensboro

"He gave me an order to report to the Surgeon General in Richmond."

Saturday March 11th 1865

I feel much refreshed this morning by the night's rest. I had a cup of tea drawn last evening which acted on me like a charm. How I bless the affection and forethought of my dear wife. It was the first time I had opened it. I had sufficient drawn to give the old lady a cup. We took tea early by ourselves. She was delighted and seemed to relish it with a true gusto. It had been many months since she had enjoyed a cup of the delightful and cherished beverage. It did me good to see the kind old soul enjoying it. Breakfast at half past seven o'clock. Heavy firing heard in the direction of Fayetteville. Last evening at dark four broken down soldiers, who had been directed to go on in advance of their commands, came in and asked for accommodations for the night. The kind old people took them all in, gave them a good supper, a comfortable bed, and breakfast this morning; and sent them on their way refreshed and encouraged, and would not receive a dime in remuneration. One poor fellow from Georgia was suffering very much from an ingrowing toe nail. The whole foot was greatly swollen and extremely painful. The old lady had his foot bathed in warm water, and, on his going to bed, had a poultice applied to it. If a cup of cold water, given in the name of the blessed Redeemer shall want its reward, shall not such acts as these, when done from pure Christian benevolence, be remembered by the great dispenser of all blessings?

I commenced my journey about half past eight o'clock, and after a weary lonely and tedious ride, arrived at a Mr. Barber's at 5 o'clock P.M. and stopped for the night. This is a regular tavern, kept by the Mail Contractor, who runs a line of hacks from Raleigh to Fayetteville. This point is thirty-six miles from Fayetteville, twenty-six from Mr. Murphy's—where I staid last night—and

Mr. Barber's Tavern, Old Stage Road at Barbour Store Road. Although overgrown around the outside, this building is nicely detailed inside. (2003)
Courtesy of Catherine Barrett Robertson

twenty-four from Raleigh. In the course of the day, I passed the Provost Guard in charge of Yankee prisoners, en route, for Raleigh.[1] Several of them, through the gross negligence of the guard, escaped last night.[2] There seemed to be no

1 **Route: The journey follows U.S. Highway 301 and North Carolina Highways 82 and 55. It traverses the scene of the Battle of Averasboro that would take place five days hence, where his sons would be involved. Mr. Barber's is located at or near the intersection of Barbour Store Road (Road 2759) and Old Stage Road (Road 1006).**

2 The guard unit was part of the 3rd Regiment of South Carolina State Troops, mostly made up of raw recruits, young men over the age of 16 who had just been mustered into service at Hamburg, S.C. in September, 1864. One of the soldiers of Company "I," John Q. Cousart, later recalled, "We arrived at Fayetteville and were hospitably entertained by the ladies of this ancient town. The writer remembers many kindnesses conferred upon him and his mess mate, John E. Lark, by these kind and patriotic ladies. Here our regiment was given charge of about five hundred prisoners captured the night before in a soiree by Hampton's cavalry on the camp of Gen. Kirkpatrick. [The Battle of Monroe's Crossroad] The writer here saw a horse (a magnificent iron grey) said to be the property of Gen. Kirkpatrick; we conducted the prisoners,

discipline in the guard, in addition to the glaring incompetency of those in command. A dash on the part of half a dozen resolute cavalry men would have surprised the whole party and released every prisoner. I passed Capt. McCorkle's naval party during the day. They came up this evening, and some of them stopped at the house. After dark Lieut. Hasel,[3] in command of some scouts and couriers, came in. He had been ordered to establish a line of couriers from this point to Genl Hardee's Head Quarters, there being a line of telegraph from here to Raleigh, where Genl Johnson now has his Head Quarters. He reports the Army and all the trains safe across the river and encamped on this side. The bridge was burned after the army had crossed. After all had passed over except a few waggons, some stragglers, lead horses and a small portion of cavalry that remained as an escort to Genls Hardee and Hampton[4] who were still in Fayetteville, the Yankee advance guard of cavalry made a dash into the Town and commenced firing on the crowd at the Market, who were hurrying on to the bridge. The confusion and rush for the bridge, at first, endangered the whole party. Genl Hardee immediately had the bridge closed, restored order and directed the crossing to be continued in an orderly manner. In the meantime, Genl Hampton formed the Stono Scouts and some other Cavalry gallantly charged and drove them from the Town. Hampton killed two Yankees with his own pistol. Duncan came safely through the fight as Lieut. Hasel saw him after the Scouts had crossed the river.

Lieut. Hasel also gave me an account of Genl Hampton's surprise of Kilpatrick near Johnsonville on Friday morning the 10th before daylight.[5] We had encamped at Johnsonville, on the night of the 8th inst. This force of Yankees was just behind us and on Thursday night occupied a position near the encampment that we had left Thursday morning. Hampton and Wheeler made a gallant dash at them on friday morning before daylight, completely surprising

---

consisting of non-commissioned officers and privates, safely to Raleigh and placed them in charge of N. C. Troops, on this march the commissioned officers among the prisoners were separated and placed in charge of a detail of officers and allowed to precede the command. They managed to make good their escape, much to the chagrin of polite Captain Broom of Fairfield who was in command of the detail." See article in *Lancaster Enterprise*, June 1, 1892, extracted in "South Carolina Regimental History Books, South Carolina Infantry Regiments," n. d., http://www.researchonline.net/sccw/southcar.htm, accessed September 10, 2010.

3   Possibly Lt. Leonard L. Hassell, listed as Leonard L. Hassell NC 12th Inf. Co. L 1st Lt., Leonard L. Hassell NC 32nd Inf., and Leonard L. Hassell NC 32nd Inf. Co. F, A 1st Lt. in Hewett, *Confederate Soldiers*.

4   Lt. Gen. Wade Hampton

5   The Battle of Monroe's Crossroad. For further reading, see Wittenberg, *The Battle of Monroe's Crossroads and the Civil War's Final Campaign* (New York, 2006).

General Wade Hampton
Library of Congress

and routing them. Their artillery and camp equipage was captured, a large number killed, between three and four hundred prisoners taken, and over one hundred and thirty prisoners, that had been taken from us, re-captured and released. Kilpatrick's baggage and horses were captured and he barely made his escape in his drawers. A woman was, also, captured in his camp in her night dress. She was either Kilpatrick's wife or his mistress, the latter doubtless. It was said that she was a Northern woman whom he had picked up in Barnwell District. She had a splendid carriage and fine pair of mules—both, doubtless, stolen property. She was turned loose to seek consolation in the caresses of her unprincipled and abandoned keeper.

Sunday March 12th 1865

Did not leave Barber's this morning until nine o'clock. Breakfast was late as he was packing up and getting ready to send off his family, stock and provisions to get them out of the way of the Yankee swarm, who were expected to sweep every thing before them like the locusts of Egypt or the modern caterpillar. Paid fifty dollars ($50) for supper, lodging, breakfast and horse feed. I ate next to the landlord's wife, at breakfast, and opposite some other ladies, who were either her daughters or sisters. They all either dipped or chewed tobacco—some of them both. A strange specimen of the femanine gender came in just before we were called to breakfast. She was a regular piney-woods sandlapper with three tallow-faced bloodless looking squallid children. She stood boldly up with her back to the fire and entered freely into the general conversation. She had a respectable quid of the weed in her mouth. This she freely masticated, and, upon turning to the fire ejected the juice with a genuine masculine grace. She warmed up when the conversation turned upon substitutes for coffee. Declared her preference for the unadulterated genuine article. When she had pure coffee, if it was but a spoonful, she want it upon this unmixed until it was out, and then tried the substitutes—but on no consideration would she mix anything with it.

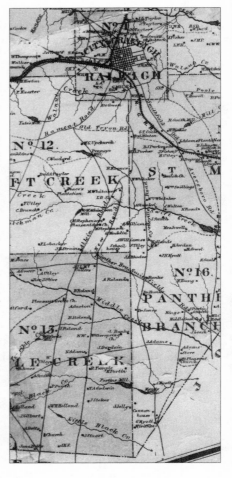

Fayetteville Road to Mrs. Banks's house and to Raleigh, N.C. Detail from Bevers Map of Wake County, 1870.
Copy furnished by Marvin L. Brown, Jr., and State Department of Archives and History, Raleigh, N.C.

She declared that, of all the suffering the war had inflicted upon her, the want of coffee was the greatest. She told me that she would work at collecting turpentine, all the winter, and then bring her miserable scrapings to the store, at this place, and barter it for coffee, be it ever so small a portion. I have no doubt, from her appearance and statement, that all she could rake and scrape was spent for tobacco, snuff and coffee. Some mourn over the loss of a fine house and splendid furniture, some over the loss of carriage and horses, some over the loss of luxurious living, and others over the loss of silks, laces and fine linen, but here was one who, in rags and poverty, felt as keenly as all those named because she could get no more coffee, and there was danger of the supply of snuff and tobacco failing. This certainly was—a specimen of the female sui generis.[6]

After passing some distance, over a terrible road, stopped at 12 o'clock in company with Capt. McCorkle's party to rest and feed my horse. As the road is very bad, I shall not attempt to get to Raleigh tonight but stop at a Mrs. Banks' about ten miles from that place.[7]

6   *Sui generis*, adjective: from Latin, meaning literally, "of its own kind"; constituting a class of its own; being the only example of its kind; unique. http://dictionary.reference.com/wordoftheday/archive/2001/06/14.html, accessed August 12, 2005.

7   **Route: The terrible road is Old Stage Road (Road 1006). Mrs. Banks's house was in the vicinity of the intersection of Banks Road (Road 2724) and Old Stage Road, possibly**

Arrived at Mrs. Banks' at 3 o'clock P.M. Like all persons on the road she was evidently expecting to be plundered by the Yankees and seems to have stripped her house of all the good furniture and bedding, leaving just sufficient to give the house and premises the appearance of belonging to a person in very moderate circumstances. She had secreted all her valuables and provisions, merely leaving sufficient to make a fair show, as she intended to remain herself. She had several sons and one son-in-law, who should have been in the regular army. They are fine-looking, hearty, robust and young. They belong to what is termed, in North Carolina, "the home guard," and I have no doubt they will guard their homes until the Yankees come, and then take their heels and skulk in some hiding place instead of meeting the foe like true men.

The old lady asked my opinion about the ultimate success of our cause. I unreservedly expressed my firm belief in our ultimate triumph, and spoke in terms of censure of those who for a respite from the present hardships of the war were willing to surrender, and go back into the old union. She replied, evidently looking upon the dark side, that she hoped we would succeed, but she always thought it was wrong to remove the old flag. God said we "must not remove the ancient landmarks."[8] This remark and an attempt to justify it by a bungling quotation from scripture, shows the superficial view that many take of this great struggle. This quotation from the Old Testament had about as much to do with the origin of our struggle as Jacob's vision had to do with the Revolution of "76". I asked her if she knew the origin of the present U. S. flag. She was under the impression that it was the same flag under which our independence was achieved in the Revolutionary War. I explained to her the mistake. This delusion has been designedly put forth by the Yankee nation in many of their illustrated histories and other works illustrating that period. In most of the pictures representing the battles and scenes of the revolution, you find the present U. S. flag occupying a prominent place. This falsehood has been carried to such a pitch that this flag is now substituted for the constitution, the bible, confession of faith and prayer book; and idolatrous kneeling to and worship of this bit of bunting are considered the only genuine test of true patriotism & Christianity.

---

at or near the site occupied by the **Marion West, Jr. family (10101 Old Stage Road), 2003.** *Personal communication, Marion West, Jr. with Thomas H. Robertson, Jr., October 27, 2003.*

8   "Remove not the ancient landmark, which thy fathers have set." *The Holy Bible*, Proverbs 22:28.

North Carolina State House
Photograph by Thomas H. Robertson, Jr., 2013

Dorothea Dix Hospital, circa 1895
Courtesy of Karl Larson

General Joseph E. Johnston
Library of Congress

Just before dark Coln Anderson,[9] commanding a Texas Brigade in Hampton's fight with Kilpatrick at Johnsonville, came up in an ambulance wounded in the thigh. He, with two others, wounded in that fight, remained all night and were sent on to Raleigh the next day. I have been suffering very much today from my old local trouble. Shall go to bed at 8 o'clock.

Monday March 13th 1865

Had a comfortable bed and good nights rest. Feel better and greatly refreshed this morning. Rose at half past six o'clock. Washed, dressed, and walked out. When I came to settle, this woman charged me $70, and did not blush to say that she would prefer ten cents in silver to the $70. I am now waiting for breakfast, after which I will set out for Raleigh. The road is said to be worse than any I have passed over. The road yesterday lay over a succession of high hills, stiff red clay cropping out which rendered them almost impassable.[10] The hills, sometimes, almost rose into mountains. The valleys between them are usually traversed by clear streams, rolling over beautiful beds of waterworn pebbles. The water, pure, clear and soft, is very fine. Arrived at Raleigh at 12 o'clock M. and stopped at the Yarborough House.[11] Had a tolerable dinner but it is a dirty and filthy Hotel. I reported to Genl Johnson immediately. He gave

9   Lt. Col. Paul Anderson of the 4th/8th Tennessee Cavalry (Consolidated). He was wounded at the Battle of Monroe's Crossroad. See Wittenberg, *The Battle of Monroe's Crossroads*, 247.

10 **Route: Atop one of these hills during our retracement trip in 2003, we met by happenstance Dr. and Mrs. Marvin L. Brown, when we stopped in at their obviously historic residence, a house called Edenwood at 7620 Old Stage Road. Dr. Brown was a retired history professor from North Carolina State University, as it turned out. He encouraged us to edit Dr. Robertson's journal for publication and introduced us to the staff of the North Carolina Archives by sending our working draft to them. He also sent us a fine map of Wake County, circa 1870, details of which are presented as two of the map illustrations in this work.**

11 The Yarborough House, on Fayetteville Street, three blocks south of the State Capitol.

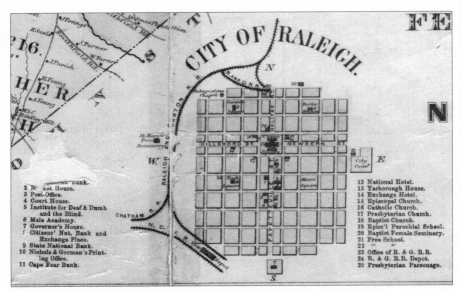

City of Raleigh. Inset from Bevers Map of Wake County, 1870.
Copy furnished by Marvin L. Brown, Jr., and State Department of Archives and History, Raleigh, N.C.

me an order to report to the Surgeon General in Richmond; I shall probably leave tomorrow at 1 o'clock P.M. Genl Johnson informed me that Mjr Willis[12] was in Charlotte with Genl Beauregard. I wrote to Henry and mailed the letter this evening.[13]

12 Maj. Edward Willis, quartermaster. Edward Willis (1834-1910) was born in Charleston, but had spent his childhood and youth in Augusta, Georgia, where he as a youngster was very likely acquainted with Dr. Robertson's family. He moved to Charleston and became chief clerk of the shipping company John Fraser & Company. Owned by George A. Trenholm, this firm became a major participant in blockade running. After South Carolina's secession, Willis had gone to England as a purchasing agent, bought arms, and sent them back to South Carolina, where they were used by a company of militia to prevent the *Star of the West* from provisioning Fort Sumter. Pvt. James L. Robertson was serving in one of the militia companies, the Vigilant Rifles. The blockade runner *Major E. Willis* was been named for him. See ArchiveGrid: Edward Willis papers, 1864-1891. University of South Carolina—South Caroliniana Library, http://beta.worldcat.org/archivegrid/record.php?id=43579481&contributor=207&archiven ame=University+of+South+Carolina+-+South+Caroliniana+Library, accessed October 22, 2012; Ethel Nepveux, "The Economist," in *Confederate Historical Association of Belgium News*, www.chab-belgium.com/pdf/english/Economist.pdf, accessed October 22, 2012; listed as E. Willis Beauregard's Staff Maj. Ch. QM, Edward Willis Gen. and Staff Adj. Gen. Dept. PACS Col., and Edward Willis Capt. in Hewett, *Confederate Soldiers*.

13 Dr. Robertson probably sent the letter to his son Henry Clay Robertson in Augusta and missed him there, because "H. C. Robertson" appears in list of "Undelivered Messages" in *Augusta Chronicle & Sentinel*, April 22, 1865.

General Pierre G. T. Beauregard
Library of Congress

Tuesday, March 14th 1865

Remained in Raleigh today, as there was no train at 1 o'clock. I shall leave at 12 o'clock tonight, and am determined not to sleep another night in this Hotel if I can help it, for never to my recollection, have I occupied so filthy a bed. If I do not contract the itch it will be a wonder. I wrote to Righton, Jimmy and Duncan today, and sent the letters from Genl Johnson's Head-quarters.

Raleigh is rather a miserable looking place. The State House is a fine building—pure Doric and situated in a commanding position. There are a few handsome residences in the suburbs with fine grounds and handsome gardens. The Lunatic Asylum is a fine building and occupies a beautiful hill near the city. This is the residence of Holden the Yankee traitor who publishes a rank Union and submission paper here.[14] I fear the majority of people of Raleigh would rejoice to see Sherman run up the U. S. flag on the dome of the State House.

14 William Woods Holden (1818-1892), publisher and editor of the *Standard* newspaper. The paper was known by several variations on that name over time. It was called the *Semi-weekly Standard* at the time of Robertson's comments and through April 24, 1865, when it changed to the *Daily Standard*. Holden was always a controversial figure. Active in Democratic political circles before the war, he first opposed secession for North Carolina, but ultimately voted for it when the fighting began. He became the avowed leader of the state's "peace movement," advocating that it was far better to make an honorable peace rather than being forced to accept unconditional surrender. He espoused overthrowing the agrarian aristocratic rule in the South to create a progressive state for the welfare of the masses. He was denounced as a traitor for such views. He ran for governor on the peace platform in 1864 against sitting Governor Zebulon G. Vance, and was defeated. Holden lived in one of Surgeon Robertson's "few handsome residences" in Raleigh, a colonial frame residence that he built in 1852 at the corner of Hargett and McDowell Streets. It had one of the first bathtubs in the city and was noted for its sunken garden. Immediately after the war President Andrew Johnson appointed him Provisional Governor of North Carolina on May 29, 1865. Holden became a Republican, and was elected governor in 1868. As the Reconstruction period was winding down, he was impeached and removed from office in 1871, whereupon he returned to the newspaper business. See *Chronicling America: Historic American Newspapers*, The Library of Congress, Raleigh,

Genl Beauregard arrived here this afternoon. He looks quite well. I had a few moments' conversation with him. He informed me that Henry was in Augusta and well. The hotel charge was $115 for myself and servant from dinner yesterday to tea this evening.

Coln Pickett,[15] Genl. Hardee's inspector General, who was sick, sent for me to see him at the residence of Judge Sanders. Mrs. Sanders—the Judge was not at home—insisted on my remaining to tea with the family. I found them very pleasant. Judge Sanders was formerly Minister from the U. S. to Spain.[16] Mrs. Sanders was a Miss Johnson[17] from Charleston, a daughter of Wm. Johnson,[18] a brother of old Dr. Johnson[19]—A dear wife, a very handsome and interesting lady, a single daughter, young, blooming, handsome and intelligent, and Miss L'Angle,[20] Mrs. Tobins Sister—and old acquaintance—formed the

---

N.C. newspapers, http://chroniclingamerica.loc.gov, accessed September 1, 2010; see also William S. Powell, ed., *Dictionary of North Carolina Biography* (University of North Carolina Press, 1979-1996), reprinted in http://docsouth.unc.edu/browse/bios/pn0000761_bio.html, accessed September 1, 2010.

15 Col. W. D. Pickett, listed as W. D. Pickett, Hardee's Corps Lt. Col., AIG. in Hewett, *Confederate Soldiers.*

16 Romulus Mitchell Saunders (1791-1867). Judge Saunders lived at "Elmwood" on Boylan Avenue in Raleigh. He was a prominent North Carolina lawyer and politician, who held many varied offices, including North Carolina State Legislator, United States Congressman, and North Carolina Superior Court Judge. In 1846, President James Polk appointed him as Envoy Extraordinary and Minister Plenipotentiary to Spain, where he remained until 1850, when he was recalled at his own request. See entry for Romulus Mitchell Saunders, quoting Article # 630 by Mary Yarbrough McAden Satterfield in *The Heritage of Caswell County, North Carolina*, in http://www.rootsweb.ancestry.com/~ncccha/biographies/romulussaunders.html, accessed September 8, 2010; http://bioguide.congress.gov/scripts/biodisplay.pl?index=S000078, accessed September 8, 2010.

17 Anne Hayes Johnson, daughter of Supreme Court Justice William Johnson and second wife of Romulus Mitchell Saunders. See entry for Romulus Mitchell Saunders, http://www.rootsweb.ancestry.com/~ncccha/biographies/romulussaunders.html, accessed September 8, 2010.

18 William Johnson, Jr. (1771-1834), lawyer of South Carolina. United States Supreme Court Justice appointed by President Thomas Jefferson in 1804. See entry for William Johnson, Jr. in *South Carolina Encyclopedia*, http://www.scencyclopedia.org/johnson.htm, accessed September 8, 2010.

19 Probably Dr. Isaac Johnson. See Waring, *A History of Medicine in South Carolina*, 303.

20 Probably Miss Madeleine L'Engle. See entry for Romulus Mitchell Saunders http://www.rootsweb.ancestry.com/~ncccha/biographies/romulussaunders.html, accessed September 8, 2010; and entry for Madeleine L'Engle (1918-2007) in *Encyclopedia of World Biography*, 2004, http://www.encyclopedia.com/doc/1G2-3404707212.html, accessed September 11, 2010.

Elmwood, home of Judge Romulus Mitchell Saunders
Photograph by Thomas H. Robertson, Jr., 2013

family circle. I found them all strong and enthusiastic in the Confederate cause. I had a delightful cup of tea, and spent a very agreeable evening—one green spot amid the desolate waste over which I have passed for the last few days. Mrs. Johnson and Miss L'Angle asked me many questions about Charleston and the people, to all of which I was enabled to give them some satisfactory answers.

Wednesday, March 15th 1865

Went to the Depot at 12 o'clock last night but the train did not get off until 2 A.M.[21] Rained all day. Horrible car—filthy and crowded to suffocation. Arrived at Greensbor [sic] at 1 o'clock P.M. The Danville train does not leave until 8 P.M. Took dinner at a house near the Depot—a very good one for the times. Landlord complained that Confederate money was good for nothing—did not want it, but took care to charge me $20 for my dinner! Took my

---

21 This train was operated by the North Carolina Rail Road, from Raleigh to Greensboro, at which point it connected with Branch Rail Road to Danville. See J. C. Swayze, *Hill & Swayze's Confederate States Rail-Road & Steam-Boat Guide*, 15.

departure from this sink of mud and mire, in the Danville train, at half past five o'clock P.M.[22] Raining, blowing and cold. Arrived in Danville, some time after midnight, and fortunately found the train for Richmond waiting.[23] Huddled into a dilapidated filthy car with no cushions at backs of the seats and jammed with soldiers and negros. I wonder that the odors and filth in these crowded cars does not produce typhus, or jail fever among the travelling public.

March 16, 1865—Battle of Averasboro, North Carolina.[24]

Thursday, March 16th 1865

At daylight had only progressed eleven miles from Danville. Still raining and blowing. It commenced clearing off before midday, and it was a great relief to the respiratory organs to raise the windows and inhale the pure air. When we approached the junction of the Southern Rail Road from Petersburg, with the Richmond & Danville Road, we saw the evidences of strife in the burnt houses, tanks and bent iron. All, however, was now quiet. As we neared the James River, down which the road runs for some distance before crossing into Richmond, the granite cropped out frequently, and coal was abundant. The scenery, as you pass down the James River, just at the water's edge, is very fine. In mid summer and autumn the country must look charming. Arrived at Richmond at 1 o'clock P.M. and got to the Spotswood Hotel at 2 P.M.[25] Have not tasted a mouthful from four o'clock yesterday until half past two today except a small crablantern which I gave one dollar for on the way. I do not think it had more than a teaspoonful of dried apples in it.[26] Shaved, which I had not done since leaving Cheraw except once at Raleigh. Washed, and dressed for dinner. Had a tolerable dinner with a fruit lether apron pudding for desert. Shall report to the Surgeon General tomorrow. Aside from the numerous officers and men in the streets and at the Hotels, Richmond looks as unlike a besieged city as Columbia or

22 This train was operated by the Branch Rail Road from Greensboro to Danville, at which point it connected with Richmond & Danville Rail Road. See Swayze, *Hill & Swayze's Confederate States Rail-Road & Steam-Boat Guide*, 28.

23 This train was operated by the Richmond & Danville Rail Road. See Swayze, *Hill & Swayze's Confederate States Rail-Road & Steam-Boat Guide*, 28.

24 Swanson, *Atlas of the Civil War*, 108.

25 "SPOTSWOOD HOTEL.—Corner Main and Eighth Streets, Jos. H. Crenshaw, Proprietor." See Swayze, *Hill & Swayze's Confederate States Rail-Road & Steam-Boat Guide*, 5.

26 The crablantern is a nineteenth-century, semi-circular apple pastry, baked or fried, similar to the modern fried pie.

Crablanterns

Have not tasted a mouthful from four o'clock yesterday until half past two today except a small crablantern which I gave one dollar for on the way. I do not think it had more than a teaspoonful of dried apples in it.

Surgeon F. M. Robertson,
March 16, 1865

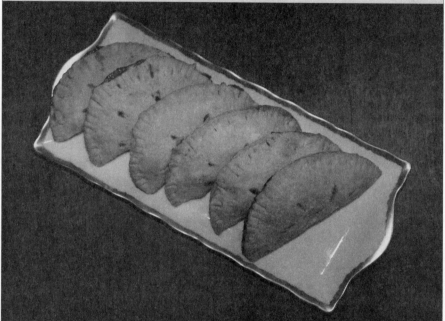

Crablanterns
Thomas H. Robertson, Jr., 2012

The crablantern is a spicy, nineteenth-century apple pie or pastry, baked or fried, common in the South during the Civil War era.[1] Its shape resembles the shell of an Atlantic blue crab, and pastry slits are reminiscent of those in a tin candle lantern. A reasonable modern reproduction of this tasty snack may be made using the following recipe:[2]

Continued on page 89

1. Besides Surgeon Robertson's description, another Civil War era source refers to this pastry treat as ". . . Crablantern or half moon pies 50 cents apeace & ct. but I don't buy any [at] such prices." in Thos. W. Hendricks to Moses Hendricks, March 25th, 1863. "The Cherished Letters, 1863," http: //freepages.genealogy.rootsweb.com/~mysouthernfamily/THECHERISHEDLETTERS1863.htm, accessed July 7, 2004.

2. Based roughly upon a recipe for Amish Half Moon Pies in *Annie's Quick and Easy Amish Recipes*, n. d., www.anniesrecipes.com/Kitchen/amish-recipes/amish-half-moon-pies-recipe.htm, accessed July 6, 2004; altered by Thomas H. Robertson, Jr., based on kitchen testing.

Surgeon General Samuel Preston Moore
Courtesy of Waring Historical Library,
Medical University of South Carolina.

Augusta, in a time of profound peace. There was some fighting in the vicinity yesterday but I was unable to ascertain the facts in relation to it. In fact I have determined not to burden these notes with the various reported incidents that float about from day to day. The official telegrams give the true state of matters.

I have a small and comfortable room, but a filthy bed. I know my dearest wife would grieve if she could only look upon the dirty sheets. One shudders as he gets into bed just as he would at the idea of a cold shower bath on a frosty morning in December.

Friday March 17th 1865

Reported to the Surgeon General at 10 o'clock this morning. He was polite and not by any means rude. I took a seat and had a long chat with him. Upon receiving my communication from Florence enclosing Holbrooks[27] resignation and stating that I could not get to Columbia, the board was dissolved[28] and Dr.

---

27 John Edwards Holbrook, M.D. (1794-1871). He was head of the board of Medical Examiners, presumably assuming the chair following the resignation of Board President Dr. Eli Geddings, M.D. on February 7, 1865. These men were 70 and 68 years old, respectively. Dr. Holbrook was also an accomplished naturalist, having published books on snakes, *North American Herpetology*, in 1842, and fishes, *Ichthyology of South Carolina*, in 1855. See *South Carolina Historical Magazine*, vol. 111, nos. 1-2, January-April 2010, 99.

28 Special Order No. 42/15, February 20, 1865, revoked Special Order # 4, Par. # 10, January 6, 1862, which had originally constituted an Army Medical Board, including Surgeon F. M. Robertson, to convene at Charleston. See *Compiled Service Records*, Confed. Gen. & Staff officers, for F. M. Robertson, Microfilm Roll # 214, S. C. Department of Archives and History, Columbia.

Continued from page 87

2 double-crust pie pastry sets (homemade or store-bought), chilled
2 cups dried apples, loose (one 5-ounce package)
1 cup water
1/16 teaspoon salt
½ cup sugar
1 small orange, grated zest, and squeezed juice
2 Tablespoons butter
1 ½ teaspoons cinnamon
1 egg, beaten
2 Tablespoons water

Prepare the pastry and roll out thin (1/16 to 1/8 inch thick, to yield 4 rounds per pastry, if using the store-bought kind). Cut into five inch circles and stack in waxed paper layers. Gather scraps, knead, and re-roll. Refrigerate in air tight wrapping until ready to bake.

Chop the dried apple slices into halves and boil them in 1 cup water and the 1/16 teaspoon salt, covered, until the apples are soft. Add sugar, orange zest and juice, butter, and cinnamon. Simmer slowly until the liquid thickens. Allow the filling to cool. It may be refrigerated until ready to bake.

Make an egg wash of beaten egg and 2 Tablespoons of water. Moisten the edges of each pastry round with the egg wash. Place a small portion (a heaping Tablespoon, more or less) of the filling in the middle of each pastry, avoiding the edges. Fold the pastry over the filling into a semi-circular shape and pinch the edges tightly together, or crimp with fork tines, curling slightly upward to retard leakage. Make three short slits in the top pastry with a sharp knife. Transfer the crablanterns immediately to an ungreased baking pan lined with parchment paper. Bake in the center of a preheated 350-degree oven for about 25 to 35 minutes, until golden brown.

May be served immediately or at room temperature. Also, may be kept refrigerated for later warming. Good with a scoop of vanilla ice cream, or just plain.

Makes about 14 to18 five-inch crablanterns.

Miles[29] and myself ordered to report to Crowell[30] for hospital duty. I told him it was probable I should not be able to find Dr. Crowell. He directed me to go to Chester, and if I could not find Crowell, to report back to him by letter. He voluntarily told me that, as I had been broken up in all my family arrangements, I could take as much time as I desired to arrange my affairs. He gave me transportation to Chester. I wrote my dear wife a short open letter—all that was admissible, through Coln Ould,[31] the commissioner of exchange, to go by way

29 Francis Turquand Miles, M.D. (1827-1903). See Waring, *A History of Medicine in South Carolina*, 267-8.

30 Dr. N. S. Crowell, Medical Director of hospitals in Charleston. See Waring, *A History of Medicine in South Carolina*, 128.

31 Robert Ould, Gen. and Staff, Exch. Agent, as listed in Hewett, *Confederate Soldiers*.

of New York, by the flag of truce boat. God grant that it may get to her. Called upon the paymaster and Quarter Master, and drew my pay up to the lst of March and commutation for quarters and fuel up to the day I left Charleston. This was a lucky hit.

Saturday, March 18th 1865

Settled my bill at the Spotswood, which was $105 for self and servant, and left Richmond yesterday evening at half past six o'clock. Cars literally packed, inside and out, with returned prisoners, who have just arrived by the flag of truce boat. Fell in company with Mr. Baggot from our City[32] who had been in prison sixteen months, also Lieut. Hopkins[33] and Mr. Williams,[34] both of Charleston, who had just been released. I was indebted to them for a seat. When the cars were opened, Williams & Hopkins rushed in, secured seats and then hoisted the window and drew Baggott and myself through it into the car. Without a resort to this expedient, I should have been left in Richmond another night. Henry, with our baggage, barely got on the platform of one of the cars. After crossing the river, another car was put on and he was enabled to get a comfortable seat. Had a most uncomfortable night, and was compelled to take a miserable dirty box car at Danville.[35] I find I have taken a severe cold, and am now suffering with an excruciating headache. We arrived at Greensboro at 4 o'clock P.M. Although we made the connection, I am too sick to go on tonight. I am sure I cannot stand another night in the uncomfortable, filthy and crowded cars. If I feel better, I will resume my journey tomorrow.

I stopped at the house near the depot where they charged me $20 for a dinner on Thursday. There was no other chance, as I did not know a living soul in the place. I had a cup of my dear wife's tea drawn and relished it very much. I shall be compelled to take a miserable bed in a small dirty room with two strangers in two other beds. Henry will sleep at my bedside. He is a most true and faithful companion.

---

32 Not further identified.

33 Possibly J. A. Hopkins or a son; listed as James Hopkins SC 9th Inf. Co. B Lt. in Hewett, *Confederate Soldiers*; J. A. Hopkins owned property in Charleston at 2 Adgers South Wharf, which was occupied by slaves. See *Census of the City of Charleston, South Carolina for the Year 1861*, 224, accessed October 13, 2012.

34 Not further identified.

35 This train was operated by the Branch Rail Road. See Swayze, *Hill & Swayze's Confederate States Rail-Road & Steam-Boat Guide*, 28.

The Battle of Averasboro

As Francis Marion Robertson traveled the Fayetteville to Raleigh road on Saturday, March 11, 1865, little did he know that he was traversing the scene of a fierce battle that would take place five days hence. At least one of his sons, 2nd Lt. James L. Robertson, would be involved and would end up wounded.

Lieutenant General William J. Hardee's command followed the same route, a day or two's march behind the surgeon. They evacuated Fayetteville on March 10-11, 1865, burning the bridge over the Cape Fear River as they left.[1] The force consisted of about 6,000 men and was made up mainly of Georgia and South Carolina troops, including a large proportion of heavy artillery soldiers and some garrison infantrymen whose fighting experience had been manning coastal forts and heavy gun batteries. Converted entirely to infantry after the evacuation of Charleston, they received their foot soldier training while on the march.[2] "Red infantrymen," the Yankees called them, because of the red collars and cuffs on their gray uniforms that distinguished them as artillerymen.[3]

A North Carolina unit, composed of parts of the Fayetteville Arsenal Battalion, known locally as the Armory Guard, joined Hardee's army at Fayetteville, and was assigned to Brig. Gen. Stephen Elliott's brigade. This unit of upwards of 200 men was comprised mostly of workers at the Fayetteville Arsenal and Armory under the command of Capt. Armand L. DeRosset, Lt. James L. Robertson's second cousin.[4]

Upon the approach of the Union army to Fayetteville, the other remaining men of the Armory Guard, under the command of Lt. Col. Frederick L. Childs, had dismantled the important machinery of the arsenal and moved it to the coal mines on Deep River at Egypt. Subsequently, the arsenal buildings themselves were demolished by the Federals.[5]

Hardee's main objective was to join forces with remnants of the other Confederate commands in the Deep South, who were converging on central North Carolina to form the Army of the South under the command of Gen. Joseph E. Johnston. In addition to Hardee's Corps, these forces included the Army of Tennessee under Lt. Gen. Alexander P. Stewart; Maj. Gen. Robert F. Hoke's Division from the Army of Northern Virginia, assigned to Gen. Braxton Bragg's Department of North

1 Bradley, *Last Stand in the Carolinas: The Battle of Bentonville*, 105-9.

2 Joseph E. Johnston, General, C.S.A., *Narrative of Military Operations Directed during the Late War between the States*, (New York, 1874), Appendix: W. J. Hardee, "Memoranda of the Operations of my Corps, while under the command of General J. E. Johnston, in the Dalton and Atlanta, and North Carolina Campaigns, 582. General Hardee stated that he had 6,000 effectives of foot soldiers, plus part of General Wheeler's cavalry.

3 Sion H. Harrington III and John Hairr, *Eyewitnesses to Averasboro, Volume 1: The Confederates*, (Erwin, NC, 2001), 11, 38.

4 Louis H. Manarin, comp., *North Carolina Troops 1861-1865, A Roster*, (Raleigh, 1971, second printing with addenda, 1989), Vol. III, 342, 347, 678-9. The portion of the Armory Guard that joined Hardee's corps was Company B of the 2nd Battalion N.C. Local Defense Troops and some men of the other companies. Company B had been detailed to the coast to assist in the defense of Fort Anderson and the City of Wilmington. After the fall of Wilmington on February 20-21, 1865, the company assisted in obstructing the Cape Fear River and then returned to Fayetteville. See also *Eyewitnesses to Averasboro, Volume 1*, 31-2.

5 Angley, et al., *Sherman's March through North Carolina: A Chronology*, 24; Bradley, *Bentonville*, 480n.

Carolina, retreating from Wilmington; and Lt. Gen. Wade Hampton's cavalry command.[6] Time was needed to effect the convergence, and Johnston was unsure of the Union army's destination. The major railroad towns were obvious objectives; but, were the Yankees headed toward Raleigh or to Goldsboro?[7]

The Federals under Gen. William T. Sherman moved north from Fayetteville in two separate wings along roughly parallel roads about twenty miles apart.[8] The Left Wing, commanded by Maj. Gen. Henry W. Slocum, consisted of the XX and XIV Corps, supported by Bvt. Maj. Gen. Judson Kilpatrick's cavalry.[9] Sherman himself was with the Left Wing, which moved north along the Fayetteville-Raleigh road, after having completed a pontoon crossing of the Cape Fear River on March 14, 1865, near the site of the bridge burned by the Confederates three days earlier.[10]

Hardee determined to buy some time by making a stand where the road passed through a narrow neck of land between the swollen Cape Fear and Black Rivers, at a point south of where the roads to Raleigh and Goldsboro divided.[11] He formed his forces into three lines of defense about two miles wide at right angles to the Fayetteville-Raleigh road, flanked by the river swamps on both sides. He positioned his untested "red infantry" troops on the first line behind trenches and breastworks that they hastily built. The 1st South Carolina Artillery, under Col. Alfred M. Rhett, occupied the right flank with one artillery piece from Stuart's Battery in its midst. LeGardeur's Battery and Lucas's Battalion with two artillery pieces occupied the center near the road. The 1st South Carolina Infantry defended the left side marked by a pond.[12] On March 15, 1865, Hardee instructed Brig. Gen. William B. Taliaferro, commanding the first line, that he should hold the line "until it was no longer tenable, then fall back upon Elliott's line."[13] That afternoon Colonel Rhett accompanied his detachments of skirmishers a half mile in front of his main line, where he was surprised to be captured by Federal cavalry whom he mistook for friendly troops.[14]

The first significant Federal attack came at about 6:00 a.m. on March 16, 1865, beginning at the left side of the line of Rhett's Brigade. Federal cavalry under Col. Thomas J. Jordan and infantry under Col. William Hawley began the Union advance that became a series of frontal assaults on the Confederate defensive line.[15] Major Thomas A. Hugenin, commanding the 1st South Carolina In-

---

6 Bradley, *Bentonville*, 137, 437-47; Mark A. Moore, *Moore's Historical Guide to the Battle of Bentonville*, (Campbell, CA, 1997), 16.

7 *Johnston's Narrative*, 382.

8 Moore, *Moore's Guide to Bentonville*, 9.

9 Bradley, *Bentonville*, 420-23.

10 Bradley, *Bentonville*, 112.

11 Moore, *Moore's Guide to Bentonville*, 9.

12 Moore, *Moore's Guide to Bentonville*, Map, 12; "Journal of Major Thomas Abram Huguenin" in *Eyewitnesses* to Averasboro, Volume 1, Map 42, 46-7; Mark A. Smith and Wade Sokolosky, *"No Such Army Since the Days of Julius Caesar," Sherman's Carolinas Campaign: from Fayetteville to Averasboro*, (Ft. Mitchell, KY, 2005), 65.

13 Bradley, *Bentonville*, 116, 123.

14 Bradley, *Bentonville*, 116-9.

15 Bradley, *Bentonville*, 121.

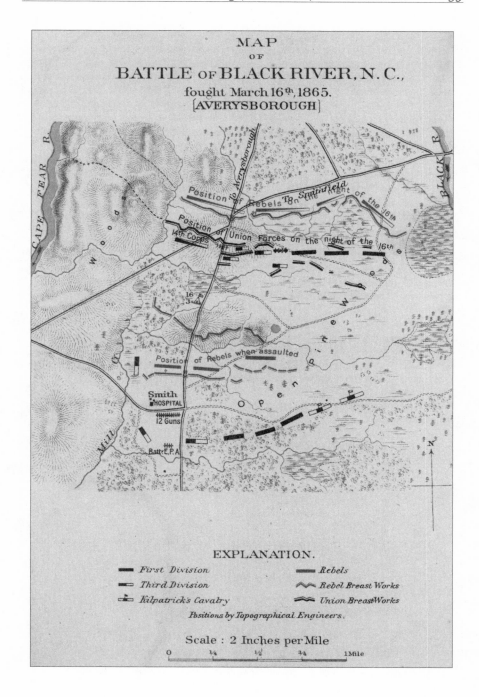

MAP
OF
BATTLE OF BLACK RIVER, N.C.,
fought March 16th, 1865.
[AVERYSBOROUGH]

EXPLANATION.

First Division		Rebels
Third Division		Rebel Breast Works
Kilpatrick's Cavalry		Union Breast Works

Positions by Topographical Engineers.

Scale : 2 Inches per Mile

0   ¼   ½   ¾   1 Mile

fantry, called for reinforcements on the Confederate left.[16] Captains McMillan King and Charles Inglesby moved their companies, Company "I" and Company "D," detached from the 1st South Carolina Artillery to reinforce the extreme left.[17] Lt. James L. Robertson served in Company "I." Captain DeRosset's Armory Guard Battalion also moved to the left of Rhett's Brigade as reinforcements near the first attack point.[18] Rhett's brigade, now commanded by Col. William B. Butler, probably with the Armory Guard, held off the Union attacks in fierce fighting for nearly five hours, until a charge around their right flank by Ohio and Illinois infantry under Col. Henry Case sent the Confederates reeling into the second tier of their defenses.[19]

The Armory Guard was one of two North Carolina forces that saw fighting at Averasboro. The battalion was in the thick of heavy fighting on either the first or second lines of battle, or both. When Capt. Armand L. DeRosset found his men being slowly pressed back, he asked Colonel Butler commanding Rhett's brigade nearby for orders, as General Elliott was too far away to report to hurriedly. Butler replied that he had no orders to give him. In conjunction with a Georgia battalion commander on his right, DeRosset determined to charge and retake their previous position. He was forming his men for the counter attack when he was shot through the lungs and fell almost at Butler's feet.[20]

The second line of battle, under the command of Brig. Gen. Stephen Elliott, soon also became untenable. Fearful of being flanked by Union cavalry, General Hardee ordered the division commander General Taliaferro to withdraw the Confederate forces to the third and main line of defense.

While heavy fighting raged along the third line, Maj. Gen. Joseph Wheeler and his Corps of cavalry arrived on the battlefield. General Hardee directed him to extend the right side of the line to the Cape Fear River. Dismounted and serving as infantry, part of the corps took a strong position behind a deep ravine, where they repulsed a Union attempt to turn the right flank. The rest of the Confederates held the third line firmly until nightfall, although heavy skirmishing and Federal artillery fire continued after dark.[21]

General Hardee determined to withdraw his troops under cover of darkness. The men built large campfires as if to be cooking supper and warming themselves, then crept away on all fours, not speaking above a whisper. As the fires died down in the early morning hours, the Federals inched forward and by daybreak discovered the ruse.[22] By this time Hardee's Corps was well on its way east toward Elevation on the route to Goldsboro.

16 "Journal of Major Thomas Abram Hugenin, His Account of the Battle of Averasboro," in *Eyewitnesses to Averasboro*, Volume 1, 47.

17 Capt. Charles Inglesby, *Historical Sketch of the First Regiment of South Carolina Artillery. (Regulars.)*, n.d., [after 1893], 16.

18 Capt. Graham Daves, "The Battle of Averasboro," in *Eyewitnesses to Averasboro, Volume 1*, 31-3.

19 Smith and Sokolosky, *Sherman's Carolinas Campaign*, 101-4.

20 Daves, "The Battle of Averasboro," in *Eyewitnesses to Averasboro, Volume 1*, 31-3.

21 Moore, *Moore's Guide to Bentonville*, 131-5; Bradley, *Bentonville*, 125-8; Smith and Sokolosky, *Sherman's Carolinas Campaign*, 115-6.

22 Bradley, *Bentonville*, 132-4.

The John Smith House, Oak Grove, after removal to a site fronting
the highway and renovation (2013).
Courtesy of Walt Smith

The Confederate losses at Averasboro were approximately 500 men, plus prisoners, while those of Sherman's command were placed at 554 by one report, 682 by another, and estimated by captured Union soldiers to have been 3000.[23] The 1st South Carolina Artillery took the brunt of the Confederate casualties. By the end of the day they had lost 215 killed, wounded, or captured, out of the 458 they had brought into the battle.[24] 2nd Lt. James L. Robertson was one of the wounded, having taken a minie ball through the leg.

As Hardee's Corps withdrew, many of the wounded were left behind at field hospitals in the several Smith family houses on and near the battlefield. Captain DeRosset and Lieutenant Robertson likely received medical attention either at "Oak Grove," John Smith's plantation house located a short distance south of the Confederate first line of battle, or at "Lebanon," home of his brother Farquhard Smith, situated just north of Hardee's third line of defense.[25]

Farquhard Smith's eighteen-year-old daughter Janie described the scene at "Lebanon" in a letter to her friend Janie Robeson:

23 *Johnston's Narrative*, 583; John G. Barrett, *Sherman's March Through the Carolinas*, (Chapel Hill, 1956), 155.

24 Bradley, *Bentonville*, 132; Angley, et al., *Sherman's March through North Carolina*, 37.

25 The field hospital set up at "Oak Grove" became enveloped by the Federal forces at the outset of the battle, and wounded of both sides were cared for by Union surgeons there. See Smith and Sokolosky, *Sherman's Carolinas Campaign*, 109.

The infirmary was here and oh it makes me shudder when I think of the awful sights I witnessed that morning. Ambulance after ambulance drove up with our wounded. One half of the house was prepared for the soldiers, but owing to the close proximity of the enemy they only sent in the sick, but every barn and out house was full and under every shed and tree the tables were carried for amputating the limbs. I just felt like my heart would break when I would see our brave men rushing into battle and then coming back so mangled. The scene beggars description, the blood lay in puddles in the grove, the groans of the dying and the complaints of those undergoing amputation was horrible, the painful impression has seared my very heart, I can never forget it.[26]

According to tradition, Captain DeRosset intervened with a surgeon somewhere that day to spare Lieutenant Robertson's leg from amputation, a procedure that was the usual medical treatment to avoid gangrene in a patient's extremities. Whether or not this story is true, Lt. Jimmie Robertson must have been impressed by the North Carolina captain, because he later named one

The Farquhard Smith House, Lebanon (2003)
Courtesy of Catherine Barrett Robertson

26 Janie Smith to Janie Wright Robeson of Ashwood plantation in Bladen County, N.C., "Where Home Used to be. Apr. 12th, 1865," original in the Mrs. Thomas H. Webb Collection, North Carolina Department of Archives and History; quoted in part in *Eyewitnesses to Averasboro, Volume 1*, 99-108; quoted also as "Janie Smith Letter," n. d., www.averasboro.com/JANIE%20SMITH520LETTERS.htm, accessed October 31, 2004; quoted also as being dated April 12, 1865 in Barrett, *Sherman's March Through the Carolinas*, 155-6; Janie Wright Robeson (1846-1919) was the daughter of John Alexander Robeson of Ashwood plantation in Bladen County, North Carolina, and married Edwin Turner MacKethan (1840-1888) in 1867. Edwin Robeson MacKethan III to Thomas H. Robertson, Jr., November 21, 2004.

of his sons after him, Armand DeRosset Robertson.[27] Captain DeRosset himself was thought to be a hopeless case. He was left for dead and wound up in the field hospital where he was captured and paroled by Union troops. He eventually recovered, however, due to the skill of a Federal surgeon and to the nursing care of kind friends who came through both the Confederate and Union lines from Raleigh under a safe conduct pass from General Beauregard.[28]

The battle at Aversaboro was a classic delaying action, fought at a strategically selected place where Hardee could check Sherman's progress no matter whether his destination was Raleigh or Goldsboro. Hardee's troops viewed their success in holding off a force five times their size as a Confederate victory at a time when they badly needed a morale boost. The Union army's movements the following day confirmed that Sherman was headed toward Goldsboro. Most importantly, Hardee's stand gained valuable time that allowed General Johnston to marshal all of his available Confederate forces to fight what would turn out to be the final battle of the Civil War at Bentonville, North Carolina, three days later.[29]

27 Armand DeRosset Robertson (1885-1960), called Derry.

28 Staff Capt. Graham Daves obtained the safe pass from General Beauregard. Captain Daves was DeRosset's brother in law, married to his sister Alice DeRosset. See Capt. Graham Daves, "The Battle of Averasboro," in *Eyewitnesses to Averasboro, Volume 1*, 33 and Historical Data Systems, comp., *American Civil War Soldiers* [database on-line], (Provo, UT, USA: Ancestry.com Operations Inc. 1999); See letter: J. Wheeler, Major-General to Lieut. Gen. W. J. Hardee, Averasborough, March 17, 1865, 9:05 a.m.: "I do not think the enemy will go farther toward Raleigh than where the road turns off to Smithfield. Colonel Ashby has sent off all the wounded which could travel and has left rations for such as were not able to travel." See *OR*, v. 47, pt. 1, 1127; Clement A. Evans, *Confederate Military History*, (Atlanta, 1899), digital edition, http://archive. org/stream/confedmilhist04evanrich#page/, 467-70 accessed December 12, 2012, 467-70; James Sprunt, *Chronicles of the Cape Fear River, 1660-1916*, second edition, (Raleigh, 1916; reprint edition, Wilmington, 1992), 292-4; Bradley, *Bentonville*, 134-5; Barrett, Sherman's March Through the Carolinas, 155-7; Angley, *Sherman's March through North Carolina*, 37-8.

29 Bradley, *Bentonville*, 114-5, 132; *Eyewitnesses to Averasboro, Volume 1*, 11.

Chapter Four

Chester, Newberry, and Augusta

"We are troubled on every side, yet not distressed."

March 19–23, 1865—Battle of Bentonville, North Carolina.[1]

Sunday, March 19th 1865

Had

a very sick night. Considerable fever and headache. Coughed and expectorated freely. At one time I concluded not to get up, and remain in bed for the day; but when I looked at the dirty room and filthy bed, I determined to make an effort and get up. I got up, and after dressing, felt better. The Raleigh train is expected at half past eight o'clock A.M. and will leave for Charlotte at ten minutes past nine. I determined to take the train for Charlotte.[2] I heard a rumor last night that there had been a fight between Hardee's and some portion of Sherman's forces, and that Coln Alfred Rhett had been killed. It gave me great anxiety, as Jimmy is in Rhett's Brigade. I went to the office of the agent and found that the Raleigh train was three hours behind time, and would probably not leave before one or two o'clock P.M. I wished to go to Church, but as the hour of arrival and departure of the train was uncertain, I remained at the Hotel.

The Raleigh train arrived at one o'clock P.M. and, to my surprise, I found Jimmy on board, with a number of others, wounded. There had been a severe engagement near Averysboro about twenty-eight miles from Fayetteville on

---

1 Swanson, *Atlas of the Civil War*, 108.

2 This train was operated by the North Carolina Rail Road. See Swayze, *Hill & Swayze's Confederate States Rail-Road & Steam-Boat Guide*, 15.

Thursday the 16th inst. lasting about six hours. Rhett's Brigade, composed of the lst South Carolina Regular Artillery, the lst South Carolina Regular Infantry and Lucas' Battalion[3] were principally engaged.

Johnson determined to make a stand at this point with Hardee's corps, to give time for the concentration of Beauregards and Braggs[4] forces at Smithfield. Skirmishing commenced on Wednesday afternoon the 15th and continued until dark. During the skirmishing on Wednesday evening Coln Rhett rode out beyond the skirmish line for the purpose of making a reconnaisance. As he never returned there was no doubt of his capture. On Thursday morning the enemy advanced in force driving in two lines of skirmishing on to our main line. The Brigade fought gallantly, and repulsed the enemy handsomely, though with considerable loss in officers and men killed and wounded. Jimmy was wounded by a minie ball passing obliquely through the calf of the left leg. The wound is painful but, I trust, not dangerous. I am too thankful to that good Providence that has spared his life in a contest in which so many have fallen to rise no more. It was providential that I was detained here, as it will enable me to take him on with me to Chester, and take charge of his case myself. Lieuts. Fickling[5] and Mikell,[6] Mr. Jenkins Mikell's son, determined to go on with us. Fickling was wounded in the leg below the knee, and Mikell in the foot, by a fragment of shell.

We arrived at Salisbury after dark. Could not get into a Hospital or Hotel, and it was too late to seek admission into a private house, and we were compelled to pass the night, without supper, under the Rail Road shed on a filthy floor. To add to our troubles and vexation, as we were getting out of the cars, some scoundrel under cover of the darkness of the night, stole Jimmy's valise, with all his clothes except what he had on, including his commission and sash.

3   Lucas's South Carolina Battalion of Rhett's Brigade; Bradley, *Bentonville*, 444; listed as SC Hvy. Arty 15th (Lucas') Bn. in Hewett, *Confederate Soldiers*.

4   Gen. Braxton Bragg, Department of North Carolina.

5   1st Lt. Eldred S. Fickling, Co. G, First South Carolina Artillery. Resident of Beaufort, S.C., wounded at Averasboro, March 16, 1865, the same day as Jimmy Robertson. See Capt. Charles Inglesby, "Historical Sketch of the First Regiment of South Carolina Artillery (Regulars)," n. d. [circa 1895], 27; listed as Eldred S. Fickling SC 1st Arty. Co. D 1st Lt., Eldred S. Fickling SC Cav. Bn. Hampton Legion Co. C. in Hewett, *Confederate Soldiers*.

6   Thomas Price Mikell (1835-1873), son of I. Jenkins Mikell of Edisto Island, S.C. and his wife Emily Caroline Price. Genealogical typescript titled "Family of the Grandparents of Lyman Hall Robertson," n. d., in possession of Ethel Robertson Boyle, Conyers, Georgia 2014; listed as T. P. Mikell SC 3rd Cav. Co. I Sgt., T. P. Mikell SC 1st (Butler's) Inf. Co. K 2nd Lt. in Hewett, *Confederate Soldiers*.

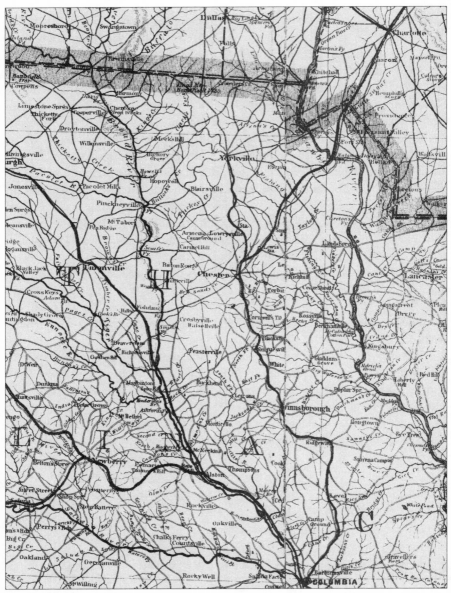

Charlotte to Chester to Ashford's Ferry to Newberry to Bauknight's (Lorick's) Ferry.
Detail from U.S. Coast Survey, 1865.
State Department of Archives and History, Raleigh, N.C.

Monday, March 20th 1865

We were up before daylight, in order to be in readiness for our extra train, which was to take Coln Goodwyn's[7] Brigade of South Carolina Militia on to Charlotte. We had a little flour and coffee. Aroused our servants, and made them extemporize an apology for a breakfast, and started at half past six o'clock. Arrived at Charlotte at one o'clock P.M. Could not get our wounded into a Hospital. Procured a room at a miserable Hotel. Lieut Fickling met his sisters here, and remained with them. Met a number of Charlestonians here, who had come out with Hardee's Army. Among them Joe Johnson,[8] who was very kind and attentive in assisting me with my charges. Things on this whole tour are in a state of great confusion. There is a great want of order and executive ability shown here. There are too many unprincipled and worthless staff officers in the different departments.

Tuesday, March 21st 1865

Started for the train this morning and was compelled to take a box car which had been used for horses.[9] The floor was covered with filth and dirty loose cotton. With a spade and an apology for a broom, we made it tolerable. It continued to rain, in the midst of which we arrived in Chester at 12 o'clock M. To my surprise, I found no Hospitals here, and could get no accommodations at the Hotels.[10] Fortunately Norman Smith[11] was here on duty, but he was in

7 Listed as A.D. Goodwyn SC 2nd Inf. Lt. Col. in Hewett, *Confederate Soldiers.*

8 Probably Dr. Joseph Johnson. See Waring, M.D., *A History of Medicine in South Carolina*, 39, 93, 321.

9 This train was operated by Charlotte & South Carolina Rail Road, from Charlotte to Chester. See Swayze, *Hill & Swayze's Confederate States Rail-Road & Steam-Boat Guide*, 15-16.

10 Coincidentally, Mary Boykin Chestnut, the famous diarist from Dixie, also travelled from Charlotte to Chester on the same day as Surgeon Robertson by a train, "overloaded with paroled prisoners. Heaven helped us—a kind mail agent took us with two other forlorn women, into his comfortable clean mail car," she wrote. In Chester she resided at Mrs. Da Vega's house, now designated as 126 Main Street (2004), where she remained until May 1, 1865. F. M. Robertson lodged nearby in Chester until April 12, 1865. See *A Walking Tour of Historic Chester, SC,* Chester County Historical Society, n.d., 14; C. Vann Woodward, ed., *Mary Chestnut's Civil War*, (New Haven and London, 1981), 765, 800.

11 Maj. Norman Wallace Smith served as chief of transportation at Chester Court House. He was a nephew of F. M. Robertson and Henrietta Toomer Righton Robertson, the son of her sister Katharine Fullerton Righton Smith and brother-in-law William Smith; listed as Norman W. Smith Gen. & Staff Maj. QM. in Hewett, *Confederate Soldiers*; Letter: Jon' Miller to A. R.

camp about a mile from the Town. I learned from him that Gillespie and his wife[12] were in Chester at Mrs. Patterson's—my old friend, Mary Jane Gage,[13] and also that my good and ever kind friend Mrs. Kennedy[14] and her daughter Lonie[15] were residing here. Both sent invitations for me to stay with them. Mrs. Kennedy would take no excuse nor relinquish her claim, so Jimmy and myself soon found ourselves in a comfortable home like room at the house of her son-in-law Mr. Martin.[16] I went to see Mary and Mrs. Patterson in the afternoon and explained the reasons why we went to Mrs. Kennedy's. What cause for thankfulness! How good is our Heavenly Father, in the hour of our extremity,

---

Lawrence, Esq., April 3, 1865, "Jonathan M. Miller legal papers, 1860-1872," Collections of South Carolina Historical Society, SCHS call number 431.02(M)31.

12 Mr. and Mrs. Alfred Gillespie, who were neighbors of F. M. Robertson in Charleston, where they lived two doors down at 5 Maiden Lane in a house owned by the Estate of Robert F. Henry. See *Charleston Census, 1861*, 135, accessed October 14, 2012.

13 Mary Jane Gage Patterson (1827-1881), sister of F. M. Robertson's medical acquaintance and horse breeder Dr. James McKibbin Gage (1813-1855) of Union, South Carolina. She was the wife of Giles Jared Patterson (1827-1891), who was a lawyer and teacher in Chester Male Academy. See James Gage McKibbin Papers, Southern Historical Collection, #1812-z, University of North Carolina at Chapel Hill; Letter: Ann Davidson Marion (Mrs. Malcolm L. Marion, Jr.) to Thomas H. Robertson, Jr., September 30, 2004 in possession of the author (2014); U.S. Census, 1860, Chester, S.C., 75-B; Joshua Hilary Hudson, LL.D., *Sketches and Reminiscences*, (Columbia, SC, 1903), 17, 22, 129.

14 Catherine Evans Kennedy (b. ca. 1785), native of Abbeville, S. C. and wife of Maj. John Kennedy (ca. 1773-1867), who was known as the "Father of Chesterville." He was a farmer and was twice elected sheriff of Chester County. Letter: Ann Davidson Marion (Mrs. Malcolm L. Marion, Jr.) to Thomas H. Robertson, Jr., September 30, 2004 containing genealogical chart, "Descendants of Unknown Kennedy," Mrs. Malcolm L. Marion, Jr., September 30, 2004 and biographical sketch of Maj. and Mrs. John Kennedy from p. 152 of unidentified published source; Mrs. Kennedy's given name is listed as "Margaret," apparently erroneously, in the 1860 Census. See *U.S. Census, 1860*, Chester, S.C., 92; Mrs. Kennedy was F. M. Robertson's "step-second cousin" by the marriage of their great grandparents Lucretia Towns Robertson and Tscharner DeGraffenreid. Letter: Catherine B. Robertson to Thomas H. Robertson, Jr., July 11, 2014.

15 Pauline "Pelona" Kennedy (b. ca. 1855, d. 1869) was actually the granddaughter of Mrs. Kennedy. Her parents were Richard E. and Sarah DeGraffenreid Kennedy, who had died in 1855 and 1860 respectively. Genealogical chart, "Descendants of Unknown Kennedy," Mrs. Malcolm L. Marion, Jr., September 30, 2004.

16 Probably J. W. Martin (b. ca. 1834), listed as living in the household of Maj. Jno. Kennedy, 1860. *U.S. Census 1860*, Chester, S.C., 92. How Martin is related to Mrs. Kennedy as her son in law has not been established. **Route: The site of the home and tavern of Maj. John Kennedy is at 101 Main Street, occupied by the Richmond Nail Building (2004).** F. M. Robertson stayed with Mrs. Kennedy for about three weeks almost directly across the street from the diarist Mary Boykin Chestnut. Although each kept a daily journal, the entries of each are entirely different, and neither mentions the other.

NAIL BUILDING (1873)

NAIL'S VARIETY STORE WAS HERE UNTIL THE 1920'S. ORIGINALLY, THIS WAS THE HOME AND TAVERN OF MAJ. JOHN KENNEDY, A LANDMARK FOR TRAVELERS FROM C 1800 UNTIL HIS DEATH IN 1867. IN 1807, AARON BURR APPEALED TO THE LOCAL CITIZENS FOR RESCUE AT THIS SITE.

Marker of the site of Mr. and Mrs. John Kennedy's House, on the main town square, Chester (2004).
Courtesy of Catherine Barrett Robertson

to cast us upon the bounty and kindness of dear old friends. "Bless the Lord, O my soul: and all that is within me, bless his holy name. Bless the Lord, O my soul, and forget not all his benefits."[17]

Wednesday, March 22nd, 1865

News of another battle between Sherman and Johnson came today. Genl Lee's dispatch says that Johnson attacked and routed him on Sunday the 19th but no particulars of the casualties.[18] Received a telegram from Dr. Miles today informing me that he was in Columbia, and that the archives of the Board were safe. I wrote him immediately. Nothing from the dear ones in Charleston.

Received a telegram from Lewis[19] at Columbia, announcing the sad intelligence of sister Mary's[20] death on the 8th of this month. How much she will be missed by her husband and family. Another link is broken in our domestic chain, and we are admonished by the near approach of the King of terrors to be in readiness, as we know not when the moment of our summons

17 *The Holy Bible*, Psalm 103, 1-2.

18 The Battle of Bentonville, for further reading see Mark L. Bradley, *Last Stand in the Carolinas: The Battle of Bentonville* (Campbell, CA, 1996).

19 Lewis Ford Robertson (1825-1904), lawyer, brother of F. M. Robertson, named after Dr. Lewis DeSaussure Ford, F.M. Robertson's medical preceptor in Augusta, Georgia. Lewis Robertson was living at 5 Limehouse Street, Charleston. *See Charleston Census, 1861*, 130.

20 Mary Ann Robertson Boggs (Mrs. Archibald Boggs) (1808-1865), died March 8, 1865, Augusta, Georgia. Her son was Brig. Gen. William Robertson Boggs. For further information on Gen. Boggs, see *Military Reminiscences of Gen. Wm. R. Boggs, C.S.A.*, Electronic Edition, (University of North Carolina at Chapel Hill, 1997), http://docsouth.unc.edu/boggs/ boggs. html, accessed September 20, 2003.

may come. Watch and pray![21] I saw a number of Charleston friends here. Like myself they are without any information from home.

Thursday, March 23rd 1865

Nothing of importance today. Various little rumors.

Friday March 24th 1865

Jimmy suffered very much from his wound last night. Had fever with considerable swelling of his leg.

Saturday, March 25th 1865

Jimmy suffered very much all day yesterday, but rested better last night. He is free from fever this morning, the swelling has subsided, and the wound is suppurating.[22] Received another telegram from Dr. Miles requesting a copy of our orders, as he had heard nothing from Richmond. He also expressed a desire to serve with me. I sent him the order. As I have heard nothing from Crowell, I reported back to the Surgeon General yesterday and requested to be ordered to Augusta. I shall await an answer here, with Jimmy.

Sunday, March 26th 1865

Jimmy had a bad night, until I gave him half a grain of sulphate of morphine. He then rested well, but had considerable fever during the night. The wound is suppurating freely at both orifices, but there is an erysipelatous blush[23] for some distance around the orifice of exit which I do not like.

Mrs. Kennedy and myself went to the Presbyterian Church this morning, and the Rev. Mr. Douglass[24] preached a good practical sermon from the eleventh chapter of Hebrews, last clause of the fourth verse: "And by it he being

---

21 *The Holy Bible*, passim, Matthew, 26, 41.

22 *Suppurating* means discharging pus.

23 *Erysipelas* is an intense local deep-red inflammation of the skin, known now in modern times to be caused by a streptococcal bacterial infection.

24 The Reverend James Douglas (1827-1904) of nearby Blackstock, S. C. See Rev. E. C. Scott, D.D., *Ministerial Directory of the Presbyterian Church, U. S., 1861-1941, Revised and supplemented 1942-1950,* (Atlanta, GA, 1950), 192.

dead yet speaketh." Gillespie came to see us in the afternoon and brought Jimmy a letter from Lizzie Fanning. Mr. Fanning[25] kindly invited Jimmy to come and stay at his house. His house escaped fire and pillage, and I understand that my silver is safe.

Monday, March 27th 1865

Nothing of interest today. Jimmy is better.

Tuesday, March 28th 1865

Major Willis[26] arrived here today for the purpose of sending forward 6000 troops that had come through from Augusta under Lieut Genl S. D. Lee.[27] A gentleman informed him that Maj. Justice,[28] Dr. Coppin[29] and my son Henry were at Broad River with the waggons and horses, and would be in Chester in the morning. Jimmy continues to improve, and is about the house on his crutches. Miles has been ordered to report for temporary duty to the Treasury Department. He told me it would make no difference in Henry's position.[30]

25 Lizzie was Jimmy's first cousin, next door neighbor, and contemporary, Elizabeth Righton Fanning (b 1844), about 21 years old. Frederick DeVeau Fanning (1806-1869), brother-in-law of F. M. Robertson. He was married to Henrietta Toomer Righton Robertson's sister, Elizabeth Fullerton Righton. The Fannings lived between the Robertsons and the Gillespies at 3 Maiden Lane. See *Charleston Census*, 1861, 135.

26 Maj. Edward Willis, Quartermaster.

27 Lt. Gen. Stephen D. Lee.

28 Probably Andrew S. Justice, listed as Andrew S. A. Justice Gen. & Staff Capt. ACS and A.S. Justice Gen. & Staff Capt. ACS. in Hewett, *Confederate Soldiers*.

29 There is no Coppin listed in Hewett, *Confederate Soldiers* nor in the *Charleston Census, 1861*. The doctor's name is definitely spelled "Coppin" in the original diary, but the person could possibly be Dr. Armory Coffin (1814-1884) of Charleston and Aiken, South Carolina. See Waring, *A History of Medicine in South Carolina*, 215. Or he could be Armory Coffin, Jr., SC Lt. Arty. Parker's Co. (Marion Arty.) Sgt. Maj., A. Coffin SC Bn. St. Cadets Co. A Adj., or W. H. Coffin Gen. & Staff Surg., as listed in Hewett, *Confederate Soldiers*.

30 Exactly what Henry Robertson's position was is unclear. He is serving a duty "with waggons and horses," presumably under the direction of Maj. Norman Smith, the chief of transportation and his first cousin. The duty must also have been within the purview of both Surgeon Miles as a physician and Maj. Willis as a quartermaster in some way. He is probably serving with or in the 7th South Carolina Reserves in this campaign, or perhaps 15th South Carolina Infantry (Regulars). He had previously been medically discharged from the army following his wounding at Fort Sumter in 1863.

Wednesday, March 29th 1865

The Major got about 2000 of the troops off this morning upon three trains. The others will take the cars at Rock Hill, some distance above this. The Major left, with the first train, for Charlotte. Henry came into town this morning in advance of his party. He looks remarkably well, and is in fine health. Norman telegraphed Major Willis to know what Henry should do. He replied, directing him to remain with Norman until he returned. Henry gave me all the news about Mr. Mikell's family.[31] He paid them a visit from Augusta and remained there ten days. He told me all about Mary and little Frank.[32] It was truly gratifying to hear from them. Mary saved everything. Mr. Mikell lost all his provisions except what he had secreted. A few of his negroes went off, but some of them returned. They took his horses and carriage with the driver and all his poultry. His house was not burned.[33]

Henry gave me an account of sister Mary's sickness and death. He was on a visit to his wife, and returned just in time to attend her funeral. It is probable she died from the bursting of an ovarian abscess in the peritonial cavity. When I last saw her she complained to me of a difficulty in that vicinity; and upon examination, I came to the conclusion that there was something wrong about that region. She was perfectly sensible to the last, and departed in the triumphs

31 Isaac Jenkins Mikell, Henry Clay Robertson's father-in-law. The family moved as refugees from their plantation home at Peters Point on Edisto Island, first to Aiken and then to the Forks of the Edisto River in Orangeburg County. See I. Jenkins Mikell, *Rumbling of the Chariot Wheels: Doings and Misdoings in the Barefooted Period of a Boy's Life on a Southern Plantation* (Columbia, SC, 1923), 26, 53, 56, 79-81. Mikell, the elder, also owned a handsome house in Charleston at 24 Rutledge Street. See *Census of the City of Charleston, South Carolina for the Year 1861*, 199.

32 Henry's wife Mary Elizabeth Mikell Robertson (1842-1924) and their son Francis Marion Robertson (b. October 27, 1864).

33 "Every family in the [slave] 'Village' had been given, a few days before the passing of the Army, six weeks rations in advance, as we rightly thought that their possessions would not be molested by the enemy, and they lived on that. All other provisions, cotton and the other movable articles of any value, were either carried off or destroyed. Father, with his usual forethought which in the past had helped him in his moderate success, provided against just such a contingency. He had built on a small island in the swamp, surrounded by water about five feet deep, a large corn crib, holding about a thousand bushels of corn, which he filled. This crib was made of green cypress logs and covered with green shingles, entirely noncombustible. He then flatted, or lightered, over to this island the corn, after which he destroyed the lighter and the trick was done. It would not burn, it could not be carted away, the water was too deep. And there it remained to support his people, and many a poor soldier's family who had nothing to live on." See Mikell, *Rumbling of the Chariot Wheels*, 110-1.

of faith. When informed by the Rev. Dr. Wilson[34] that she could not recover, she received the information with calmness, and requested to be left alone for a time. She said she was prepared for the announcement, as it was not unexpected to her. She called in all the members of the family, and addressed each one separately. She then spoke of the great struggle in which our country was contending, expressed confidence in the final success of the cause, and, just before expiring, offered a most fervent prayer for her suffering and bleeding country. How blessed is the death of those who expire with an unclouded faith in Jesus. It gives courage to the timid, hope to the doubtful, and strength to the weak.

Thursday, March 30th 1865

Went to bed with a wretched sick headache last night. Rather better this morning. I attribute it to the constant use of coffee twice a day since I have been here. Mrs. Kennedy will have her coffee—sometimes three times a day—and of the very best kind. I shall quit it, at least, except for breakfast. It is raining and blowing this morning and has the appearance of continuing for some days.

Friday March 31st 1865

I passed a very uncomfortable day yesterday. I abstained from coffee, had a good night's rest, and feel better this morning. Contrary to appearances yesterday, it is a mild, clear and beautifully bright day. But, alas! Alas! there is no brightness for me. All is still dark and uncertain before me. No intelligence from my dear wife and the loved ones in Charleston. When I recall the happy days I have passed with her and my dear children, the domestic comforts so profusely scattered around us and ask myself, shall these return? Shall I again fold her in my arms and press her to my throbbing heart—once more enjoy the happiness of seeing my dear children and grandchildren, with joyous and happy faces, seated around our peaceful fireside? I sink into gloom and sadness. But I am

---

34 The Reverend Joseph Ruggles Wilson (1822-1903), pastor of First Presbyterian Church, Augusta, Georgia, 1858-1870, and father of Thomas Woodrow Wilson, president of the United States. President Wilson included a remembrance of Augusta and the Civil War in a speech about Abraham Lincoln that he delivered in 1909: "My earliest recollection is of standing at my father's gateway in Augusta, Georgia, when I was four years old, and hearing someone pass and say that Mr. Lincoln was elected and there was to be war. Catching the intense tones of his excited voice, I remember running to ask my father what it meant." See Erick D. Montgomery, "Historical Considerations," in *Research Study: The Boyhood Home of President Woodrow Wilson, Augusta, Georgia*, by Norman Davenport Askins, P.C. Architect, copy in office of Historic Augusta, Inc.

admonished that these are sacrifices which thousands have made, and are now making. Yes, many who were so unfortunate as to be in the line of Sherman's deadly march are in a far worse condition. Then, let me arouse from this despondency and look to that Providence without whose knowledge even a sparrow falls not to the ground, that Almighty arm, whose strength can scatter our foes in a moment, and bring down those fierce judgments for which their ungodly and fiendish deeds so loudly call.

April 1, 2010—Battle of Five Forks, Virginia.[35]

Saturday, Apl. 1st 1865

Jimmy went out a short distance yesterday afternoon on his crutches. He had a severe chill last night, followed by high fever, with headache, extreme restlessness, and disturbed sleep. The effort and exposure brought back the erysipalatous inflammation of the leg. I confined him to bed, today, and dressed the whole inflamed surface with compresses, saturated with cold water, and a bandage applied with uniform pressure from the toes to the knee.

A large number of ladies, employed in the Treasury Department, arrived in the cars[36] this afternoon from Charlotte. They are, for the most part, refugees from the sea coast of South Carolina. They are following the Note Bureau, which, since the burning of Columbia, is to be established in Greenville.[37] It was

---

35 Swanson, *Atlas of the Civil War*, 110.

36 The cars are railroad cars.

37 Back on April 18, 1864, Secretary of the Treasury Christopher G. Memminger had instructed Sanders G. Jamison, Chief of the Treasury-Note Bureau, to establish a Note Bureau at Columbia, South Carolina, in addition to the facilities at Richmond, to print and engrave treasury notes (paper money) and prepare them for use. The clerks, mostly women, were charged with numbering, trimming, and signing the treasury notes. At the peak of its operation on August 2, 1864, Jamison wrote then Treasury Secretary Trenholm that the Treasury-Note Bureau employed a total of 249 ladies for these tasks. "But with Grant's imperiling of the Confederate capital and Sherman's march through Carolina having turned eastward, it was decided to move the remains of the Treasury-Note Bureau and the printing establishment of Evans and Cogswell [from burned-out Columbia] to Greenville. By March 16, the salvaged equipment had reached Chester, and on March 30, W. F. Miller and Stephen Duncan, principal clerks in the Bureau, were ordered to 'go to Greenville, S. C., and ascertain both the practicality of procuring accommodations for the female clerks, and the necessity of continuing them in the service of the Department.' . . . Nine females and five male clerks were furnished transportation to Greenville, but before the Treasury-Note Bureau could be put into operation, the Confederacy had collapsed." See Richard Cecil Todd, *Confederate Finance*, (Athens, 1954), Google Books edition, 85-90, 215. http://books.google.com/books?id=MVc1DTf4zsEC& printsec=frontcover&dq=confederate+finance&source=bl&ots=A90yBc0xr-&sig=wI3-kQ

sad to see these delicate females accustomed to all the comforts and bounties of a rich planting region, reduced to this service for a scanty subsistence. They were to be conveyed from this point to Newberry Court House, where they would take the cars for Greenville. There were no carriages to meet them—no four horse stagecoaches to whisk them along, even, with the old time mail speed. They were too thankful to pack their baggage into a common, dirty and dilapidated Quartermaster's waggon, drawn by four miserable mules; and, then, get in themselves, and journey for several days, at a snales pace, over roads as bad as they could be, not to be positively impassable, and probably be compelled to camp out at night.

When I witness these scenes, and think of those who have been robbed and insulted by the low and vulgar sweepings of European and northern dens and prisons; their houses burnt over their heads by the vile Yankee plunderers; I find my heart swelling with indignation and wrath, and, at the moment, wish for an opportunity to visit the perpetrators of such deeds with summary vengeance. But I am sure these feelings are wrong, for vengeance belongeth, alone, with God. "Vengeance is mine; I will repay saith the Lord."[38] That they deserve severe and unmitigated judgments for their wanton deeds of cruelty and outrage, all must admit. But the time and mode belongs to that God, whose judgments slumber not.

While Jimmy—poor fellow—tossed and groaned during the night, I thought of our dear home—the unremitting care of my dear devoted wife in hours of sickness. Though he has every attention and every comfort that the kindest of friends can contribute, yet a mother's soothing voice and tender touch are wanting. These constitute a balm and comfort to the wounded soldier which a stranger cannot supply. Thank God, as the day wore away, he appeared much better, and the inflammation and pain had greatly subsided by dark, and the prospects of a quiet night are bright. My servant Scott, as Jimmy calls him, is ever faithful, attentive and kind. All devotion to us both, gets up at night, no matter how often he is called, and administers to all of Jimmy's wants. He certainly is the most faithful and devoted creature. I can never forget him, and to my last moment, will share my rations with him.[39]

---

oWpgcT-WTKyktpoAPcrdY&hl=en&ei=BUSATKWoLsP68AbS1rz4AQ&sa=X&oi=book result&ct=result&resnum=2&ved=0CBYQ6AEwAQ#v=onepage&q&f=false,   accessed September 2, 2010.

38 *The Holy Bible*, Romans 12:19.

39 One of the unwritten set of manners and taboos in the South was that master and servant ate meals separately at different tables. Therefore, Surgeon Robertson's statement that he will share meals with Henry Sutcliff is a graceful thought.

April 2, 1865—Richmond, Virginia was evacuated. President Davis and the remainder of the Confederate government left at 11 p.m. by train bound for Danville.[40]

Sunday, Apl. 2d 1865

Jimmy had a comfortable night—no return of chill or fever. The wound looks well, this morning, and the inflammation has subsided very much. Reapplied the wet compresses and adjusted a clean bandage.

Henry came down from his camp, after breakfast. Shaved, washed and put on a clean shirt. We went to the Presbyterian Church together. Heard an excellent practical sermon from the Rev. Mr. Anderson,[41] who formerly preached in Yorkville, but is now voluntarily devoting himself to the soldiers. Text, 2nd Timothy, lst Chapter and 10th verse: "But is now made manifest by the appearing of our Saviour Jesus Christ, who hath abolished death, and hath brought life and immortality to light through the gospel." His principle object was to show that Christ had subdued our last great enemy, death, and, that, through Him, the sinner might escape eternal death. I did not go out in the afternoon, but remained at home with Jimmy.

Monday, Apl. 3d 1865

Jimmy's wound continues to improve. No orders in answer to my communication to the Surgeon General. I shall look every day, unless the communication is cut between this and Richmond. There are rumors of a raid by Sherman from east Tennessee, or Charlotte or Salisbury.[42]

---

40 Swanson, *Atlas of the Civil War*, 110.

41 The Reverend John Monroe Anderson (1821-1879), chaplain in Confederate service 1861-1865. See Scott, *Ministerial Directory of the Presbyterian Church, U. S.*, 14.

42 This was the beginning of Stoneman's Raid. In late March and early April, 1865, Maj. Gen. George Stoneman led his 6,000 Union cavalry troops on a raid that began in east Tennessee and extended through parts of North Carolina and Virginia. He did raid and burn much of Salisbury, including its warehouses, Confederate military supplies, and vacant prisoner of war camp, but those events did not happen until April 12-13, 1865, about nine to ten days following this diary entry. On April 3, 1865, Stoneman's cavalry troops had just crossed the North Carolina line into middle Virginia. See Swanson, *Atlas of the Civil War*, 108-110.

Tuesday, Apl. 4th 1865

No telegraphic communication with Richmond today. Still without orders. Jimmy is improving rapidly—walked out a short distance today, on his crutches. Not one word of intelligence from Charleston.

Wednesday, Apl. 5th 1865

A press dispatch, to the editor of the "South Carolinian," which is now published in this place, was received last night, announcing the fact that President Davis and the heads of Department had arrived in Danville on the 3rd inst.; that, after three days hard fighting, Grant had broken through Genl Lee lines near Petersburg and Richmond had been evacuated. Saw the announcement of the death of Thomas Barrett in Augusta. Poor fellow, I waitend [sic] on him when he was married, and knew him well.[43] He was completely devoted to the world, and had amassed a good fortune. I hope he had, in his last days, turned his thoughts to a world of more enduring happiness than the wealth of this life can afford.

Received a communication from the Surgeon General informing me that Surgeon Crowell was in Columbia, and I must report to him. I telegraphed Crowell immediately, and requested him to order me to Augusta.

Thursday, Apl. 6th 1865

The report of the evacuation of Richmond was confirmed today. The mere occupation of Richmond by the enemy is nothing, but its suddenness and the defeat of a portion of our army, with the inevitable loss of life, and wounded and capture of prisoners, makes it a disaster. This again shows the want of decision of character and delay in our authorities. The time to have placed

---

43 Thomas Samuel Barrett (August 10, 1808-April 2, 1865). F. M. Robertson "waitend on him" when he married Mary Savannah Glascock (April 5, 1814-September 17, 1880), daughter of Gen. Thomas Glascock, on April 16, 1830, in Augusta, Georgia. Barrett was a druggist in firm of Barrett & Carter, 291 Broad Street, Augusta, and he lived at the corner of Broad and Elbert (4th) Streets. Coincidentally, Thomas S. Barrett and F. M. Robertson are both great-great-grandfathers of the author, Thomas H. Robertson, Jr., maternal and paternal, respectively. See Adelaide Rossignal Barnes, "Genealogical Studies," typescript in possession of Thomas Heard Robertson, Jr., 2012; *Directory for the City of Augusta, and Business Advertiser for 1859; Macon Telegraph*, September 25, 1830, 3.

Richmond in a proper position, was in 1862, when Genl Lee had driven McClellan's[44] army from the peninsular.

The Archives of the Confederacy and all the public property, in its most comprehensive signification, had been removed, and Richmond was truly the seat of the Confederate government in name only. It was necessary, then to defend it as a point of honor. That defense was not only successful, but resulted in the breaking up of the Yankee army and disgrace of its commander. Instead of removing the Archives back to Richmond, a more central and distant point should have been selected, for the temporary seat of government, and Richmond should have been suffered to remain, as other similar cities were throughout the Confederacy, and occupied and defended simply for its intrinsic worth, and not as the capital of the Confederacy. Its defense, as such, has exhausted our country of men and subsistence. Given up at that time, Genl Lee would have been free and untrammeled, with his magnificent and victorious army, and could then have sought, and met the enemy with every advantage. All admit that it should have been evacuated some months since. If this be admitted, how much stronger the reason for its abandonment at the time I mention. Charleston was evacuated too late to save our Rail Road communication. At the proper time, its evacuation would have arrested and, probably, defeated Sherman, and saved the devastation of Georgia, South Carolina, and a portion of North Carolina. Richmond has been held until its evacuation became a crushing disaster. Nothing positive has been heard from Genl Lee's army. Received no response to my telegram of yesterday, to Dr. Crowell. I fear he is not in Columbia, and I shall be delayed in being assigned to duty. I think the Surgeon Genl not only an incompetent man, but an obstinate and illtempered creature. I should not regret to hear that he had been left in the hands of the Yankees in the evacuation of Richmond.

Friday, Apl. 7th 1865

Still further confirmation of the disaster before Petersburg, and the evacuation of Richmond. No particulars. The President still at Danville. The Surgeon General is at Charlotte. Mrs. Davis is occupying a small house in Charlotte, but rooms have been engaged for her at the Hotel, hear, [sic] for some time, and are still held subject to her orders. The President has published an address to the people. It is warm, patriotic, and determined in its tone. If his other qualifications were equal to his patriotism and firmness, I should have no

---

44 Union Maj. Gen. George B. McClellan.

fears as to his future course. But it cannot be denied that mistakes and blunders, most pertinaciously persevered in have brought us to our present gloomy position. I will, however, say no more.

Our invaders are in the hands of the Lord and he can bring their works to an end. "Fret not thyself because of evil doers, neither be thou angry against the workers of iniquity. They shall soon be cut down like the grass, and wither as the green herb. Trust in the Lord and do good, so shalt thou dwell in the land, and verily thou shalt be fed. Delight thyself in the Lord, and he shall give thee the desires of thine heart. Commit thy ways unto the Lord; trust also in him, and he shall bring it to pass."[45]

Saturday, Apl. 8th 1865

A large number of refugees from Richmond and Petersburg arrived in the Charlotte train today, Government officers, Senators and members of Congress—Many of them with families and an immense amount of baggage. What a leveller war is. All had to take the same mode of conveyance—a common quartermasters waggon. I saw a few moments since, Senator Wigfall's[46] family crammed into one, with as little ceremony as a camp woman and her brats would have been pitched in. Officers just from Raleigh state that Genl Johnson had given notice to the authorities of that city, that he would uncover it with his troops today and fall back to Hillsboro. His army will be united with Lee's army. It is now evident that Grant[47] was reinforced by Schofield[48] and a part of Sherman's army. This accounts for breaking Lee's line.

Received a telegram from Surgeon Crowell informing me that orders sending me to duty in Augusta have been sent me by mail. I presume I shall receive them in a day or two, when I will be off with Norman Smith. I am very thankful that my request has been granted. I trust I shall be able to make myself more comfortable there than in many places to which I might have been sent. Besides it will give me a better chance of communicating with my dear wife, from whom I am still without any information.

---

45 *The Holy Bible*, Psalm 37:1-5.

46 Louis Trezevant Wigfall (1816-1874), native of Edgefield County, S.C., Confederate senator from Texas. See James O. Farmer, PhD, et al., *The Story of Edgefield* (The Edgefield Historical Society, 2009), 93.

47 Gen. Ulysses S. Grant.

48 Gen. John M. Schofield.

April 9, 1865—General Robert E. Lee surrenders the Army of Northern Virginia to General Ulysses S. Grant at Appomattox Courthouse, Virginia.[49]

Saturday Apl 9th 1865[50]

Did not go to church this morning as there was no service in the Presbyterian Church. How hard it is in the army to keep this day as it should be observed. It should be a day of sacred rest and meditation. How many delightful Sabbaths have I passed when, with my dearest wife and beloved children, I could go to the Sanctuary, and worship in our humble manner, the Great Redeemer, with "none to molest or make us afraid." But, now how full of grief and trepidation are our hours of prayer and meditation. An exile from my home, with no intelligence from those loved ones who are in the enemies lines, my mind is constantly agitated and troubled with doubts and fears. Their hearts, too, must be a prey to untold anxieties and fears in relation to the safety of the boys and myself. What suspense! What anguish! Oh! that we may have grace to say with St. Paul,[51] "We are troubled on every side, yet not distressed. We are perplexed, but not in despair; persecuted, but not forsaken; cast down, but not destroyed; always bearing about in the body, the dying of the Lord Jesus, that the life also of Jesus might be made manifest in our body."[52]

Went to the Presbyterian Church in the afternoon, and heard the pastor, the Rev. Mr. White.[53] I did not hear his text, but, from what I could gather from some parts of his discourse, I presume it was from that part of Chronicles which gives an account of the death of Uzzia in an attempt to remove the Ark from the house of Obededom. His manner was unpleasant and not calculated to edify.

49 Swanson, *Atlas of the Civil War*, 110.

50 Actually it was Sunday, April 9, 1865.

51 Robertson wrote first and then struck out, "the Psalmist."

52 *The Holy Bible*, II Corinthians, 4: 8-10. Coincidentally, Robertson enters this quotation about being ". . . troubled on every side, yet not distressed" on the very day of Gen. Robert E. Lee's surrender of the Army of Northern Virginia.

53 The Reverend James E. White, pastor of Purity Church 1853-1873. See Scott, *Ministerial Directory of the Presbyterian Church, U. S.*, 765.

Monday, Apl. 10th 1865

It commenced raining last evening, and has continued, at intervals, all day. It is very unpleasant, here, in rainy months. The soil is stiff red clay, with a mixture of lime. It is very destructive to shoes. There is no news from the front, and no particulars of the fight before Petersburg. I understand from Norman Smith, that Genl Lovel is to be here, on his way to Columbia, tomorrow. It is probable he is to command this Department.[54] We are now ready to leave as soon as my orders arrive. No intelligence from my dear ones in Charleston.

Tuesday, Apl. 11th 1865

Have determined, unless something transpires to prevent, to leave in the morning. If my orders do not come today, they can be sent after me. Called to see Mrs. Patterson this morning and bid her goodbye. Gillespie and his wife left for Union on Saturday. She is very kind and seems to be very much attached to our family. Jimmy and myself dined with them a few days since. Wrote to Righton and Duncan yesterday, and to my brother Lewis this morning. It has continued to rain in showers during the day.

Reports of a raid upon Sumter—one report is that citizens have been shot and the Town burnt.[55] Its truth would not surprise me, as there seems to be no energy or system with those in authority in this state. Dr. Miles arrived here this afternoon, en route to report to the Surgeon General. He tells me that the boxcar bringing a portion of our Archives and my books and instruments, has never come to hand.

I cannot find terms sufficiently strong to express my gratitude to this good and kind family for their kindness to Jimmy and myself. Brothers or sons could not have received more devoted care and unremitting attention. We have been

---

54 Maj. Gen. Mansfield Lovell (1822-1884), graduate of West Point, 1842. On March 23, 1865, General Johnston wrote to Gen. Robert E. Lee requesting that Maj. Gen. Lovell be ordered to report to him, adding, "I regard him equal to our best major-generals." On April 7, 1865, General Johnston assigned General Lovell to command in the State of South Carolina. See *OR*, v. 47, pt. 2, 1454, pt. 3, 765, 688.

55 The attack became known as Potter's Raid. "On April 9, 1865, the day that Robert E. Lee surrendered at Appomattox Court House, Federal troops under Gen. Edward E. Potter occupied Sumter. They destroyed railroad property (locomotives, cars, shops, store houses, the freight depot), burned cotton and the jail, ransacked businesses and looted homes. . . ." From Sumter County Historical Commission Marker, "Potter's Raid," 2009, located in Sumter, South Carolina, described in "The Historical Marker Database," for "Military Post/Potter's Raid Marker," updated February 23, 2010, http://www.hmdb.org/Marker.asp?Marker=27832, accessed September 11, 2010.

here three weeks with a servant, and not one cent compensation will they take. We have occupied the best room in the house, and I am sure, in Mrs. Martin's precarious state of health, have put them to serious inconvenience. All I can say is, may the blessing of God rest upon them all. May He shield them from our merciless and savage invaders who war alike upon the female, the child and the male. In the hour of peril, may He cover them with the palm of His hand as with a shield.

While I write, another kind female friend—Mrs. Patterson—has sent in a basket of eatables for us to carry on our journey. Oh that our men were all such patriots and heroes as our women. Then no conscript law would be necessary, no enrolling officers would be known; but, with one mighty rush, like the angry waves of the ocean, our invaders would be swept from our soil.

Norman Smith has just passed, and tells us to be ready by eight o'clock in the morning. My orders, by mail, have not arrived. I have telegraphed Dr. Crowell to send them here by telegraph, or duplicates of them to Augusta by the first courier.

Wednesday, Apl. 12th 1865

Our friends gave us an early and sumptuous breakfast this morning. The waggon was at the door at 8 o'clock A.M. for our luggage. The Buggy which is to carry Jimmy and the young ladies arrived at the same time. We bid farewell to our kind friends who seemed pained to part with us. All but Norman Smith and myself left Chester at 9 o'clock A.M. After waiting until 11 o'clock without receiving any telegram from Dr. Crowell, we started at 11 o'clock. Our party consisted of Jimmy, the two Misses Patterson,[56] and Miss Aldrich[57] in the Buggy. Maj. Burtody[58] of the Artillery, Capt. Clarke[59] of the Quartermaster

---

56 Probably Adora Eugenia Patterson (b. 1843) and Mildred Anna Patterson (b. 1839), both sisters of Giles Patterson. William Terrell Lewis, *Genealogy of the Lewis Family in America: from the middle of the seventeenth century down to the present time*, http://www.ebooksread.com/authors-eng/ nicholas-barbon/genealogy-of-the-lewis-family-in-america-from-the-middle-of-the-seventee nth-cen-iuo/page-27-genealogy-of-the-lewis-family-in-america-from-the-middle-of-the-seve nteenth-cen-iuo.shtml, accessed January 12, 2013.

57 Possibly Anna Aldrich (b. ca. 1848), daughter of James Thomas Aldrich (1819-1875) of Barnwell, South Carolina, or his nieces Rosa (b. 1842) or Sara (b. 1846).

58 Maj. Thomas D. Bertody; listed as Bertody, Thomas D., GA Hvy. Arty. 22nd Bn. Co. A, Capt., in Hewett, *Confederate Soldiers*; Major Bertody of Twenty-second Georgia Battalion, *OR*, v. 47, 1086.

59 Probably Clark, John, G. GA Gen & Staff, Capt., AQM. as listed in Hewett, *Confederate Soldiers*.

Mr. Stephens's [actually Robert M. Stephenson's] House (2004)
Courtesy of Catherine Barrett Robertson

Department, Norman Smith, Lawton Miller[60] and myself on horseback. Josiah Axson[61] and my son Henry alternately on foot and in the waggon. My servant, Henry, Capt. Clarke's servant and the teamster.[62]

As we passed out of Chester, we met a long train of provisions going on to Genl Johnson's Army. It extended several miles, and it was some time before we succeeded in passing them. The first nine miles of the road was very hilly and bad, having been terribly cut up during the recent rains, by the government trains passing between Newberry and Chester. The face of the country presents a pleasing and beautiful prospect, from the summit of the various hills over

60 Alexander Lawton Miller (1848-1934), grand-nephew of F. M. Robertson and future brother-in-law of James Lawrence Robertson.

61 Josiah Mikell Axson (b. 1838, Charleston, S.C.), Norman W. Smith's brother-in-law. Smith had married Julia Martin Axson (b. ca. 1827) on February 5, 1857. Email, Erick Montgomery to Thomas H. Robertson, Jr., December 10, 2012. Probably Axson, J. M. SC 5th Cav. Co. E. as listed in Hewett, *Confederate Soldiers*.

62 **Route: The entourage followed Ashford Street and Ashford Ferry Road (S-16). The road changes names to Douglass Road near Sandy Creek (still numbered S-16). In Fairfield County the name becomes Old Douglass Road (S-22).**

which we are passing. The houses and plantations give evidence of wealth and refinement. Most of the houses are well built and commodious—neatly planted with fine orchards, large gardens and, tastefully laid out grounds with flowers, evergreens, and shrubbery—many with splendid groves of native oaks.

Just before leaving Chester, news was received that Sherman had cut the Rail Road at High Point, and had taken and burnt Salisbury.[63]

Thursday, 13th Apl 1865

Encamped about eighteen miles from Chester last night. Procured accommodations for the young ladies, in a comfortable house with a kind family. They also gave Jimmy and myself a bed. This was the residence of a Mr. Stephens.[64] The ladies and Jimmy took supper, had lodging and breakfast, and were only charged $5 apiece. I took my meals in camp and they would take nothing for my bed. They even made an apology for charging the ladies and Jimmy, by stating that they were compelled to take in and accommodate so many soldiers that they found it necessary to make some charges to those who were able to pay, in order to replace the provisions consumed.

Started, in the rain, this morning at 7 o'clock.[65] The ladies were stowed away in the waggon, and Jimmy and the boys took the buggy which had no top. I managed to keep dry with my overcoat and an indian rubber cloth over my legs. I came on to Ashfords ferry on Broad River, in advance of the party.[66] Walked my horse twelve miles in three hours, which brought me to the ferry at 10 o'clock A. M. Passed a number of fine houses today. Plantations all look well and florishing. We touched the track of Kilpatrick's raiders today. The desolation, which marked the course of Sherman's Army, is called the "burnt

---

63 Stoneman's Raid. For further details, see footnote under the April 3, 1865 diary entry.

64 "Mr. Stephens" is Robert Murdock Stevenson, whose house was nine years old in 1865. Stevenson was called "Long Robin" Stevenson and was six feet nine inches tall. He was a promoter and stockholder of the first railroad from Columbia to Charlotte. See Julian Stevenson Bolick, *A Fairfield Sketchbook* (Clinton, SC, 1963), 200-2. **Route: The current address is 5394 Old Douglass Road, Blackstock, SC. Garland Painter was the incumbent owner in 2004.**

65 **Route: The route for this rainy day's ride extends along Harden Road (S-346), where the bridge over the West Fork of Little River was currently out of service (2004); thence, in turn, along roads S-204, S-18, State Route 215, and State Route 34 to the site of Ashford's Ferry over the Broad River.**

66 Ashford's Ferry was established 1796 by William Lyles. It became known as Ashfords in 1807 and was the most important ferry on the Broad River. See Thomas H. Pope, *The History of Newberry County, South Carolina, Volume One 1749-1860* (Columbia, SC, 1973), 129.

Milestones

We crossed the river and continued our march until 5 o'clock P.M. which brought us within eight miles and a half of Newberry Court House. We have made 19 1/2 miles today, besides crossing the ferry.

Surgeon F. M. Robertson
April 13, 1865

Surgeon Robertson's journal entries often include an accounting of the number of miles that he traveled on that day. In retracing the diarist's footsteps, the author found that his distances are surprisingly accurate when compared to the actual lengths between landmarks that are still identifiable. How was he able to be so precise?

It seems logical that the answer lies in the placement of markers along the roads. We found square granite milestones still standing in place at four locations along the route to support this hypothesis. All of these were situated on the grounds of antebellum buildings, three houses and one courthouse, where owners have preserved them as a part of the historic settings.[1]

The markers are generally located on the right side of the route in the direction of increasing mileage, which extends from south to north beginning at the southernmost political boundary of a county, district, or state. This is the same pattern that is used by departments of transportation for highway mile markers today.

Milestone 20, located in the front yard of the historic Pine House at the intersection of U.S. Highway 25 and S.C. Highway 121 in present day Trenton, passed by the diarist's party on April 16, 1865. (2004)
Courtesy of Catherine Barrett Robertson

1. The milestone designations that our retracement party found in 2004 include a granite marker at old Newberry District Courthouse, South Carolina, passed by F. M. Robertson's party on April 14, 1865; Milestone 2 on George Loop, Newberry County, South Carolina, 2 miles north of Bauknight's Ferry over the Saluda River, also passed on April 14, 1865; Milestone 20 in the front yard of Pine House, owned by Mr. and Mrs. Bettis C. Rainsford, Jr., 2014, located at Pine House Crossroads, the intersection of U. S. Highway 25 and S. C. Highway 121 in present day Trenton, passed on April 16, 1865; Milestone 15 located at 2671 Edgefield Road opposite Padgett Road, 2004, passed on April 16, 1865, situated 15 miles from the Savannah River bridge at the now dead town of Hamburg, South Carolina, opposite Augusta, Georgia. Milestone 15 has been removed between 2004 and 2014.

Thomas B. Wadlington (Keitt) House
Image courtesy of South Carolina Department of Archives and History

district." I passed one place marked by six stacks of blackened chimneys, the work of these merciless vandals. Language cannot express the untold miseries that have been left in the tracks of these unfeeling and unprincipled wretches. The record is in heaven.

I stopped at the ferry, and as there was a government forge and a forage master there, I gave my horse some fodder and had his hind shoes tightened. The waggon, buggy and remainder of the party came up at half past one P.M. We crossed the river and continued our march until 5 o'clock P.M. which brought us within eight miles and a half of Newberry Court House. We have made 19 1/2 miles today, besides crossing the ferry. The rain ceased in the course of the morning, and the rest of the day was pleasant and clear. We obtained accommodations for the ladies at Dr. Rutherford's[67] about half a mile

---

67 "Liberty Hill," home of Dr. Thomas Brooks Rutherford (d. 1865). Dr. Rutherford's house later burned and was replaced by the "Nance House," built by former governor William H. Gist (Governor of South Carolina 1858-1860) for his son Richard. Gist bought the land at an auction after the death of Dr. Rutherford in 1865, who was possessed of 732 acres. The Liberty Hill house burned down about that time. Personal communication with Dot and Don Secor, the encumbent residents, October 2, 2004. See S. C. Department of Archives and History, National Register of Historic Places inventory form, Site No. 668, 6/12/85. Dr. Rutherford was elected on May 21, 1860 as a delegate to the South Carolina Democratic Convention from Newberry. See Pope, *The History of Newberry County Volume One*, 209. **Route: Located at 337**

from our encampment, which is in a grove of Mr. Wadlington's near a fine spring. Mr. Wadlington accommodated me with a bed.[68] Found the people all in a state of alarm and excitement about the raids at Sumter and in the vicinity of Columbia. Each one expected to be the next victim.

April 14, 1865—Abraham Lincoln assassinated at Ford's Theater, Washington, D.C.[69]

Friday, 14th Apl 1865

Took and early breakfast in camp, and left with Mjr. Burtody and Capt. Clarke at 1/4 before 6 o'clock, and arrived in the village of Newberry at 8 o'clock A.M. We remained in Newberry until the balance of the party arrived. Norman, Jimmy and the ladies remained in the village to have some repairs done to the buggy, and we left with the waggon at 11 1/2 o'clock A.M. and arrived at Bauknight's ferry on the Saluda River at 3 P.M., at which point the buggy overtook us.[70]

Rutherford Road, the foundations of Liberty Hill were still visible in the front yard of the Nance House, 2004.

68 Thomas Bauskett Wadlington (1821-1882), planter, lawyer, widower. The substantial Greek Revival house was about six years old in 1865. See S. C. Department of Archives and History, National Register of Historic Places inventory form, Site. No. 674, 5/21/85; John Belton O'Neal and John A. Chapman, *The Annals of Newberry*, (Newberry, SC, 1892), Google Books edition, accessed December 22, 2012, 574-5. **Route: The house was used as a fraternity house for TKE of Newberry College from the 1970s until it burned in 1989. The site is located on southwest corner of the intersection of SC 34 and U. S. Highway 176, which was named Keitt's Crossroads, following Mr. Wadlington's death, for the husband of Wadlington's sister and heir, Carolina Mary James Wadlington Keitt (Mrs. Ellison Summerfield Keitt). The high brick foundation and chimneys of the house were still standing in 2004. The site still encompasses a fine grove of trees, including one very large oak tree. An adjacent low area may once have contained a spring. Mr. Wadlington is buried in the adjoining cemetery of Enoree Baptist Church, previously known as Bauskett Church.**

69 Swanson, *Atlas of the Civil War*, 110.

70 **Route: The party followed State Route 395, Deadfall Road (S-83), and George Loop (West), on which granite Milepost No. 2 stood in the front yard of the Ozziee George residence in 2004. This point is 2 miles north of the ferry over the Saluda River. Thence, the route extends either along Davenport Road or George Road through private property to the site of Bauknight's Ferry, shown on some maps as Lorick's Ferry.** In 1852, William Bouknight was given the franchise for the ferry over the Saluda River for ten years. Previously, the ferry had been known variously as Boatner's, Waldo's, Lorick's, and Huiett's Ferry. See Pope, *The History of Newberry County, Volume One*, 127-8.

Crossed and encamped two miles from the river.[71] I made an effort to get the ladies accommodated at Mr. Bauknight's, but he could not take them as there was a Methodist Quarterly meeting near, and he expected the Presiding Elder and a sufficient number of preachers to stay all night with him, to fill all his rooms.

I made another effort to get accommodations for them about two miles further on. This was at a Mr. Perry's, a wealthy planter. His wife was not only rude, but positively insulting. As the comfort of the young ladies was the question at issue, I brought all my powers of persuasion to bear without showing any resentment at the rudeness of the hostess. She recommended us to go further. I told her that this was impossible as we had then gone beyond the limit of our days journey, and wound up by telling her if she still refused to accommodate them, that, for the first time in the progress of our journey, the ladies would be compelled to camp out and sleep in the woods. This appeal appeared to awaken a little of that latent feeling of female sympathy, which had, hitherto lain dormant. She said she would see what could be done. Upon this declaration I caused the ladies to alight from the buggy and walk into the house. I turned them over to the little fat woman, with keen eyes, a pinched mean nose, upturned chin and thin lips (she smoked and dipped) and made a hasty, if not disorderly, retreat to our encampment.[72]

In contrast to this, Mjr. Burtody, Capt. Clarke, and myself obtained a lunch of a lady near Newberry at a ladys house. She had an infant at the breast and several other children. She had, a few months previous, lost her husband in the army. She let us have a dozen eggs, and gave us bacon a[nd] greens, with an abundance of milk and clabber. She did not wish to charge anything, but we compelled her to receive compensation.

Soon after supper, it commenced raining, but by throwing another fly over that already pitched, we managed to keep dry.

Saturday, Apl. 15th 1865

It ceased raining about 12 o'clock last night. This morning was dark, cloudy, and threatening. I learned from the young ladies, this morning, that the

---

71 **Route: South of Bauknight's Ferry, the route leads through private property to the intersection of Bethany School House Road (S-129) and Road S-145, called Perry's Crossroads, 2004, about 2 miles from the Saluda River.**

72 **Route: The campsite was located near the intersection of Bethany School House Road (S-129) and Road S-44.**

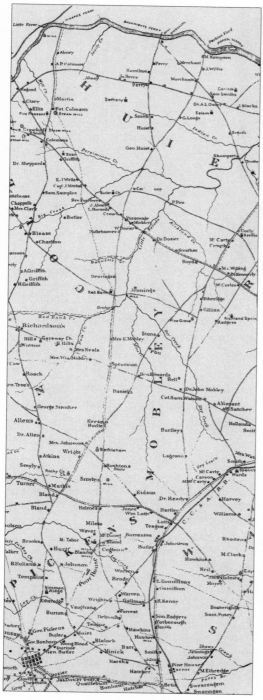

Bauknight's Ferry to Colonel Smyley's
house and Pine House crossroad.
Detail from Boles, Map of Edgefield
County, 1871.
*Courtesy of Thompkins Library of Old
Edgefield District Genealogical Society*

hostess softened down very much after seeing and conversing with them—confessed that she had been extremely rude and professed sorrow for her conduct. She asked them who I was and regretted that I did not return to the house that she might have had an opportunity of expressing her regrets in person. She told them that they were indebted to my earnest appeal, for she never saw a man so hard to get rid of in all her life.

Started this morning at 7 o'clock. The clouds soon cleared off and the day turned out to be very pleasant. Exchanged salt for some chickens and eggs on the way. We can get anything the people have for salt.

In consequence of Mjr. Burtody, Capt. Clarke and myself going ahead every morning and getting a lunch about 12 o'clock, the ladies have styled us the buttermilk

Road through hills near Col. Smyley's
Plantation (2004)
Catherine Barrett Robertson

rangers.[73] Today we went ahead and stopped at a Dr. Mobleys, about 12 miles from our camping ground, and asked for a lunch. The gentleman was not at home, but the good lady requested us to come in.[74] We did so. She had our horses fed, and in the course of half an hour called us in, not to lunch, but to dinner. The dinner consisted of boiled bacon and turnip greens, fried ham and eggs, irish potatoes with butter, sweet potatoes, salad dressed with egg and vinegar, corn and wheat bread, fine light fritters and syrup, with and abundance of butter and buttermilk. The Buttermilk rangers felt, as they mounted their horses, that they had foraged to some purpose today. She did not wish to charge anything, but we insisted, and compelled her to receive compensation.

We completed 20 miles by 3 o'clock P.M. and stopped just as a thunder shower was coming up.[75] Coln Smiley, a kind gentleman, took the whole party

73 Route: The "buttermilk rangers" likely traveled along S-129 and Jersey Trail (S-401) and Denny Highway (State Route 194) changing to State Route 121 in the present day town of Saluda (formerly called Red Bank) (2004).

74 William Simkins Mobley, M.D. (1809-1866). Member of the South Carolina legislature 1854-1866. He kept his doctor's office near the house and was "...very popular both as neighbor and physician." Mrs. Mobley was Susannah Neal Mobley. See John A. Chapman, *History of Edgefield County from the Earliest Settlements to 1897* (Newberry, SC, 1897), 101; "The Descendants of Dr. John Richard Mobley, Sr. and Lucretia Simkins," compiled by Johnson Bland Mobley, Jr., privately published, (Columbia, SC, 1991). **Route: The Dr. Mobley place was probably located on State Route 121 just north of Lenny's Lane, 2004.**

75 Route: The last part of the twenty miles included State Route 121, Church Road (S-119), and an unimproved dirt road now crossing private property to the intersection of Road S-190 and Weaver Road (S-18). The old Colonel Smyley place is at or near this intersection.

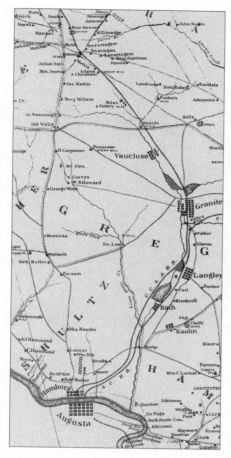

Pine House Crossroad to Augusta, Georgia.
Detail from Boles Map of
Edgefield County, 1871.
*Courtesy of Thompkins Library of Old Edgefield
District Genealogical Society.*

in and allowed our waggon and horses to bivouac under his gin house.[76] My son Henry was taken with a severe chill on the road today. He had a high fever and raging headache when we arrived at Coln Smileys. I had him put to bed immediately, and gave him a cup of warm tea, which, thanks to the forethought of my blessed wife, I had with me. I felt very uneasy about him, and made arrangements to sleep with him, in order to watch his symptoms carefully.

Sunday, Apl. 16th 1865

Henry suffered very much during the night, but his fever went off towards morning, and he was enabled to proceed with us in the wagon. Coln Smiley accommodated the entire party last night, and would not charge a cent. In fact we could not urge him, under any considerations, to receive anything, and after seeing that the more we urged the matter, the more painful it was to him, we desisted, and left his hospitable mansion with a thousand thanks and good wishes. The Yankees have not visited him, and we sincerely trust he may never fall a sacrifice to the lawless and inhuman pack of plunderers. The first

---

76 Col. James C. Smyley (1820-1872), a planter by business and occupation, respected native of Edgefield County, Colonel of Militia, delegate to South Carolina Secession Convention and signer of Ordinance of Secession, December 20, 1860. See Chapman, *History of Edgefield County*, 236.

Hamburg, South Carolina and Augusta, Georgia. Detail of Bird's Eye View of Augusta, 1872.
Courtesy of Augusta Museum of History

five miles of the road was very bad.[77] Stiff clay hills. A stratified rock crops out abundantly. It is evidently clay slate in its character. The laminae are thin and lie perpendicular. After the first five miles the clay hills and stratified rocks almost entirely disappeared, and the country gradually assumed a sandy level appearance with extensive pine forests—collectively called the piney woods region. The sandy road was good in consequence of the beating rain of yesterday, and we made excellent progress.[78] We determined to push on for Augusta, and made but a brief stop in the middle of the day.[79] We reached the

[77] Route: The five miles of bad road follows Weaver Road (S-18) to the intersection of State Route 23.

[78] Route: South of State Route 23, the road name changes to Woodyard Road (still numbered S-18).

[79] Route: The stop was probably at or near Pine House Crossroads in present day Trenton. Milepost No. 20 stands in front of the residence called the Pine House, the property of Mr. and Mrs. Bettis C. Rainsford, Jr., (2014). From this point the route continues along State Route 121, U.S. Highway 25, Old Edgefield Road, Martintown Road (U.S. Highway 25), Aiken-Augusta Highway (U.S. Highways 1 and 25); and,

range of hills overlooking Augusta a little before six o'clock P.M. and at six we crossed the bridge, having made thirty miles today. Henry continued better through the day, although very feeble from the fatigue of riding in the waggon. Jimmy stood the journey admirably and was delighted to get among kind friends and relatives.

I have continued these notes up to this point, only for the perusal of my dear wife hoping that they may some day reach her and serve to fill up, in some measure, that blank which our separation has occasioned.[80]

I have been now over a week in Augusta, and have found kind friends every where. Henry had a return of his chill and fever the morning after our arrival in Augusta. He was very sick for several days, but by close watching and prompt attention his fever finally gave way and he is again out and about his business.

I shall make no comment, at present, upon the Sad condition of our cause, but leave it in the hands of God who works in His own mysterious ways. Oh that He may preserve my darling wife and dear children, and bring us together again.

thence, over the **Fifth Street Bridge to Augusta, Georgia. This last part follows the old high road east of the now dead town of Hamburg.**

80 The statement that he has "continued these notes . . . only for the perusal of my dear wife." does not seem to be entirely true. Dr. Robertson included in his journal a lot of family connection information that his wife would have already known.

Epilogue

The prayer with which Dr. Robertson ends his narrative asking for the safe reunion of his family was answered soon afterward. The one about the sad condition of the Southern cause and God's mysterious ways has taken a little longer.

On April 26, 1865, Gen. Joseph E. Johnston surrendered the remnant of his army of about 30,000 troops to Gen. William T. Sherman at Bennett's farmhouse near Durham's Station, North Carolina. The same day President Jefferson Davis met with his Cabinet in Charlotte and agreed to depart later in the day with the goal of reaching the lands west of the Mississippi River.[1]

The group traveled on to Abbeville, South Carolina, and thence to Washington, Georgia, where they arrived on May 2, 1865, with a small detachment of soldiers and a wagon train carrying gold and government documents. President Davis lodged and dined with Dr. John Joseph Robertson, younger brother of Francis Marion Robertson, at the local Branch of the Bank of Georgia, where Dr. Robertson was the cashier and occupied a spacious residence with his family upstairs.[2] On May 3, the remnant of the Confederate

---

1 Wilson Angley, Jerry L. Cross, and Michael Hill, *Sherman's March through North Carolina: A Chronology*, (Raleigh, 1995), 83, 86, 93; Swanson, *Atlas of the Civil War*, 110.

2 John Joseph Robertson, M.D. (1819-1873), brother of Francis Marion Robertson; graduate of Medical College of South Carolina; bank cashier in Washington, Georgia; planter in Wilkes County, Georgia; and signer of State of Georgia Ordinance of Secession representing Wilkes County, Georgia, along with Robert Toombs. See original printed copy of ordinance in possession of Thomas H. Robertson, Jr., Augusta, Georgia (2014), "Republic of Georgia, Ordinance of Secession, Passed Jan'ry 19, 1861, with the Names of the Signers, . . . George W. Crawford of Richmond, President, Milledgeville, January 22, 1861," (Augusta, Georgia:

Cabinet met at the bank and then dispersed. The pursuing Federal troops arrived in Washington the following day. President Davis got as far as Irwinville, Georgia, where he was captured on May 9, 1865. His captors brought him by wagon and railroad through Macon, Atlanta, and Augusta, then down the Savannah River by boat, and up the coast by ship to the North where he was imprisoned for two years. As for the Confederate gold, although stories, myths, and studies about its fate abound, it has never been found.[3]

The "sad condition" of the Southern cause carried on through the postwar time called Reconstruction. Although the Reconstruction period officially lasted only about twelve years, until 1877, its economic effects remained much longer, with financial vestiges still evident a hundred years later. The former wealth of the South, which had been largely based upon agriculture and slave labor, was almost totally lost. The losses, which included the immense cost of the war effort, the large investments in slaves, and the worthless monetary system, led to general poverty of the populace that took several generations from which to recover. A New South finally did emerge, based on manufacturing and other new endeavors. These efforts brought a measure of prosperity in time, but they were chiefly financed by Northern capitalists to whom much of the profits also accrued.[4]

Those Southerners who would have had the financial means to start over were the ones most hampered by the terms of Reconstruction. In addition to the former Confederate political and military leaders, those who owned property valued at over $20,000 were not included in the general amnesty and had to apply for special pardon from President Andrew Johnson to become United States citizens again. For instance, F. M. Robertson's nephew Jonathan Meyer Miller, a planter of Augusta, Georgia, and Beech Island, South Carolina,

Constitutionalist Steam Press, 1861); William C. Davis, ed., *Diary of a Confederate Soldier: John S. Jackman of the Orphan Brigade*, (Columbia, 1997), 167.

3   Robert M. Willingham, Jr., *The History of Wilkes County, Georgia* (Washington, GA, 2002), 175-182.

4   "The Lost Cause," a pervasive southern philosophy that emerged during the post war years, is often viewed by modern historical scholars with some contempt, even ridicule in some cases. The philosophy contained some myths, to be sure; but it was real to those who had experienced the war and its aftermath. With the lack of surviving men, the Lost Cause was championed by the overwhelmingly female white population. "Look back to glory" was a common attitude that was born of the military defeat and the nearly total loss of money. Genteel poverty was accepted, even pervasive, among formerly affluent white families. What could they hang onto that was positive? They ended up with neither an independent country, nor military victory, nor money, to say nothing of the men lost or crippled. Beyond their surviving household goods, they found value in their good family names, their heritage, their religion, and a reverence for their lost struggle for independence, however mythical those things may have formerly been.

Parole pass of Major Joseph Righton Robertson
Collection of Thomas H. Robertson, Jr.

who had invested heavily in plantations and slaves, applied for such a special pardon in August, 1865. As in the case of most planters, the value of the slaves he had owned exceeded by many times the value of the farm land he planted. The loss of the human chattel as part of the collateral for loans often led to financial disaster for debtor and creditor alike. In Miller's case, for example, the aftermath of the war left him in serious financial straits, and he had to sell his 775-acre Goodale plantation in 1871 to satisfy debts owed to his creditors. His debts also included a $1000 note, still unpaid in 1872, for the purchase of a ten-year-old mulatto slave named Albert from A. R. Laurence of Iredell County, North Carolina in December of 1860.[5]

5 President Andrew Johnson, Amnesty Proclamation, May 29, 1865, http://itwsewanee.edu/reconstruction/html/docs/andrewj.html, accessed December 28, 2008; Case Files of Applications from Former Confederates for Presidential Pardons ("Amnesty Papers"), 1865-1867, Microfilm Roll 21 (Washington: The National Archives, 1976).); National Register of Historic Places, Inventory-Nomination Form for Fitzsimons-Hampton-Harris House [Goodale plantation house], Items 7 and 8; Jonathan Meyer Miller at one time or another owned at least three plantations: Ardis and White House in Beech Island, S.C. and Goodale in Richmond County, Georgia. He also operated the Sand Bar Ferry over the Savannah River between them; "Simons & Simons case records, I, 1819-1878," SCHS Call Number 431.02 (I), which include the related "Jonathan M. Miller legal papers, 1860-1872," SCHS Call Number: 431.02(M) 31, in collections of South Carolina Historical Society; Thomas Heard Robertson, Jr., *Albert: History and Reflections on Slavery and Its Aftermath*, unpublished manuscript in possession of the author, 2015, passim.

The Robertson family was soon reunited after the war, and they fared better than most in surviving it. In fact, it is remarkable that a father and five sons would all live through the fighting, with only two of them as wounded casualties.

The oldest son, William Francis, followed his father's medical footsteps in Charleston, becoming Chair of Obstetrics and Diseases of Women and Children at the Medical College in 1867. Sadly, he, his wife Lydia, and one of their three daughters all died in 1875, leaving their two other small children to be adopted by two of his brothers.[6]

Joseph Righton Robertson was paroled as a part of General Johnston's army at Greensboro, North Carolina, on May 2, 1865. He had married Constantia Whitridge Taylor just before the war started and had seen the birth of their first child in 1860. They had two more children during the conflict, out of an eventual total of eight. Immediately after the war he reentered mercantile life in Charleston, beginning as a bookkeeper and advancing to a partnership with the firms of Geo. W. Williams & Co., Robertson, Taylor & Co., and their succeeding concerns. He served as president of Ashepoo Phosphate Company and was a trustee of the Medical College of South Carolina for many years.[7]

Henry Clay Robertson returned to Charleston after the war, where he was in charge of Atlantic Wharves under Mr. Trenholm for several years. Later he began work as a commission merchant with his brother's firm, Robertson, Taylor & Williams, cotton factors. Although he became one of the junior partners, he withdrew and went to work in manufacturing, eventually becoming treasurer and general manager of Newberry Cotton Mills, Newberry, South Carolina, after 1883.[8]

---

6   Waring, *A History of Medicine in South Carolina*, 291; Robertson Family Records by Joseph Righton Robertson, Sr. and Jr., of Spartanburg, from the estate of Constance Sevier Robertson, in possession of Thomas H. Robertson, Jr., 2014 (hereinafter cited Joseph Righton Robertson, Sr. and Jr. genealogical papers).

7   Joseph Righton Robertson Sr. and Jr. Genealogical papers: Descendants list and the obituary of Maj. Jos. R. Robertson. Joseph Righton Robertson's employer and partner George W. Williams had been a City Alderman of Charleston during the war, and it had fallen to him to surrender the City to the Federals, after the Confederate evacuation, at the Atlantic (Mills) Wharf at 10:00 am on February 18, 1865. He bore a note from Mayor Macbeth that read: "The military authorities of the Confederate States have evacuated the city. I have remained to enforce law and preserve order until you take such steps as you may think best." See Burton, *The Siege of Charleston*, 319.

8   Genealogical typescript titled, "Family Register, Lyman Hall Robertson and Constance Truxton Robertson," n. d., in possession of Ethel Robertson Boyle, Conyers, Georgia, 2004; [South Carolina] State Department of Agriculture, Commerce, and Immigration, *Handbook of South Carolina, 1907* (Columbia, 1907), 460. Henry Clay Robertson's employer, George Alfred

James L. Robertson,
New York, August 16, 1869.
Collection of Thomas H. Robertson, Jr.

Jimmie (James Lawrence Robertson) recovered from the leg wound he had received at Averasboro and finished his degree in classical languages at the College of Charleston in 1869. Seeking work, he traveled north and was employed for a time in New York, but soon returned to the South. He married Jonathan Miller's daughter Katharine Smith Miller, his cousin, on November 24, 1870, at Ardis in Beech Island, South Carolina, near Augusta, Georgia, his original home. By 1880 he was employed as a farmer, living with his wife Kitty and their young family in Beech Island. He subsequently moved to Augusta, where he served as a vestryman of Saint Paul's Church for eighteen years. He changed occupations to cotton textile manufacturing, ultimately becoming secretary and treasurer of Langley Manufacturing Company, Langley, South Carolina. In 1885, the couple named the youngest of their six children Armand deRosset Robertson in honor of the cousin whom Jimmie had encountered at the Battle of Averasboro twenty years before.[9]

Trenholm (1807-1876), had been a major figure in the Confederacy as one of the originators and most successful practitioners of blockade running. He also took over as Secretary of the Treasury of the Confederate States government in June, 1864, just as the currency was collapsing. Trenholm is widely believed to be the model upon whom author Margaret Mitchell based her character Rhett Butler in her novel *Gone with the Wind*. He received a pardon in 1866 and faced bankruptcy and financial disaster upon his return to Charleston. In 1870, he reorganized his companies under the name of George A. Trenholm & Son and rebuilt a large personal fortune. See Rosen, *Confederate Charleston*, 81, 151, 162; Stephen R. Wise, *Lifeline of the Confederacy: Blockade Running During the Civil War* (University of South Carolina Press, 1988), 46-7, 150-1; Dr. E. Lee Spence, *Treasures of the Confederate Coast: The Real Rhett Butler & Other Revelations* (Charleston, 1995), 9-36; North Carolina Office of Archives and History, George A. Trenholm, Marker P-52 Text and Essay, http://www.ncmarkers.com/print_marker.aspx?id=P-52, accessed October 22, 2012.

9 Joseph Righton Robertson Sr. and Jr. genealogical papers; Joseph Righton Robertson, M.D., "Robertson 1826-1932," ca. 1932, 2pp., 2, typescript in possession of Thomas H.

Stock Certificate signed by Jas. L. Robertson as Secretary, October 25, 1911.
From original in possession of Clayton P. Boardman

Duncan Clinch Robertson was paroled on May 1, 1865, with his South Carolina Cavalry unit and the rest of General Johnston's army at Greensboro, North Carolina. In 1869 he was working with his brother Henry in Charleston harbor on the wharf under Major Willis. On April 20, 1876, at Edisto Island, he married Mary Caroline Mikell, half-sister of his brother Henry's wife.[10]

Robertson, Jr., 2014; Photograph of James Lawrence Robertson taken by C. D. Fredricks & Co., 587 Broadway, New York, inscribed on reverse, "New York Aug 16th 1869," and in a different hand, "Coz. Jas. L. Robertson, Aunt Hennie's son," in possession of Thomas H. Robertson, Jr., 2014; the entry in New York City directory for 1870: "Robertson, James, mer[chant], 443 Water [Street], h[ouse] 254 W. 54th" could be James Lawrence Robertson. He was not found in the census for 1870 in Charleston nor New York. He was not living in his father's household in Charleston at the time of the census of 1870. See email message: Frank Thompson (of New York) to Thomas H. Robertson, Jr., December 11, 2008; Katharine Smith Miller was his first cousin once removed; Wm. K. Miller, *History of St. Paul's Episcopal Church, Augusta, Georgia* (Augusta: privately published by W. K. Miller at the request of the Vestry, 1945), 73; Original stock certificates of Langley Manufacturing Company signed by Jas. L. Robertson as Sec'y and by Thomas Barrett as President dated 1911 and 1913 and issued to John W. Dickey, in possession of Clayton P. Boardman III, 2008.

10 *Compiled Service Records* for Duncan C. Robertson; Joseph Righton Robertson Sr. and Jr. genealogical papers; Letter: John Meyer Miller to Margaret Smith Miller, October 14, 1869, in Thomas Heard Robertson, Jr., *Miller Family Letters 1837 to 1894*, second edition, privately published, June, 1994, copy in Reese Library, Georgia Regents University, Augusta. Maj. Edward Willis was General Beauregard's Quartermaster in Charleston during the war and was Henry Clay Robertson's supervisor in the latter days of the conflict, as Surgeon F. M.

Daughter Henrietta Marion Robertson had married Henry Kollock Silliman, but soon died from cholera morbus and complications of a premature childbirth on July 18, 1865, at age 25.[11]

Henry Sutcliff, Dr. Robertson's servant, is unusual among African-American slaves in that he had both a given name and a published surname. He continued to live in Charleston into the 1900s, first as a domestic servant and later as a laborer and a porter. He was married in December, 1869. In July, 1870, he was living with the Mitchell household of dressmakers and washers in the Fourth Ward of the City.[12]

As for the family patriarch, Francis Marion Robertson returned to Charleston to his wife Henrietta with whom he would share a long post-bellum existence. Their house on Maiden Lane survived the shelling and the silver was safe, as he told us in his diary. The city was shambles, and so was what remained of the Medical College. All of its records had been lost during the war, its building bombed by shells, its museum robbed, and even the furniture stolen. To cover expenses, the school assessed each returning faculty member $100,

Robertson's journal indicates. At the outset of the war, Willis had been blockade runner George A. Trenholm's chief clerk and purchasing agent and was involved through his several trading companies in procuring support materials for the army. In the aftermath, Willis was associated with Trenhom at the Atlantic Wharf. In 1866, Willis purchased the fine mansion at 24 Rutledge Avenue in 1866 from I. Jenkins Mikell, Henry and Duncan Robertson's father-in-law, for $22,000. Major Willis ultimately established the factorage firm of Willis & Chisolm. He also had the distinction of introducing Gen. Robert E. Lee on April 26, 1870 to the Chief and Board of Fire Masters of Charleston, while the general was visiting Charleston at that time. The next day the venerable general met with leading citizens of Charleston, including former Treasury Secretary Trenholm. See Rosen, *Confederate Charleston*, 162; Cunningham, *Doctors in Gray*, 297; ArchiveGrid: Edward Willis papers, 1864-1891. University of South Carolina-South Caroliniana Library, http://beta.worldcat.org/archivegrid/record.php?id=43579481&contributor=207&archivename=University+of+South+Carolina+-+South+Caroliniana+Library, accessed October 22, 2012; CCPL—Charleston County Public Library–South, Carolina, http://www.ccpl.org/content. asp?id=15649&action=detail&catID=6026&parentID=5747, accessed October 17, 2012.

11 Joseph Righton Robertson Sr. and Jr. genealogical papers; Letter: F. M. Robertson to Joseph Righton Robertson, July 27th, 1865, chronicling the circumstances of the death of the latter's sister, Henrietta Marion Robertson Silliman, original letter in Papers of Constance Sevier Robertson in possession of Thomas H. Robertson, Jr., 2014.

12 *U.S. Census, 1870.* Henry "Suttliff" is most likely Henry "Sutcliff," as his name appears in the 1870 *U.S. Census*. On July 11, 1870, he is listed as being a black male, employed as a domestic servant, who cannot read nor write, and who is living with a group of five mulatto women named Mitchell, ranging in age from 8 to 36 years old, and one mulatto female named Moffitt, age 16. The oldest, Emma Mitchell, 36, is listed as a mantua maker [dressmaker]. It is unclear as to whether or not one of these women is his new wife. The search for Henry Sutcliff in the *U.S. Census, 1880* has been fruitless. The Charleston city directories list him as Henry Sutcliffe in 1886, a laborer living at 106 Anson, and in 1905, as a porter residing at 3 Beresford.

The Sticks: Leading staff, Fort Sumter flagstaff, and State Bank baluster.
Collection of Catherine Barrett Robertson. Photograph by Thomas H. Robertson, Jr., 2013

The Sticks: Three Mementos of Southern Independence, Sought and Lost

When F. M. Robertson introduced Whig Senator Henry Clay to the citizens of Augusta, Georgia, during his run for the presidency in 1844, William T. Gould marshaled the procession to the podium using a gold-tipped black baton, or leading staff. This symbol of authority had its historical roots in the fasces or beating sticks of ancient Rome, used to clear the way for important figures to pass through. The same rod saw service on June 29, 1864, in the hand of Col. Charles A. Platt,

Continued on page 137

Memorial tablet to Lt. Gen./Bishop Leonidas Polk at Saint Paul's Church, Augusta, Georgia, the site of his funeral and first burial. His remains were removed to New Orleans in the 1940s.
Photograph by Thomas H. Robertson, Jr., 2013

Henrietta Toomer Righton Robertson
Collection of Thomas H. Robertson, Jr.

and supplemented those funds first by selling the College's surviving wax model collection and subsequently by taking out a bank loan. In November 1865, the school reopened for an enrollment of 34 students and with Dr. Robertson serving as Assistant Professor of Obstetrics. By the Fall of 1867 he had been promoted to Professor of Obstetrics and Diseases of Women and Children, and the next year to Dean of the Medical School, a position he held until 1873 when he retired from the college.[13]

Both before and after the war, he lectured, wrote and published papers on a variety of topics, mostly in medical and religious journals. For instance, he had a keen interest in the disease yellow fever and presented reports in 1839 and 1858 on the subject. He did not believe that the disease was contagious, and he was so firmly of this opinion that he went so far as to swallow, by means of a capsule, some of the black vomit to prove it. The germ theory of disease causation had not been accepted then and the means of transmission of this

Francis Marion Robertson, M.D.
Collection of Thomas H. Robertson, Jr.

13 Waring, *A History of Medicine in South Carolina*, 143-146, 290-291.

Flagstaff of Fort Sumter, cut down by
Confederate artillery fire at 1:00 p.m.
on April 13, 1861.
*Image from the collections of the South Carolina
Historical Society*

Continued from page 135

Acting Marshall, at the head of the funeral procession from Augusta's City Hall to Saint Paul's Church for Bishop-Lt. Gen. Leonidas Polk, who had been killed by Federal artillery fire at Pine Mountain, Georgia on June 14, 1864. The baton appeared again on October 31, 1878 at the unveiling ceremony for the Confederate Monument on Broad Street in Augusta, when James C. C. Black was marshal of the day. Capt. F. Edgeworth Eve used it once more with John Clark as marshal of the Confederate Memorial Day procession that included Governor Gordon on April 26, 1887.[1]

The firing on Fort Sumter in Charleston harbor on April 12, 1861, signaled the beginning of the Civil War, and the fall of its flagstaff the next day created a business opportunity for souvenir creators and seekers to mark the momentous event. Charleston jeweler Spencer & Teague made "studs, Sleeve Buttons and trinkets of part of the flag Staff at Fort Sumter to be kept as tokens and mementos. . . . we can't make them fast enough to supply the demand." General P. G. T. Beauregard, who had ordered the bombardment, obtained a gold-headed walking stick made from the wood of the flag staff. Surgeon F. M. Robertson procured a similar cane with a silver cap engraved, "Flag Staff of Fort Sumter, Shot away during the Bombardment, April 13th 1861."[2]

The end of the Civil War was also marked by creators of mementos. The State Bank of Georgia building in Washington, Georgia, yielded at least one souvenir. Surgeon F. M. Robertson's brother, Dr. John Joseph Robertson and his wife hosted the fleeing Jefferson Davis, Mrs. Davis, and a remnant of Confederate Cabinet there on May 3, 1865. J. J. Robertson was cashier of the bank and lived there with his family. Later, following the failure of the bank, the building was converted to a private residence by Benjamin W. Heard, and eventually acquired a new name, the Heard House.

Continued on page 139

1. Wm. T. Gould to J. C. C. Black, Esq., October 29, 1878, including later annotation about Capt. Eve, original letter in possession of Catherine Barrett Robertson, 2013; Catherine B. R. Smith, "Death and Funerals of Bishop-General Leonidas Polk, including His Interment at St. Paul's Church, Augusta, Georgia, June 29, 1864," Valdosta State College, November 18, 1981, typescript copy in possession of Thomas H. Robertson, Jr., 2014; *The Augusta Chronicle*, October 31, 1878, April 26, 1887, and May 11, 1908.

2. Katherine W. Giles, "God Be the Judge between Us!": Final Steps in the March to Civil War, January –April 1861," *Carologue*, Vol. 26, No. 4, (Spring 2011), 13; Greg Goebel, "Spring 1861: You Will Want only Strike A Hornet's Nest," *In the Public Domain*, v. 1, chapter 2.0 of 89 (March 1, 2006), 5, http://www.vectorsite.net/twcw_02.html, accessed July 25, 2006; Beauregard's souvenir cane is pictured in John E. Stanchak, *Civil War* (New York: Dorling Kindersley Publishing, Inc., 2000), 15; F. M. Robertson's cane is in possession of Catherine Barrett Robertson, 2013; Andrew Pickens Butler, who moved to Louisiana after the war, also had a prized memento, "a walking stick made from the flagstaff that rose from one of the walls of Fort Sumter, when it was fired upon at the beginning of the war." See http://ftp.rootsweb.com/pub /usgenweb/ la/bossier/bios/butlerap.txt, accessed December 6, 2004.

dreaded malady was, of course, far from being discovered at this time.[14]

Among the contributions he made to the advancement of his profession, Dr. Robertson introduced a modification of Hodges's obstetrical forceps that proved useful to practitioners and published a paper on the subject in 1872.[15]

Robertson lectured strongly against the "evolution hypothesis" of Charles Darwin in an 1880 address before the South Carolina Medical Association, of which he was president. The arguments on this subject soon raged within the theological seminary of the Presbyterian Church at Columbia. The prominent professor of natural science there, the Reverend Dr. James Woodrow,[16] uncle of future President Woodrow Wilson, delivered an address on evolution before the alumni association in 1884. In doing so, he helped fan the embers of a debate that continues to the present day. Woodrow summarized his belief that

> the doctrine of Evolution in itself . . . is not . . . religious or irreligious, theistic or atheistic, yet . . . recognizing that it is God's PLAN OF CREATION, instead of being tempted to put away thoughts of him, as I contemplate this wondrous series of events, caused and controlled by the power and wisdom of the Lord God Almighty, I am led with profounder reverence and admiration to give glory and honor to him that sits on the throne, who liveth for ever and ever. . ."

F. M. Robertson provided a terse commentary in a note handwritten at the bottom margin of his own copy of the Woodrow address: "The voice is Jacob's voice, but the hands are the hands of Esau."[17]

Robertson remained active in politics after the war, now with the Democratic Party. He was chairman of the Democratic Convention in 1879

---

14 Joseph Righton Robertson, M.D., "Robertson 1826-1932," 2. Dr. J. R. Robertson recorded the black vomit experiment and went on to write, "and it was not until the year 1900 that Carrol, Lazear and Reed conducted their memorable experiments [with mosquitoes] in Cuba, definitely establishing the cause of this dreaded malady"; F. M. Robertson, M.D., "Remarks on the Black Vomit of Yellow Fever, Augusta, Ga., October 10, 1839," *Medical Examiner*, Vol. II, No. 42, (Philadelphia, October 18, 1839), 51; Charles C. Jones, Jr., and Salem Dutcher, *Memorial History of Augusta, Georgia*, (Syracuse, NY, 1890), 255-6; [F. M. Robertson, I. P. Garvin, and P. F. Eve], "A Report of the Origin and Cause of The Late Epidemic in Augusta, Ga., Submitted to a Meeting of the Physicians of Augusta, Ga., on the 10th of December, 1839, Re-Printed by Order of Council, November, 1877," (Augusta, GA, 1877), copy in Georgia Regents University, Augusta, Reese Library Special Collections.

15 Obituary of Francis Marion Robertson M.D., 1806-1892, by the Reverend Dr. John Forrest of Charleston, S.C., *Transactions of South Carolina Medical Association,* 1893, 16-19.

16 The Reverend James Woodrow (1828-1907).

17 "Evolution by Woodrow, Girardeau, Armstrong and Robertson," n. d., hardcover collection of reprinted articles and addresses in possession of Thomas H. Robertson, Jr., 2014.

Silver head of F. M. Robertson's walking cane made from the Fort Sumter flagstaff. *Collection of Catherine Barrett Robertson. Photograph by Thomas H. Robertson, Jr., 2013*

Continued from page 137

In spite of efforts by the Daughters of the Confederacy to save the Heard House, Wilkes County, its owner in 1904, advertised it for sale and demolition. W. A. Slaton of Washington secured one of the mahogany stairway balusters from the impending wreckage and had it made into a walking cane, which he presented to attorney Joseph B. Cumming of Augusta. Cumming's descendants ultimately passed the walking cane along to Thomas Heard Robertson, because of a supposed family connection between donee and the acquired name of the Heard House. The actual genealogical connection

Continued on page 141

State Bank of Georgia Building, Washington, Georgia Branch
Courtesy of Georgia Archives, Vanishing Georgia Collection, wlk001

that nominated W. A. Courtenay for Mayor of Charleston—"a stormy gathering, over which he presided with consummate skill and tact."[18]

He continued to serve as Dean of the Medical College until he retired from the school in 1873. He kept up his medical practice, serving as the medical representative on the Charleston Board of Health in 1875 and as Consulting Physician to Roper Hospital until 1881 when he retired from medicine completely. He spent the remainder of his days in literary and philosophical studies until his death on July 15, 1892, at age 86.[19]

The Reverend Dr. John Forrest, writing a memorial resolution published by the South Carolina Medical Association, praised his "strong religious convictions" and the "lustre of his faith," together with a "native strength of character with him that commanded . . . a reverence accorded to few." There was no doubt who was in charge. These traits led to his nickname "Field Marshal," from his soldierly bearing, military career, and the coincidence of his initials.[20]

He obviously did not keep his 1836 promise to his wife Henrietta "to wipe my hands of military matters."[21] And although he states at the conclusion of his journal that he is writing the diary of this odyssey for her benefit, its pages contain subject matter and observations that would obviously be of interest to a

18 Obituary of Francis Marion Robertson, M.D., copy and typescript in Waring Historical Library files, Medical University of South Carolina; William Ashmead Courtenay (1831-1908), Mayor of Charleston 1879-1887. Founder of Newry, South Carolina, 1893, where he built a cotton mill. http://192.220.96.192/was/htm, accessed December 10, 2008.

19 Obituary of Francis Marion Robertson, M.D., copy and typescript in Waring Historical Library files, Medical University of South Carolina; *The Revised Ordinances of the City of Charleston Relative to the Health Department and the Acts of the General Assembly Relating Thereto* (Charleston, 1875), personal copy embossed "F. M. Robertson, M. D." on the cover, in possession of Thomas H. Robertson, Jr., 2014.

20 Obituary of Francis Marion Robertson M.D., 1806-1892, by the Reverend Dr. John Forrest of Charleston, S.C., *Transactions of South Carolina Medical Association*, 1893, 16-19; "Your grandfather [F. M. Robertson] was a stern man, but not unreasonable and I liked him," more especially during his later years, when he had his grandchildren around him and had softened much in manner. He was always the best dressed man I knew, Always drove a stylish and fast horse in pursuit of his profession." See Letter, W[illiam] R[obertson] Boggs to Miss Pamela Robertson, February 18, 1900, copy in possession of Thomas H. Robertson, Jr., 2014.

21 Francis Marion Robertson to Henrietta Toomer Righton Robertson, March 17, 1836. See Thomas Heard Robertson, Jr., "The Richmond Blues in the Second Seminole War: Letters of Captain Francis Marion Robertson, M.D.," in *Military Collector & Historian*, Volume 54, No. 2, Summer 2002. Original letter in Collection of Augusta Richmond County Historical Society, Special Collections, Reese Library, Georgia Regents University, Augusta.

wider audience. Henrietta and Francis must have recognized this larger value, as they preserved the journal for posterity—now to the benefit of readers one hundred fifty years later.

Continued from page 139

with the commemorated Cabinet event at the Old State Bank building turned out not to be a Heard at all, but a different forebear, Heard Robertson's great-great uncle, Dr. John Joseph Robertson.[3]

3. "[Heard House] has been commonly used by writers in describing our old bank building, but the Daughters of the Confedercy [sic], after giving the matter due consideration have passed resolutions adopting the original title, namely, "Old State Bank", for the reason that giving it another name is misleading. General B. W. Heard purchased the property long after the war, and was in no way connected with the meeting of the last cabinet within its walls . . . ." See "The Heard House: The Fame of Washington's Historic Building," Mrs. T. M. Green, Historian, U. D. C., 1899, copy of typescript in possession of Thomas H. Robertson, Jr., 2014; The State Bank Building was originally built in 1819. See Joyce Perkerson Poole, *A Heard Family Record-Based History* (Baltimore, 2005), 386; *The Washington Chronicle*, April 25, 1904; Bryan Cumming (son of Joseph B. Cumming) to undesignated addressee, December, 1942, original letter attached to the baluster walking stick in possession of Catherine Barrett Robertson, 2014.

Partial Robertson Genealogical Chart

Relatives of Francis Marion Robertson, M.D.

Including Four Generations through 1865.
Individuals mentioned in the Journal are distinguished by bold text.

William Robertson 1786-1859
m. Pamela Moseley 1789-1837

    2. Surg. Francis Marion Robertson, M.D. 1806-1892
    m. Henrietta Toomer Righton 1805–1873

        3. Asst. Surg. William Francis Robertson, M.D. 1834–1875
        m. Lydia Murray Clark

        3. Maj. Joseph Righton Robertson 1836–1916
        m. Constantia (Lily) Whitridge Taylor

            4. John Frederick Robertson 1860-1919
            4. Henry Clarence Robertson 1862-
            4. James Taylor Robertson 1865-1866

        3. Henrietta Marion Robertson 1839-1865
        m. Henry K. Silliman

        3. Pvt. Henry Clay Robertson 1841-1892
        m. Mary Elizabeth Mikell 1842-1924

            4. Francis Marion Robertson 1864-

        3. Lt. James Lawrence Robertson 1843-1922
        m. Katharine (Kitty) Smith Miller 1845-1931

        3. Pvt. Duncan Clinch Robertson 1845-1898
        m. Mary Caroline Mikell

    2. Mary Ann Robertson 1808-1865
    m. Archibald Boggs 1801-1870

        3. Gen. William Robertson Boggs 1829-
        m. Mary Sophia Symington

        3. Robert Boggs 1832-
        m. Eliza Jane Innerarity

3. Archibald Pickens Boggs 1834-1887
   m. Martha Bruce Turpin
3. Pamela Robertson Boggs 1836-
   m. Joshua Willingham Butt
3. Catherine Joyner Boggs 1839-
   m. John Decatur Butt

2. William Alexander Robertson 1817-1858
m. Mary Louisa Walton
   3. Robert Walton Robertson

2. John Joseph Robertson 1819-1873
m. Elizabeth Felix Gilbert Hay

2. Lucretia Catherine Robertson 1822-1869
m. Richard W. Joyner

2. Lewis Ford Robertson 1825-1904
m. Sarah Twells 1825-1894

2. James Walthall Robertson 1830-1911
m. Anne Heard Parks

Partial Righton Genealogical Chart

Relatives of Mrs. Francis Marion Robertson (Henrietta Toomer Righton)

Including Four Generations through 1865.
Individuals mentioned in the Journal are distinguished by bold text.

Joseph Righton 1762-1847
m. Elizabeth Fullerton 1768-1855
- **2. Henrietta Toomer Righton 1805-1873**
  m. **Surg. Francis Marion Robertson, M.D. 1806-1892**
  - **3. Asst. Surg. William Francis Robertson, M.D. 1834-1875**
    m. Lydia Murray Clark
  - **3. Maj. Joseph Righton Robertson 1836-1916**
    m. Constantia (Lily) Whitridge Taylor
    - 4. John Frederick Robertson 1860-1919
      m. Emmie Lenora Mickle
    - 4. Henry Clarence Robertson 1862-
      m. Ella Josephine Pope
    - 4. James Taylor Robertson 1865-1866
  - **3. Henrietta Marion Robertson 1839-1865**
    m. Henry K. Silliman
  - **3. Pvt. Henry Clay Robertson 1841-1892**
    m. Mary Elizabeth Mikell 1842-1924
    - 4. Francis Marion Robertson 1864-
  - **3. Lt. James Lawrence Robertson* 1843-1922**
    m. Katharine (Kitty) Smith Miller* 1845-1931
  - **3. Pvt. Duncan Clinch Robertson 1845-1898**
    m. Mary Caroline Mikell
- **2. Jane Elizabeth Righton Abt. 1790-**
  m. Samuel Yates, Jr.
- **2. Katharine (Kitty) Fullerton Righton 1799-1843**
  m. William Smith 1793-1877

   3. Margaret J. Smith 1824-1895
      m. Jonathan Meyer Miller 1810-1912
         4. William Wallace Miller 1843-1910
         4. Katharine (Kitty) Smith Miller* 1845-1931
            m. James Lawrence Robertson* 1843-1922
         4. John Meyer Miller 1846-1872
         4. Alexander Lawton Miller 1848-1934
         4. Anselm Irvin Miller 1849-1880
         4. Elizabeth Moore Miller 1851-1881
         4. George Twiggs Miller 1853-1944
         4. Emily Jones Miller 1855-1913
         4. Annie Righton Miller 1857-1934
         4. Norman Peter Miller 1859-1937
   3. Brig. Gen. William Duncan Smith 1825-1862
      m. Georgia King
   3. Maj. Norman Wallace Smith 1830-
      m. Julia Martin Axson 1827-
   3. Sophia Edwards Smith 1834-
      m. John Gardiner Richards 1828-1914
   3. Elizabeth Smith 1837-
      m. Bender Nail Miller 1834-
2. Elizabeth Fullerton Righton
   m. Frederick DeVeau Fanning 1806-1869
      3. Elizabeth Righton Fanning 1844-

*Katharine Smith Miller and James Lawrence Robertson were first cousins, once removed.

Appendix C

An Interview with Author
Thomas Heard Robertson, Jr.

SB: How are you related to Surgeon Robertson?

TR: Francis Marion Robertson is my great-great-grandfather. My Robertson family line through him includes citizen-soldiers of six generations in every major American war, from a lieutenant in the Continental Army in the Revolutionary War through my father's service with the last United States horse cavalry unit in World War II.

SB: How did you come to edit the journal?

TR: This branch of my family never throws anything away! That's been both a blessing and a curse for me. I have ended up with a basement full of papers and other stuff, including a little 1950s-vintage, nylon stocking box that contains Dr. F. M. Robertson's thin leather-bound diary. I found the little inherited volume fascinating because the surgeon recorded daily his journey through four states over three months time near the end of the Civil War.

SB: That in itself makes it uncommon.

TR: It does. His entries cover both the Southern military responses to the Federal invasion and the everyday events of the people he encountered along the way. I do not know of another similar eyewitness account of this length and depth during those final weeks of the Confederacy in the Deep South. There may be one, but I don't know of it.

SB: Civil War students and many people today know a little something about Sherman's March to the Sea through Georgia, but not much about his subsequent Carolinas Campaign, which this journal discusses.

TR: It is still quite overlooked, which puzzles me, although that is beginning to change. The campaign was tough for the local people—it meted out much more punishing effects than many realize. My level of knowledge was about equal to history of Sherman's campaigns and the end of the war. The people and events of the diary led me to a much deeper understanding of the chaotic end of the Southern Confederacy in that part of the South.

SB: What surprised you the most as you read the journal for the first time?

TR: As I read through the surgeon's narrative the first time, I realized there were important stories threaded inside that needed to be shared and further explored. I was surprised at the detail of his daily accounts, and the intimacy with which he described the generals and political figures. I later figured out that Dr. Robertson really did know the generals and politicians personally, through his various previous associations with them as a West Point cadet, political activist, and Presbyterian church leader.

SB: You utilized extensive footnotes and sidebars within the text on a wide variety of subjects. Why?

TR: Every time I have read the diary I gleaned something new out of it, probably because the doctor made many subtle references here and there to subjects that he and his audience at the time would have already understood. They all would have known about the people and events of the time, and he did not have to retell them. In my case, I needed to know those background stories to fully understand the diary. So I decided to include as much additional information as possible in the footnotes—probably more than the usual academic references—to explain or complement the text. A few things were either too long for footnotes or seemed better suited as stand-alone subjects, so I presented them as sidebars. They cover a potpourri of topics, from the politics of the Radical Republicans vs. Abraham Lincoln to a recipe for a then-popular apple pie, and even songs with their musical scores. These subjects are mentioned in passing by the surgeon, but I have tried to make them come alive for the modern reader so they could see and understand his world as he did.

SB: Anything in particular surprise you during your research?

TR: Yes. Imagine my astonishment when I discovered that newly elected President Abraham Lincoln had used a letter from Dr. F. M. Robertson as evidence to imprison the former Clerk of the United States House of Representatives for suspicion of treason! I ran across the text of the letter in the Official Records of the United States and Confederate Armies. In February 1861, Robertson wrote to his former Whig Party acquaintance Samuel J. Anderson, who was then living in New York. In this letter, he described the political and economic situation in South Carolina and the national crisis symbolically brewing at Fort Sumter. That cast suspicion on Anderson and he was jailed in August 1861. His Republican captors released him a few months later after he took an oath of allegiance to the United States.

SB: Your Prologue and Epilogue offer a lot of background on the war in the Charleston area prior to the opening of the diary and what happened afterward. Why did you make them as comprehensive as you did?

TR: When I started, I had aimed merely to set the stage for the opening diary narrative, which begins with the evacuation of Charleston by the Confederate army in February 1865. I also intended to give only the basic background of the surgeon himself and to introduce some of the characters who would be mentioned in the diary. But, as I did the research on these subjects, particularly the doctor's relatives (who included his five sons in Confederate service), I found that most of them were involved in one important turning point of the war or another, from the very beginning to the very end. So I decided to include their stories. Taken together, they illustrate pretty well what was going on in the Deep South, both before and after the time frame of the journal.

SB: Tell us about the events following Sherman's march north through the Carolinas. What type of coverage will readers discover here?

TR: The Epilogue depicts the postwar time frame mostly by telling the stories of what happened to the surgeon and his immediate family after the fighting was over. One thing I was amazed to find out was that Dr. Robertson's younger brother, Dr. John Joseph Robertson, hosted the fleeing President Jefferson Davis, Mrs. Davis, and part of the Confederate Cabinet overnight on May 2, 1865, at the local branch of the Bank of Georgia in Washington, Georgia. J. J. Robertson was cashier of the bank and lived upstairs with his wife and family. Davis and the remnant Confederate Cabinet met at the bank the next morning and dispersed just before Federal troops entered the town in pursuit.

SB: Can you give readers an idea of some of the battles and other events discussed in the journal?

TR: Surgeon Robertson mentions several battles and skirmishes in his journal, including the Battle of Monroe's Crossroads, fought near Johnsonville where Robertson had camped with a branch of General Hardee's army just two days before. The doctor seems to enjoy telling us that Union General Kilpatrick was completely surprised by the Confederate attack before daylight, and "barely made his escape in his drawers. A woman was, also, captured in his camp in her night dress. . . . his mistress . . . doubtless.''

I have also included an account of the Battle of Averasboro as a sidebar. The Confederates made a strategic defensive stand there, and the doctor's son Jimmy was wounded by a minie ball. General Hardee executed the engagement as a classic delaying action, at a strategic pinch point between two rivers that were both in flood stage. His troops considered the battle a Confederate victory, because they had successfully held off a much-larger Union force at a time when they badly needed a morale boost. Hardee's stand gained valuable time that allowed his commander, General Joe Johnston, to marshal all of the available Confederate forces to fight what would turn out to be the final large battle in North Carolina at Bentonville three days later.

SB: You retraced the diarist's route. How was that effort helpful in your work?

TR: In 2003 and 2004, my sisters and I followed the actual route that our ancestor took and wrote about so long ago. We covered hundreds of miles and found it remarkable that we could follow in his footsteps fairly precisely. Many of the country roads, houses, and landmarks mentioned in the diary were still there after nearly 150 years. We also heard the stories of Sherman's march still alive in the minds of people we met along the way. Beside that, standing on the battleground where our great-grandfather Jimmy Robertson was shot just days before the end of the war was a pretty powerful experience. For me, following the diary on the ground made me realize the broader value of the history of that time all the more, and convinced me that I really did have to share that history with others by editing the journal for publication.

SB: We are glad you did. Thank you for your time, Mr. Robertson.

TR: You're welcome.

Bibliography

Books and Articles

Angley, Wilson, Jerry L. Cross, and Michael Hill, *Sherman's March through North Carolina, A Chronology*, Raleigh: North Carolina Department of Cultural Resources, Division of Archives and History, 1995.

Bailey, Albert Edward, *The Gospel in Hymns: Backgrounds and Interpretations*, New York: Charles Scribner's Sons, 1950.

Barrett, John G., *Sherman's March through the Carolinas*, Chapel Hill: The University of North Carolina Press, 1956.

Barrett, John Gilchrist, *North Carolina as a Civil War Battleground 1861-1865*, Raleigh: North Carolina Department of Cultural Resources, Division of Archives and History, 2003.

The Holy Bible, Authorized King James Version, London: Eyre and Spottiswoode, Limited.

Boggs, William R., Gen., *Military Reminiscences of Gen. Wm. R. Boggs, C.S.A.*, Electronic edition, University of North Carolina at Chapel Hill: 1997, http://docsouth.unc.edu/boggs/boggs.html, accessed September 20, 2003.

Bolick, Julian Stevenson, *A Fairfield Sketchbook*, Clinton, SC: Jacobs Brothers, 1963.

Bollet, Alfred Jay, M.D., *Civil War Medicine: Challenges and Triumphs*, Tucson: Galen Press, Ltd., 2002.

Boylston, Raymond P., Jr., *Battle of Aiken*, Raleigh: Boylston Enterprises, 2003.

——, Butler's Brigade: *That Fighting Civil War Cavalry Brigade from South Carolina*, Raleigh: Jarrett Press & Publications, Inc., 2001.

——, *Edisto Rebels at Charleston*, Raleigh: Boylston Enterprises, 2003.

Bradley, Mark L., *Last Stand in the Carolinas: The Battle of Bentonville*, Campbell, California: Savas Woodbury Publishers, 1996.

Bragg, C. L., Charles D. Ross, Gordon A. Blaker, Stephanie A. T. Jacobe, and Theodore P. Savas, *Never for Want of Powder: the Confederate Powder Works in Augusta, Georgia*, Columbia: The University of South Carolina Press, 2007.

Brennan, Patrick, *Secessionville: Assault on Charleston*, Campbell, California: Savas Publishing Company, 1996.

Brown, Russell K., "Augusta's 'Pet Company': The Washington Light Artillery," in *Richmond County History*, v. 26, no. 2, Winter 1996.

Burton, E. Milby, *The Siege of Charleston, 1861-1865*. Columbia, South Carolina: University of South Carolina Press, 1970.

Calhoun, David B., *Cloud of Witnesses: The Story of First Presbyterian Church*, Augusta, Georgia 1804-2004, United States of America, 2004.

Campbell, Jacqueline Glass, *When Sherman Marched North from the Sea: Resistance on the Confederate Home Front*, Chapel Hill: The University of North Carolina Press, 2003.

Carmichael, Emmet B., "Richard Fraser Michel," in *Alabama Journal of Medical Science*, v. 2, no.2, 1965.

Cashin, Edward J., *The Story of Augusta*, Augusta: Richmond County Board of Education, 1980.

Chapman, John A., *History of Edgefield County from the Earliest Settlements to 1897*, Newberry, SC: Elbert H. Aull, 1897.

The Revised Ordinances of the City of Charleston Relative to the Health Department and the Acts of the General Assembly Relating Thereto, Charleston: The News and Courier Job Presses, 1875, personal copy embossed "F. M. Robertson, M. D." on the cover, in possession of Thomas Heard Robertson, Jr., 2012.

Chisholm, J. J., *A Manual of Military Surgery for Use of Surgeons in the Confederate Army*, Richmond: West & Johnston, 1861.

Confederate States of America. War Dept. Regulations for the Medical Department of the C. S. Army. University of North Carolina, Documenting the American South, electronic edition of *Regulations for the Medical Department of the C. S. Army*, Richmond: Ritchie & Dunnavant, Printers, 1862. http://docsouth.unc.edu/imls/regulations/regulations.html..

Cunningham, H. H., *Doctors in Gray: The Confederate Medical Service*. Second edition. Baton Rouge: Louisiana State University Press, 1983.

Dammann, Gordon, *Pictorial Encyclopedia of Civil War Medical Instruments and Equipment*, Volume I, Missoula, Montana: Pictorial Histories Publishing Company, 1983.

Davis, William C., ed., *Diary of a Confederate Soldier: John S. Jackman of the Orphan Brigade*, Columbia: University of South Carolina Press, 1997.

Evans, Clement A, *Confederate Military History*, (Atlanta: Confederate Publishing Company, 1899), digital edition, http://archive.org/stream/confedmilhist04evanrich#page/, accessed December 12, 2012.

Farmer, James O., PhD, et al., *The Story of Edgefield*, Edgefield, South Carolina: The Edgefield Historical Society, 2009.

Fonvielle, Chris E., Jr., *The Wilmington Campaign: Last Rays of Departing Hope*, Campbell, California: Savas Publishing Company, 1997.

Gadski, Mary Ellen. *The History of the DeRosset House: A research report presented to Historic Wilmington Foundation, Inc.* 2 parts. n.d. ca. 1981. Copy in New Hanover County Library, Wilmington, North Carolina.

Giles, Katherine W., "God Be the Judge between Us!": Final Steps in the March to Civil War, January–April 1861," *Carologue*, Vol. 26, No. 4, (Spring 2011).

Glatthaar, Joseph T., *The March to the Sea and Beyond: Sherman's Troops in the Savannah and Carolinas Campaigns*, Baton Rouge: Louisiana State University Press, 1995.

Green, Carol C., *Chimborazo: The Confederacy's Largest Hospital*, Knoxville: The University of Tennessee Press, 2004.

Harrington, Sion H. III, and John Hairr, *Eyewitnesses to Averasboro, Volume 1: The Confederates*, Erwin, North Carolina: Averasboro Press, 2001.

Hay Melba Porter, and Carol Rearden, ed., *The Papers of Henry Clay: Volume 10, Candidate, Compromiser, Elder Statesman January 1, 1844–June 29, 1852*, Google Books edition, Lexington, KY: University of Kentucky Press, 1991.

Heath, George, Parish *Psalmody: A Collection of Psalms and Hymns for Public Worship*, [Presbyterian Church in the United States] Philadelphia: Perkins & Purves, 1844, Google Books edition, accessed August 29, 2010.

Hewett, Janet B., ed., *The Roster of Confederate Soldiers 1861-1865*, 16 volumes, Wilmington, NC: Broadfoot Publishing Company, 1995.

Hill, Barbara Lynch, *Summerville: A Sesquicentennial Edition of the history of The Flower Town in the Pines*, West Columbia, South Carolina: Wentworth Printing, 1998.

Holcomb, Brent, ed., *St. David's Parish, South Carolina, Minutes of the Vestry 1768-1832 Parish Register 1819-1924*, Easley, SC: The Southern Historical Press.

Horn, Stanley F., *The Army of Tennessee: A Military History*, Indianapolis: The Bobbs-Merrill Company, 1941.

Hudson, Joshua Hilary, LL.D., *Sketches and Reminiscences*, Columbia: The State Company, 1903.

Inglesby, Charles, Capt., *Historical Sketch of the First Regiment of South Carolina Artillery (Regulars)*, n.d., [circa 1895]. Copy in collections of South Carolina Historical Society.

Johnson, Lucille Miller, *Hometown Heritage*, Fayetteville: Col. Rowan Chapter, Daughters of the American Revolution, 1978.

Johnston, Joseph E., General, C.S.A., *Narrative of Military Operations Directed during the Late War between the States*, New York: D. Appleton and Company, 1874, including Appendix: W. J. Hardee, "Memoranda of the Operations of my Corps, while under the command of General J. E. Johnston in the Dalton and Atlanta, and North Carolina Campaigns."

Jones, Charles C., Jr., and Salem Dutcher, *Memorial History of Augusta, Georgia*, Syracuse, New York: D. Mason & Co., 1890.

Lamon, Ward Hill, *Recollections of Abraham Lincoln, 1847-1865*, Chicago: A. C. McClurg and Company, 1895, Google Books edition, 2005, accessed August 10, 2010.

Lesser, Charles H., *Relic of the Lost Cause: The Story of South Carolina's Ordinance of Secession*, 2nd edition, Columbia: University of South Carolina Press, 1996.

Manarin, Louis H., comp., *North Carolina Troops 1861-1865, A Roster*, Raleigh: State Division of Archives and History, 1971, second printing with addenda, 1989, Vol. III.

May, John Amasa and Joan Reynolds Faunt, *South Carolina Secedes*, Columbia: University of South Carolina Press, 1960.

Merrill, Adeline Godfrey Pringle, ed., *All in One Southern Family, Volume II: Life in Cheraw*, Charleston, 1996.

Mikell, I. Jenkins, *Rumbling of the Chariot Wheels: Doings and Misdoings in the Barefooted Period of a Boy's Life on a Southern Plantation*, Columbia, 1923.

Miller, Wm. K., *History of St. Paul's Episcopal Church, Augusta, Georgia*, Augusta: privately published by W. K. Miller at the request of the Vestry, 1945.

Mills, Robert, *Atlas of the State of South Carolina, 1825*, reprint edition, with an introduction by Gene Waddell, Easley, South Carolina: Southern Historical Press, 1980.

Mobley, Johnson Bland, comp., "The Descendants of Dr. John Richard Mobley, Sr. and Lucretia Simkins," privately published, Columbia, 1991.

Moore, Mark A., *Moore's Historical Guide to the Battle of Bentonville*, Campbell, California: Savas Publishing Company, 1997.

Murphy, John M., M.D., and Howard Michael Madaus, *Confederate Rifles & Muskets: Infantry Small Arms Manufactured in the Southern Confederacy, 1861-1865*, Newport Beach, California: Graphic Publishers, 1996.

Nelson, Larry E., *Sherman's March through the Upper Pee Dee Region of South Carolina*. Florence, South Carolina: Pee Dee Heritage Center, 2001.

——, "Sherman at Cheraw," *South Carolina Historical Magazine*, Vol. 100, No. 4, October, 1999, 328-54.

Oates, John A., *The Story of Fayetteville and The Upper Cape Fear*, Charlotte: The Dowd Press, 1950.

O'Neal, John Belton and John A. Chapman, *The Annals of Newberry*, Newberry, S. C.: Aull & Houseal, 1892, Google Books edition, accessed December 22, 2012.

Phelps, W. Chris, *The Bombardment of Charleston 1863-1865*. Gretna, Louisiana: Pelican Publishing Company, 2002.

——, *Charlestonians in War*, Gretna, Louisiana: Pelican Publishing Company, 2004.

Poole, Joyce Perkerson, *A Heard Family Record-Based History*, Baltimore: Gateway Press, Inc., 2005.

Pope, Thomas H., *The History of Newberry County, South Carolina, Volume One 1749-1860*, Columbia: University of South Carolina Press, 1973.

Powell, William S., ed., Dictionary of North Carolina Biography. Chapel Hill: The University of North Carolina Press, 1979-1996, reprinted in http://docsouth.unc.edu/browse/bios/pn0000761_bio.html, accessed September 1, 2010.

Power, J. Tracy and Daniel J. Bell, *Rivers Bridge State Park Visitors Guide*, South Carolina Department of Parks, Recreation and Tourism, 1992.

Protestant Episcopal Church in the United States of America, The Hymnal of the Protestant Episcopal Church, 1940, New York: The Church Pension Fund, 1943.

Rainsford, Bettis C., et al., *The Story of Edgefield*, Edgefield: Edgefield County Historical Society, 2009.

Robertson, F. M., M.D., "Remarks on the Black Vomit of Yellow Fever, Augusta, Ga., October 10, 1839," *Medical Examiner*, Vol. II, No. 42, Philadelphia, October 18, 1839.

[Robertson, F. M., I. P. Garvin, and P. F. Eve], "A Report of the Origin and Cause of The Late Epidemic in Augusta, Ga., Submitted to a Meeting of the Physicians of Augusta, Ga., on the 10th of December, 1839, Re-Printed by Order of Council, November, 1877," Augusta, Ga.: Chronicle & Constitutionalist Book Print, 1877, copy in Georgia Regents University, Augusta, Reese Library Special Collections.

Robertson, Thomas Heard, Jr., *Miller Family Letters 1837 to 1894*, second edition, privately published, June, 1994, copy in Reese Library, Georgia Regents University, Augusta.

——, "The Richmond Blues in the Second Seminole War: Letters of Capt. Francis Marion Robertson, M.D.", *Military Collector & Historian, Journal of the Company of Military Historians*, Vol. 54, No. 2, Summer 2002, 51-63.

Roman, Alfred, *The Military Operations of General Beauregard in the War Between the States, 1861 to 1865*, 2 vol., New York: Harper & Brothers, 1884.

Rosen, Robert N., *Confederate Charleston: An Illustrated History of the City and the People During the Civil War*. Columbia: University of South Carolina Press, 1994.

—— and Richard W. Hatcher III, *Images of America: The First Shot*, Charleston: Arcadia Publishing, 2011.

Rutkow, Ira M., M.D., "Anesthesia during the Civil War," *Archives Of Surgery*, Chicago: 1960 [Arch/Surg] 1999 Jun; v. 134 (6).

Schroeder-Lein, Glenna R., *Confederate Hospitals on the Move: Samuel H. Stout and the Army of Tennessee*, Columbia: University of South Carolina Press, 1994.

Scott, E. C., Rev., D.D., *Ministerial Directory of the Presbyterian Church, U. S., 1861-1941, Revised and supplemented 1942-1950*, Atlanta, Georgia: Hubbard Printing Company 1950.

Smith, Mark A. and Wade Sokolosky, *"No Such Army Since the Days of Julius Caesar," Sherman's Carolinas Campaign: from Fayetteville to Aversaboro*, Ft. Mitchell, Kentucky: Ironclad Publishing, 2005.

[South Carolina] State Department of Agriculture, Commerce, and Immigration, *Handbook of South Carolina, 1907*, Columbia: The State Company, 1907.

Speer, Paul R. and Charles R. Gamble, *Magnitude and Frequency of Floods in the United States, Part 2-A. South Atlantic Slope Basins, James River to Savannah River, Geological Survey Water-Supply Paper 1673*, Washington: 1964.

Spence, Dr. E. Lee, *Treasures of the Confederate Coast: The Real Rhett Butler & Other Revelations*, Charleston: Narwhal Press, 1995.

Sprunt, James, *Chronicles of The Cape Fear River, 1660-1916, second edition, Raleigh: 1916, reprint edition, Wilmington: Broadfoot Publishing Company, 1992*.

Stamps, Lieutenant Colonel T. D., *Civil War Atlas to Accompany Steele's American Campaigns*, West Point, New York: Military Art and Engineering Department, United States Military Academy, 1941.

Stanchak, John E., *Civil War*, New York: Dorling Kindersley Publishing, Inc., 2000.

Stony, Samuel Gaillard, *This is Charleston*, Charleston: Carolina Art Association, Historic Charleston Foundation, and the Preservation Society of Charleston, 1970.

Strong, Ludlow Potter, et al., *List of Direct Descendants of the deRosset Family with introduction and brief notes, Compiled 1947-1948 by Ludlow Potter Strong assisted by various descendants, to supplement the "Annals of the de Rossets,"* privately published, 1948, copy in possession of Thomas H. Robertson, Jr., 2014.

Strong, Frederick deRosset, "Some Additions to the List of Direct Descendants of the deRossett Family," privately published May, 1984, copy in possession of Thomas H. Robertson, Jr., 2014.

Swanson, Mark, *Atlas of the Civil War Month by Month: Major Battles and Troop Movements*, Athens & London: The University of Georgia Press, 2004.

Swayze, J. C., *Hill & Swayze's Confederate States Rail-Road & Steam-Boat Guide*, Griffin, Georgia: Hill & Swayze, Publishers, 1862, scanned version, University of North Carolina at Chapel Hill, 2001, http:docsouth.unc.edu/imls/Swayze/Swayze.html, accessed July 24, 2010.

Todd, Richard Cecil, *Confederate Finance*, Athens: University of Georgia Press, 1954, Google Books edition, http://books.google.com/books?id=MVc1DTf4zsEC&printsec=front cover&dq=confederate+finance&source=bl&ots=A90yBc0xr-&sig=wI3-kQoWpgcT-W TKyktpoAPcrdY&hl=en&ei=BUSATKWoLsP68AbS1rz4AQ&sa=X&oi=book_result& ct=result&resnum=2&ved=0CBYQ6AEwAQ#v=onepage&q&f=false, accessed September 2, 2010.

Trowbridge, J. T., *The South: A Tour of its Battle-fields and Ruined Cities, etc.*, Hartford, Connecticut: L. Stebbins, 1866.

Virgil, *Aeneid*, Book 4.

Vogt, James R., "Map of North Carolina, 1861-1865," copy in Museum of the Cape Fear, Fayetteville, N.C.

Ware, Lowry, *Old Abbeville: Scenes of the Past of a Town Where Old Time Things are not Forgotten*, Columbia, SC: ACMAR, 1992.

Waring, Joseph Ioor, M.D., *A History of Medicine in South Carolina 1825-1900*, Columbia: The South Carolina Medical Association, 1967.

Watkins, R. A., *Directory for the City of Augusta and Business Advertiser for 1859*, Augusta, Ga.: R. A. Watkins, 1859, Google Books edition, accessed October 13, 2012.

Wilbur, C. Keith, M.D., *Civil War Medicine 1861-1865*, Old Saybrook, Connecticut: 1998.

Willingham, Robert M., Jr., *The History of Wilkes County, Georgia*, Washington, Georgia: Wilkes Publishing Company, 2002.

Wise, Stephen R., *Lifeline of the Confederacy: Blockade Running During the Civil War*, Columbia: University of South Carolina Press, 1988.

Wittenberg, Eric J., *The Battle of Monroe's Crossroads and the Civil War's Final Campaign*, New York: Savas Beatie LLC, 2006.

Woodrow, et al., "Evolution by Woodrow, Girardeau, Armstrong and Robertson," n. d., hardcover collection of reprinted articles and addresses in possession of Thomas Heard Robertson, Jr., 2014.

Internet Sources

Annie's Quick and Easy Amish Recipes, n. d., www.anniesrecipes.com/Kitchen/amish-recipes/ amish-half-moon-pies-recipe.htm, accessed July 6, 2004.

Andrew Pickens Butler, http://ftp.rootsweb.com/pub_/usgenweb/la/bossier/bios/butlerap. txt, accessed December 6, 2004.

ArchiveGrid: Edward Willis papers, 1864-1891. University of South Carolina–South Caroliniana Library, http://beta.worldcat.org/archivegrid/record.php?id=43579481&contributor=207&archivename=University+of+South+Carolina+-+South+Caroliniana+Library, accessed Oct- ober 22, 2012.

http://awt.ancestry.com/cgi-bin/igm.cgi?op=GET&db=ssassybritches&id=I04468, accessed October 12, 2003.

http://www.battleofaiken.org/history.htm, accessed October 31, 2004.

http://bioguide.congress.gov/scripts/biodisplay.pl?index=S000078, accessed September 8, 2010.

Burns, Robert, "John Anderson, My Jo," "Best Love Poems Network: Romantic poems for poetry lovers!" www.bestlovepoems.net/classic love poems/john anderson my jo robert burns, accessed August 11, 2005.

Charleston County Public Library–South, Carolina, http://www.ccpl.org/content.asp?id=15649&action=detail&catID=6026&parentID=5747, accessed October 17, 2012.

Chronicling America: Historic American Newspapers, The Library of Congress, Raleigh, N.C. newspapers. http://chroniclingamerica.loc.gov, accessed September 1, 2010.

Connor, J. T. H., "Chloroform and the Civil War," http://findarticles.com/p/articles qu3912/is 200202/ai n9408156/print?tag artBody:col1, accessed November 24, 2008.

Courtenay, William Ashmead, biographical sketch, http://192.220.96.192/was/htm, accessed December 10, 2008.

http://dictionary.reference.com/wordofthe day/archive/2001/06/14.html, accessed August 12, 2005.

http://en.wikipedia.org/wiki/David Porter McCorkle, accessed October 13, 2012.

http://www.encyclopedia.com/doc/1O214-distance.html, accessed September 8, 2010.

Encyclopedia of World Biography, 2004, entry for Madeleine L'Engle, http://www.encyclopedia.com/doc/1G2-3404707212.html, accessed September 11, 2010.

Goebel, Greg, "Spring 1861: You Will Wantonly Strike A Hornet's Nest," *In the Public Domain*, v. 1, chapter 2.0 of 89 (March 1, 2006), http://www.vectorsite.net/twcw 02.html, accessed July 25, 2006.

Thos. W. Hendricks to Moses Hendricks, March 25th, 1863. "The Cherished Letters, 1863," http://freepages.genealogy.rootsweb.com/~mysouthernfamily/THECHERISHEDLETTERS1863.htm, accessed July 7, 2004.

Historical Data Systems, comp., *American Civil War Soldiers* [database on-line], Provo, UT, USA: Ancestry.com Operations Inc, 1999.

North Carolina Office of Archives and History, George A. Trenholm, Marker P-52 Text and Essay, http://www.ncmarkers.com/print marker.aspx?id=P-52, accessed October 22, 2012.

National Park Service, *U. S. Civil War Soldiers, 1861-1865*, Provo, UT, USA: Ancestry.com Operations, Inc, 2007, accessed November 26, 2012.

Nepveux, Ethel "The Economist," in *Confederate Historical Association of Belgium News*, www.chab-belgium.com/pdf/english/Economist.pdf, accessed October 22, 2012.

North Carolina History Project, "Fayetteville and Western Plank Road," Raleigh: John Locke Foundation, 2012, http://www.northcarolinahistory.org/encyclopedia/70/entry, accessed October 12, 2012.

Register of Officers of the Confederate States Navy 1861-1865, Historical Data Systems, comp., *U. S. Civil War Soldier Records and Profiles*, Provo, UT, USA: Ancestry.com Operations, Inc, 2009, accessed November 26, 2012.

http://www.rootsweb.ancestry.com/~ncccha/biographies/romulussaunders.html, entry for Romulus Mitchell Saunders, accessed September 8, 2010.

Satterfield, Mary Yarbrough McAden, Article # 630 by in *The Heritage of Caswell County, North Carolina*, entry for Romulus Mitchell Saunders, quoted in http://www.rootsweb.ancestry.com/~ncccha/biographies/romulussaunders.html, accessed September 8, 2010.

"Sixteenth (16th) Regiment South Carolina Militia Charleston District, 4th Brigade 2d Division," n. d., http://www.geocities.com/screbels_1864/SM1660.html, accessed October 23, 2003.

"Janie Smith Letter," n. d., www.averasboro.com/JANIE%20SMITH520LETTERS.htm, accessed October 31, 2004.

South Carolina Encyclopedia, http://www.scencyclopedia.org/johnson.htm, entry for William Johnson, Jr., accessed September 8, 2010.

"South Carolina Regimental History Books, South Carolina Infantry Regiments," n. d., article from *Lancaster Enterprise*, June 1, 1892, http://www.researchonline.net/sccw/southcar.htm, accessed September 10, 2010.

Sumter County Historical Commission Marker, "Potter's Raid," 2009, located in Sumter, South Carolina, described in "The Historical Marker Database," for "Military Post/Potter's Raid Marker," updated February 23, 2010. http://www.hmdb.org/Marker.asp?Marker=27832, accessed September 11, 2010.

Manuscripts

Barnes, Adelaide Rossignal, "Genealogical Studies," typescript in possession of Thomas Heard Robertson, Jr., 2012.

Boggs, W. R., to Miss Pamela Robertson, February 18th, 1900, original in Constance Sevier Robertson papers in possession of Thomas Heard Robertson, Jr., 2010.

Cumming, Bryan to undesignated addressee, December, 1942, original letter in possession of Catherine Barrett Robertson, 2014.

"Family Register, Lyman Hall Robertson and Constance Truxton Robertson," n. d., genealogical typescript in possession of Ethel Robertson Boyle, Conyers, Georgia, 2014.

"Family Record," manuscript of Marriages, Births, Deaths, from Constance S. Robertson Estate Papers in possession of Thomas Heard Robertson, Jr., 2014.

Green, Mrs. T. M., "The Heard House: The Fame of Washington's Historic Building," Historian, U. D. C., 1899, copy of typescript in possession of Thomas H. Robertson, 2014.

James Gage McKibbin Papers, Southern Historical Collection, #1812-z, University of North Carolina at Chapel Hill.

Marion, Ann Davidson (Mrs. Malcolm L. Marion, Jr.) to Thomas H. Robertson, Jr., September 30, 2004.

Montgomery, Erick D., "Historical Considerations," in *Research Study: The Boyhood Home of President Woodrow Wilson, Augusta, Georgia*, by Norman Davenport Askins, P.C. Architect, copy in office of Historic Augusta, Inc.

Moore, Margaret Wallace Robertson, Application for membership in United Daughters of the Confederacy of Margaret Wallace Robertson Moore (Mrs. John Moore), Paper # 76, June 29, 1936.

Nixon, Araminta McDiarmid (Mrs. Cobbs G. Nixon) to Thomas H. Robertson, n.d., received October 27, 2003.

Robertson, Catherine Heard, "Corrected Line of William Robertson 1705-1774 to 1969," genealogical manuscript (with annotations by Thomas Heard Robertson), original in possession of Thomas Heard Robertson, Jr., 2014.

Robertson, Francis M., "An Inaugural Dissertation on Remittent Fever Submitted to the examination of the Dean and Professors of the Medical College of So. Ca. For the degree of

Doctor of Medicine By Francis M. Robertson of Augusta Georgia 1830," copy in Waring Historical Library, Medical University of South Carolina.

Robertson, F. M., to Joseph Righton Robertson, July 27, 1865 and August 9, 1865, originals in Constance Sevier Robertson papers in possession of Thomas Heard Robertson, Jr., 2014.

Obituary of Francis Marion Robertson, M.D., copy and typescript in Waring Historical Library files, Medical University of South Carolina.

Robertson, Joseph Righton, M.D., "Robertson 1826-1932," family history typescript in possession of Thomas Heard Robertson, Jr., 2014.

Robertson, Thomas Heard, Jr., *Albert: History and Reflections on Slavery and Its Aftermath*, unpublished manuscript in possession of the author, 2015.

Smith, Catherine B. R., "Death and Funerals of Bishop-General Leonidas Polk, including His Interment at St. Paul's Church, Augusta, Georgia, June 29, 1864," Valdosta State College, November 18, 1981, typescript copy in possession of Thomas H. Robertson 2014.

Newspapers and Periodicals

Augusta Chronicle & Sentinel, April 22, 1865.

The Cheraw Chronicle Bicentennial Edition, July 1, 1976.

Cheraw Visitors Bureau, *Guide to Cheraw Historic District*, copy in exhibits in Cheraw Lyceum Museum, Cheraw, S.C.

Confederate States Medical and Surgical Journal, September and October, 1864.

"First Presbyterian Church, Cheraw, South Carolina 175th Anniversary Service, September 21, 2003," program.

The Fayetteville Observer, July 17, 1966, narrative by Mrs. James C. (Kate Robinson) McDiarmid of North Wilkesboro.

The State Magazine, June 1987, Hetzer, Michael, "The Coal Demon of Deep River,", electronic edition, http://freepages.history.rootsweb.ancestry.com/~pfwilson/coal_demon_of_deep_river.html, accessed October 10, 2003.

Jonesborough Whig and Independent Journal, Jonesborough, Tennessee, March 27, 1844. [The search for this reference within the University of Tennessee, Knoxville, Library remains ongoing.]

Macon Telegraph, September 25, 1830.

New York Times, September 24, 1861 and December 26, 1874; http://www.hwwilson.com/Print/Facts%20Pres%20Sample.pdf, accessed November 11, 2008.

North Carolina Medical Journal, November 1995, v. 56, no. 11, Charles E. Williams, MS III, "Dr. Edmund Burke Haywood and Civil War medicine in Raleigh, North Carolina."

Savannah Republican, October, 1862, copied from *Charleston Courier*, n.d. Newspaper account of the "Death of Brig. General Wm. Duncan Smith."

The Southern Presbyterian, Charleston, S.C. July 23rd, 1859, Francis Marion Robertson, "We are Passing Away," typescript in possession of Thomas Heard Robertson, Jr., 2014.

Transactions of the South Carolina Medical Association, 1893, Obituary of Francis Marion Robertson, M.D., copies in files of Waring Historical Library, Medical University of South Carolina.

The Washington Chronicle, April 25, 1904.

Records

"Amnesty Papers," Case Files of Applications from Former Confederates for Presidential Pardons, 1865-1867, Microfilm Roll 21, Washington: The National Archives, 1976.

Amnesty Proclamation, President Andrew Johnson, May 29, 1865, http://itwsewanee.edu/reconstruction/html/docs/andrewj.html, accessed December 28, 2008.

Census of the City of Charleston, South Carolina for the Year 1861, electronic edition, http://docsouth.unc.edu/imls/census/census.html, accessed December 15, 2008.

Compiled Service Records of Confederate Soldiers Who Served in Organizations from South Carolina, various individuals, General Reference Branch, National Archives and Records Administration, Washington, D. C.

Compiled Service Records, Confederate General & Staff Officers, South Carolina Department of Archives and History, Columbia, S. C., Microfilm.

Confederate States of America. *War Dept. Regulations for the Medical Department of the C. S. Army*, Richmond: Ritchie & Dunnavant, Printers, 1862. Electronic edition. University of North Carolina, Documenting the American South, http://docsouth.unc.edu/imls/regulations/regulations.html, accessed October 20, 2003.

National Register of Historic Places, Inventory-Nomination Form for Fitzsimons-Hampton-Harris House [Goodale Plantation house], Richmond County, Georgia.

"Republic of Georgia, Ordinance of Secession, Passed Jan'ry 19, 1861, with the Names of the Signers, . . . George W. Crawford of Richmond, President, Milledgeville, January 22, 1861," Augusta, Georgia: Constitutionalist Steam Press, 1861, original printed copy in possession of Thomas Heard. Robertson, Jr., Augusta, Georgia, 2014.

"Simons & Simons case records, I, 1819-1878," SCHS Call Number 431.02 (I), including "Jonathan M. Miller legal papers, 1860-1872," SCHS Call Number: 431.02(M) 31, South Carolina Historical Society, Columbia, S. C.

S. C. Department of Archives and History, National Register of Historic Places inventory form, Site. No. 674, 5/21/85.

United States Census, 1850, 1860, 1870.

United States Military Academy, "U.S.M.A. Cadet Application Papers (1805 to 1866)," microfilm copy in West Point Library, original at National Archives and Record Service, Washington, D.C.

———, *Register of Graduates*, Classes of 1825, 1826, 1827, 1828, and 1829, including non-graduates.

The War of the Rebellion: A Compilation of the Official Records of the Union and Confederate Armies, 128 vols., Washington, DC, 1880-1901.

Index

Campbell, Thomas, 57
Cape Fear River, 6, 57, 61n, 63, 67n, 91-92, 94
Carrington, William, 43n
Carthage, North Carolina, 57-60
Case, Henry, 94
Charleston, South Carolina, 1-2, 7, 9-14, 21, 27-29, 30-30n, 35-37, 43, 55, 82n, 90-91, 102n, 103-104, 106-107, 111, 131
Charleston Board of Health, 140
Charleston Summer Medical Institute, 21, 22n
Charlotte & South Carolina Rail Road, 101n
Charlotte, North Carolina, 35, 37, 43, 82, 101, 108, 110, 112-113
Cheatham, Benjamin F., 6
Cheraw & Darlington Rail Road, 30n, 48n
Cheraw, South Carolina, 28, 30-30n, 31n, 36, 40, 42n, 44-45, 47, 48n, 51-53, 55, 59, 69, 86
USS *Chesapeake*, 24
Chester Male Academy, 102n
Chester, North Carolina, 108n, 116-118
Chestnut, Mary Boykin, 101n, 102n
Childs, Frederick L., 91
Chisholm, J. Julian, 23
Clark, John, 116-116n, 121-122, 124, 137
Clark, Lydia Murray, 143, 145
Clay, Henry, 21, 135
Clinch, Duncan L., 20, 34n
Columbia, South Carolina, 1, 29-30, 33, 35-36, 69, 103, 108, 111
Confederate States Army Medical Department, 14

Congaree River, 33
Corbett, William B., 33-33n
Courtenay, W. A., 140
Cousart, John Q., 75n
crablantern, 86-86n, 87
Crawford, George W., 9n,
Crowell, N. S., 89-89n, 111-113, 116
Cumming, Joseph B., 139
Dahlgren, John A., 11
Danville, Virginia, 85-86, 90, 110-112
Darlington Court House, 39
Darwin, Charles, 138
Daughters of the Confederacy, 139
Daves, Graham, 97n
Davis, Jefferson, 2, 7, 19, 36, 68n, 110-111, 128-129, 137
Deep River Coal Bed, 61n, 91
DeGraffenreid, Tscharner, 102n
DeRosset, Armand L., 91, 94-96, 97n
Douglas, James, 104
Duncan, A. S., 43n, 72
Duncan, Stephen, 108n
Edisto Island, 24, 106
Egypt Coal Mines, 67n,
Elliott, Stephen Jr., 47-47n, 91, 94
Eve, F. Edgeworth, 137-137n
Fanning, Elizabeth Righton, 105-105n, 146
Fanning, Frederick DeVeau, 105n, 146
Fayetteville Arsenal Battalion, 91-91n, 94
Fayetteville, North Carolina, 38, 40, 56, 59, 61-61n, 63, 67-67n, 68, 74, 75n, 76, 91
Fickling, Eldred S., 99-99n, 101
Fillmore, Millard, 9n
Five Forks, battle of, 108